York St John College
Fountains Learning Centre

⁻turn this item on or before the date stamped below,
⁻called, the loan is reduced to 10 days

STEVEN SPIE⌐

INTERVIEWS

CONVERSATIONS WITH FILMMAKERS SERIES

PETER BRUNETTE, GENERAL EDITOR

Photofest

STEVEN
SPIELBERG

INTERVIEWS

EDITED BY LESTER D. FRIEDMAN AND
BRENT NOTBOHM

UNIVERSITY PRESS OF MISSISSIPPI / JACKSON

www.upress.state.ms.us

∞

Library of Congress Cataloging-in-Publication Data

Spielberg, Steven, 1947–
    Steven Spielberg : interviews / edited by Lester D. Friedman and Brent
Notbohm.
        p.   cm. — (Conversations with filmmakers series)
    A collection of interviews by various interviewers, 1974-1999.
    Filmography : p.
    Includes index.
    ISBN 1-57806-112-1 (cloth : alk. paper) — ISBN 1-57806-113-X
(paper : alk. paper)
    1. Spielberg, Steven, 1947—Interviews.   2. Motion picture producers
and directors—United States—Interviews.   I. Friedman, Lester D.
II. Notbohm, Brent.   III. Title.   IV. Series.
PN1998.3.S65A5 2000
791.43'0233'092—dc21
    [B]   99-052479

British Library Cataloging-in-Publication Data available

CONTENTS

INTRODUCTION

FIRST, THE FACTS. STEVEN Spielberg is either the director (*E.T. The Extra-Terrestrial, Jurassic Park, Jaws, Raiders of the Lost Ark, Schindler's List, The Lost World: Jurassic Park, Saving Private Ryan, Indiana Jones and The Last Crusade*) or the producer (*Men in Black, Twister, Back to the Future*) of over one-third of the thirty highest grossing films of all time. Among the 100 best films of all time recently identified by an American Film Institute poll, five directed by Spielberg made the elite list: *Schindler's List, E.T. The Extra-Terrestrial, Jaws, Raiders of the Lost Ark,* and *Close Encounters of the Third Kind.* In fact, voters chose *Schindler's List* as the only movie from either the 1980s or 1990s for a spot in the top ten; the next most recent film, Francis Ford Coppola's *The Godfather,* was released over two decades earlier.

This unique recognition accorded Spielberg's films is even more astounding, given the fact that more highly respected modern auteurs like Woody Allen (1), Stanley Kubrick (3), Francis Ford Coppola (2), and Martin Scorsese (3) and acknowledged masters such as Charlie Chaplin (3), Orson Welles (1), and John Ford (2) failed to match Spielberg's accomplishment. Only Alfred Hitchcock, himself dismissed throughout much of his active career as a mere entertainer who created suspense yarns, approaches Spielberg with four films on the list. Equally impressive, none of these esteemed directors has a film among the top thirty grossing films of all time, *The Godfather* coming closest in 87th place. Little wonder, then, that *Time* magazine anointed Spielberg the "most influential" filmmaker of the twentieth century.

Steven Spielberg has, in effect, become a brand name. His bemused, slightly distracted smile greets us from countless glossy magazine covers and slick entertainment programs. At least twenty independent internet sites devote themselves entirely to Spielberg and his films, while various models of his computer software, CD-ROMS (including one that allows you to progress from "novice moviemaker" to "A-List Director" with guidance from Steven Spielberg) and videogames dot the cyber landscape. On the teen angst series *Dawson's Creek,* aspiring filmmaker Dawson Leery (James Van Der Beek) reveres Spielberg, transforming his closet into a movie poster shrine venerating his idol. Spielberg also has a substantial stake in television programs (including America's highest ranked series, *ER*), theme restaurants, toy lines, cartoon shows, internet companies, amusement parks, and entertainment centers—all of which bear his imprint.

On an even grander scale, the director was the creative midwife in the birthing of Hollywood's first state of the art studio in 70 years: Dream-Works SKG (formed with record mogul David Geffen and film executive Jeffrey Katzenberg) has quickly emerged as a significant financial and creative force in American moviemaking. Not surprising, therefore, Spielberg often holds the number one spot on *Forbes* magazine's annual list of the highest paid entertainers. He even achieved the dubious distinction of attracting his own obsessed stalker, a singular event in the annals of the Director's Guild of America; Jonathan Norman, who was convicted (1998) of planning to kidnap, rape, and torture Spielberg. Given the totality of his input into our national consciousness, the combined products of Spielberg's imagination represent a ubiquitous cultural force whose influence extends far beyond the confining screens of local metroplexes.

Next, the question. In light of the mountain of indisputable evidence attesting to Spielberg's financial and aesthetic achievements, why have so few cinema scholars devoted in-depth studies to his work? Partly, this dearth of intellectual work exists because academics usually prefer to wield their analytical and rhetorical skills in the service of undervalued creative artists struggling to fund their productions, not acclaimed entertainers who sit atop immense financial empires and command princely budgets for projects they chose to direct. Equally important, most film scholars contemptuously dismiss Spielberg as little more than a modern P. T. Barnum, a technically gifted and intellectually shallow showman who substitutes spectacle for substance. They feel that Spielberg (along with his pal George

Lucas) has been responsible for the two greatest sins in modern cinema history: the "Blockbuster" mentality that permeates the commercial film industry and the infantalization of contemporary movies; the former leaves little room for intellectually challenging cinematic works lacking widespread audience appeal and the latter encourages action flicks accentuating multiple explosions rather than significant subjects.

But even acknowledging these objections, it still seems quite odd that erudite books appear each year which elaborate upon the works of obscure silent film directors or examine hip filmmakers with a handful of movies to their credit, while the most successful director of all time receives scant sustained critical attention. With the exception of various essays on *Schindler's List* and a forthcoming volume in Cambridge University's Film Classic Series, the vast majority of publications about Spielberg simply recirculate biographical events or recycle behind-the-scenes accounts of his filmmaking, rarely providing more than an ardent fan's eye view of the man or his work. Only a handful of writers have sought to examine the personal qualities and communal vision which coalesced to allow this gawky outsider to morph into Hollywood's most powerful figure. A mere smattering of pieces even endeavor to analyze the components of his essential worldview, the issues which animate his most significant works, the roots of his immense acceptance, and the influence his vast spectrum of imaginative products exerts on the public consciousness.

This collection addresses these important issues by presenting a series of interviews that span Spielberg's public career from 1974 to 1999. As such, it provides insight into those persistent, often obsessive, considerations which most influence the filmmaker from his earliest projects as a budding filmmaker to his recent works as a mature artist. The contours of his development remain known to a large segment of moviegoers: Spielberg's endless fascination with filmmaking as a teenager, his precocious beginnings as a wunderkind at Universal Studios, the persistent childlike perspectives of his movies, the mass popularity his pictures attained, his struggle to move beyond adolescent films, his disheartening middle-age slump, and his artistic breakthrough with *Schindler's List*. The interviewers, themselves, often highlight the director's age (ranging from his early twenties to his mid fifties) at the time of their conversation, noting how the changes in Spielberg's personal life (marriage, fatherhood, divorce, remarriage, adoption, etc.) directly influence his movies. This chronological pattern, therefore, affords the reader a sharp sense of Spielberg's steady technical and thematic maturation, as he strives to harness his impressive moviemaking skills into the service of more complex subjects.

In the earliest interviews as well as in the most recent, Spielberg explores the various connections and conflicts between public financial success and personal artistic vision. His very first answer to David Helpern's initial question in 1974 (before the release of *Jaws* a year later) relates how he raised money to make his early movies. This preoccupation with the financial side of filming—including percentages, points, budgets, and revenues—reappears as a major component within almost every piece in the book. Spielberg himself constantly monitors his level of concern about fiscal success to chart his growth as a mature filmmaker. The more emotionally committed he is to a project, the less he cares about box office receipts or director salary. So, he reveals to Glenn Collins how he took only the minimum D.G.A. salary for directing *The Color Purple* and spent that on overages. In his exchange with Stephen Dubner some twenty-five years later, Spielberg emphasizes how his personal vision took precedence over his business acumen in making *Schindler's List,* since "he was convinced that the film would lose money even though it cost only $22 million."

Throughout his career, Spielberg clearly articulates the fundamental commandment of commercial filmmaking: making financially successful products is the currency necessary to convince studio chieftains to bankroll future projects. Perhaps even more importantly, it fulfilled a deep psychological need that reappears in most of the interviews; box office hits signified that he was pleasing people, and even further, that he was accepted by a large audience of moviegoers. Recalling a formative incident, Spielberg tells Steve Poster in 1978 how as a young teenager he screened an early film for his fellow boy scouts and got "whoops and screams and applause and everything else that made me want to do it more and more. That was sort of the raw beginning." Such immediate gratification and admiration for a kid who always felt like a geeky outsider, a boy alienated from his peers by physical limitations and Jewish culture, proved an irresistible fix of instant approval that inspired his nascent filmmaking career. This addiction became a habit that Spielberg has been rarely able to kick.

Spielberg returns to this obviously compelling image of cheering Boy Scouts in a conversation with Kenneth Turan as recently as the tail end of 1998: "For me nothing's changed from the first day when I was a twelve year old and showed an 8 millimeter movie I had made to Boy Scouts. The reaction the Boy Scout troop had and the feeling that it gave me inside is no different than the feeling I have today when an audience has the same reaction to something made by hundreds of people and for a lot of money." No matter how much his career has flourished, no matter how many Oscars he wins or box office records he breaks, a crucial part of Spielberg's psyche remains indelibly stamped by this childhood image of himself as a perpetual outsider and of filmmaking as the key to acceptance. His aesthetic sensibility, therefore, is almost always bent to his ongoing need for us to like his films—and by extension the man himself. As such, he remains obsessed with how audiences respond to his work; almost every interview contains some reference to audience expectations that the director must fulfill to deem his film, and therefore himself, as successful.

Yet, as his preoccupation with financial considerations battles constantly with his need for more personal expression, Spielberg ultimately realizes that his compulsion to please others must, at times, retreat in the face of his need to please himself, particularly with projects that strike a personal resonance within his psyche. In 1988, he tells Myra Forsberg that turning 40 caused him to reassess his work and that he needed to "please a part of me I haven't pleased before." Starting with *Empire of the Sun,* he continues in the Forsberg interview, he felt "a side that doesn't necessarily think of the audience with every thought and breath, but thinks about what I need to be satisfied." Even though he knew that *Empire of the Sun* was not a very commercial project with wide audience appeal, Spielberg discloses to Susan Royal in 1989 that he still "had to make the movie" and felt "I really want to make it for myself." Such willingness to risk commercial failure and, in his own mind personal rejection, seems a significant leap in emotional independence for a director who had previously defined success more in terms of weekly grosses than personal satisfaction.

The type of rollercoaster filmmaking which unleashes Spielberg's seemingly endless arsenal of dazzling technical skills, visual stylistics, and narrative capabilities appears prominently in the director's most flamboyant products, such as *Jaws,* the three *Raiders* films, and the two *Jurassic Park* movies. Here, to paraphrase William Blake, the road to excess leads Spielberg to the palace of box office riches. It also foregrounds the director's most ingratiating relationship with his audience, as he masterfully whips frame after frame into a pleasurable confection of sights and sounds.

As he related to Todd McCarthy in *Film Comment* (May-June 1982), one of his main concerns in this type of filmmaking was "to enthrall, entertain, take people out of their seats to get them involved—through showman-ship—in a kind of dialogue with the picture you've made. . . . I love making films that are stimulus-response, stimulus-response." Spielberg also has the uncanny skill to compartmentalize projects, evidenced in his consistent ability to labor on two strikingly dissimilar films simultaneously; thus, he created *E.T. The Extra-Terrestrial* as he was making *Raiders of the Lost Ark* and, even more surprisingly, put the finishing touches on *Jurassic Park* as he was shooting *Schindler's List*.

By the time Spielberg reaches the emotional maturity and personal secu-rity to make *Schindler's List,* he deliberately abandons the stunning array of technical tools which characterizes his most successful commercial narra-tives. "Restraint" is the word he chooses to characterize his aesthetic while making a stark, three hour, black and white film about anti-Semitism and Nazi brutality. This decision springs from a crucial realization about the character of his previous work, as he told John Richardson in 1994: "The authenticity of the story was too important to fall back on the commercial techniques that had gotten me a certain reputation in the area of craft and polish. . . . I threw a whole bunch of tools out of the toolbox. . . . I just lim-ited the utensils, so the story would be the strength of the piece." Such a statement demonstrates Spielberg, in effect, turning his back on the pow-erful techniques even his detractors characterize as his greatest gifts as a visual storyteller. During the entire process involved in *Schindler's List,* he was constantly on guard not to make scenes too *Spielbergian*—a rather amazing instance of a filmmaker internalizing, and responding to, the harsh criticism he received while carving out a very successful commercial career.

Such a desire for truthful depictions appears in *Saving Private Ryan* as well. Spielberg "deglamorizes" the technology and shoots the chaotic Omaha Beach sequence from the frightened point of view of the common soldier, endowing this segment with an authenticity not found in any other Hollywood war feature. Here, again, as Spielberg relates to Kenneth Turan, his ambitions are "noble" rather than commercial: "thanking all those guys, your grandparents and my dad, who fought in World War II." He told his crew, "Don't think of this movie as something we're going to go out and make a killing on but just as a memorial." For Spielberg, then, authentic filmmaking demands a simplification of technique. In the Omaha Beach sequence, Spielberg's model is not other war films; rather, he turns to documentaries made during World War II to find a model of realistic film-making.

Technically, Spielberg recognizes that his immense gifts for visual narratives, as well as his drive to control every aspect of the shooting process, can impede the instinctual flow of images from his imagination. In his most personal projects—*E.T. The Extra-Terrestrial, Schindler's List,* the Omaha Beach sequence in *Saving Private Ryan,* he willingly forsakes his elaborate, scene-by-scene story boards and allows more improvisational filmmaking to permeate his set. The more his films are about people and their relationships, as opposed to being driven by whiplash plots and elaborate special effects, the more Spielberg strives for the spontaneity and vitality that springs from extemporaneous shooting. Yet it is not the actual shooting of a film which he most enjoys. In fact, Spielberg constantly utilizes war metaphors to describe this process: "making a movie is like a scene of battle" (Bobrow) and it's "hand to hand combat" (Hodenfield). Throughout the making of a movie, he constantly feels "under siege" (Royal), and must "become a two-star general" (Royal). What he does enjoy remains remarkably consistent throughout the 25 year span of these interviews: finding a good story, working it out in visual images, editing after the shooting has concluded. Perhaps ironically, this very public man loves the most solitary parts of the filmmaking process far better than the communal activity he finds on the set with actors and crew members.

Steven Spielberg has been in the public eye for over a quarter of a century. His movies turn a gaudy spotlight on any subject or event he chooses to explore, whether it be sea creatures, space aliens, Nazi monsters, or dog-face soldiers. Through these interviews, we can follow his evolution from a brash young filmmaker struggling to carve out a career in Hollywood, to his spectacular triumphs in the commercial cinema, to his maturation as a middle aged director seeking to inspire his imagination with meaningful subjects. Along the way, Spielberg grapples with professional conflicts and personal demons. At times, his intense drive to create economic blockbusters clashes head on with his desire for critical respect. Similarly, his mastery of visual narrative techniques and dazzling special effects sometimes overwhelm his grasp of subtle characterizations or thematic complexity. The Steven Spielberg who emerges through these interviews is a complex amalgam of businessman and artist, of arrogance and insecurity, of shallowness and substance. For good or ill, Spielberg has emerged as a larger than life figure within American society, a cultural force that shapes our times and inhabits our dreams.

Conforming to the policy of the University Press of Mississippi in regard to its interview series, the interviews collected in this book have not been edited in any significant way. While this may result in some repetition in Spielberg's remarks, it does offer more integrity for the scholarly reader. More importantly, these repetitions, marks of the director's private obsessions, are themselves quite revealing.

We gratefully acknowledge each of the authors contributing to this collection of interviews, in addition to the students of our "Masters of Modern Cinema" class at Syracuse University, particularly Jeremy Shipp and Michael French. We also appreciate the efforts, both personal and professional, that Owen Shapiro has made on our behalf. In Syracuse, Lester thanks Rae-Ellen Kavey for her consistent support and invaluable suggestions. In Wisconsin, Brent thanks Yvonne Notbohm and Jennifer Hindman for their ever-present encouragement, love, and support.

Finally, Lester would like to make a special dedication to Tony and Lee Bucci—great friends then, even better friends now. Brent dedicates his work on this book to the memory of his father, LaVerne Notbohm (1935–1993)—we loved him well.

Lester D. Friedman and Brent Notbohm, 1 November 1999

CHRONOLOGY

1946   Born December 18 in Cincinnati, Ohio, the eldest child of Arnold and Leah Posner Spielberg.

1952   Spielberg family moves to a suburb of Camden, New Jersey, called Haddon Township.

1957   Directs his first amateur film, *The Last Train Wreck* (3 mins., 8mm). Spielberg family moves to Arcadia, Arizona.

1958–61 Directs series of increasingly complex films, including: *The Last Gunfight, A Day in the Life of Thunder, Fighter Squad, Film Noir, Scary Hollow.*

1962   *Escape to Nowhere,* a 40 minute war film which wins a filmmaking contest.

1964   *Firelight,* a 140 minute feature film directed by Spielberg, premiers in Phoenix, Arizona.
        Spielberg family moves to California, eventually living in Saratoga.

1965–69 Spielberg attends college at Long Beach State.

1966   Arnold and Leah Spielberg divorce.

1968   Directs and produces *Amblin,* a short 35 mm film which eventually (1969) wins award at Atlanta Film Festival.

1969   Sid Sheinberg, vice-president of production at Universal Studios, sees *Amblin* and offers Spielberg a seven year contract. He leaves college to become a professional director.

1969   Directs "Eyes" a segment of *Night Gallery* written by Rod Serling and starring Joan Crawford, Barry Sullivan, and Tom Bosley, which airs on November 8.

1970   Directs a segment of *Marcus Welby, M.D.* ("The Daredevil Gesture") starring Robert Young and James Brolin, which airs on March 17.

1971   Directs segments of *Night Gallery* ("Make Me Laugh"), *The Name of the Game* ("LA 2017"), *The Psychiatrist* ("The Private World of Martin Dalton"), *Columbo* ("Murder By Book"), and *Owen Marshall, Counselor at Law* ("Eulogy for a Wide Receiver").

   Duel airs as an *ABC Movie of the Weekend*. It is eventually released theatrically in Europe (with extra scenes shot by Spielberg).

1974   *The Sugarland Express.*

1975   *Jaws.*

1977   *Close Encounters of the Third Kind*, which earns Spielberg his first nomination for the Best Director Oscar.

1979   *1941.*

1981   *Raiders of the Lost Ark.*

1982   *Poltergeist*, written by Spielberg but directed by Tobe Hooper.

1982   *E.T. The Extra-Terrestrial*, for which he is nominated for the Best Director Oscar.

1983   "Kick the Can" segment of *Twilight Zone: The Movie.*

1984   *Indiana Jones and the Temple of Doom.*

1985   *The Color Purple.*

   Birth of son Max and marriage to Amy Irving.

1985   Directs two segments of *Amazing Stories* TV series ("The Mission" and "Ghost Train").

1987   *Empire of the Sun.*

   Wins the Irving G. Thalberg Memorial Award for "creative producing" by the Academy of Motion Picture Arts and Sciences.

1989   *Indiana Jones and the Last Crusade.*

Always.

Divorces Amy Irving.

1990   Birth of daughter Sasha and marriage to Kate Capshaw.

Adopts African American foster child, Theo.

1991   *Hook.*

1992   Birth of his son, Sawyer.

1993   *Jurassic Park.*

Schindler's List, which wins Academy Awards for Best Director and Best Picture.

1994   Launches new studio, Dreamworks SKG, with Jeffrey Katzenberg and David Geffen.

Establishes Survivors of the Shoah Visual History Foundation to videotape the stories of Holocaust survivors.

1996   Birth of his daughter Destry and adoption of daughter Mikaela, an African American child.

1997   *The Lost World: Jurassic Park.*

Amistad.

1998   *Saving Private Ryan,* which wins Academy Award for Best Director.

FILMOGRAPHY

As Director

1971
DUEL (TV)
Universal Pictures (aka MCA/Universal Pictures)
Distributed by: American Broadcasting Company (ABC)
Producer: George Eckstein
Director: **Steven Spielberg**
Screenplay: Richard Matheson
Cinematography: Jack A. Marta
Production Design: Robert S. Smith
Editing: Frank Morriss
Music: Billy Goldenberg
Cast: Dennis Weaver (David Mann), Jacqueline Scott (Mrs. Mann), Eddie
Firestone (Cafe Owner), Lou Frizzell (Bus Driver), Gene Dynarski (Man
in Cafe), Lucille Benson (Lady at Snakerama), Tim Herbert (Gas Station
Attendant), Charles Seel (Old Man), Shirley O'Hara (Waitress), Alexander
Lockwood (Old Man in Car), Amy Douglass (Old Woman in Car), Dick
Whittington (Radio Interviewer), Carey Loftin (The Truck Driver), Dale
Van Sickel (Car Driver)
Color
90 minutes

1974
THE SUGARLAND EXPRESS
Universal Pictures (aka MCA/Universal Pictures)

Producers: David Brown/Richard D. Zanuck
Director: **Steven Spielberg**
Screenplay: Hal Barwood/Matthew Robbins
Cinematography: Vilmos Zsigmond
Editing: Edward M. Abroms/Verna Fields
Music: John Williams
Cast: Goldie Hawn (Lou Jean Poplin), Ben Johnson (Captain Tanner),
Michael Sacks (Maxwell Slide), William Atherton (Clovis Poplin), Gregory
Walcott (Mashburn), Steve Kanaly (Jessup), Louise Latham (Mrs. Looby),
Harrison Zanuck (Baby Langston), A. L. Camp (Mr. Nocker), Jessie Lee
Fulton (Mrs. Nocker), Dean Smith (Russ Berry), Ted Grossman (Dietz)
Color
110 minutes

1975
JAWS
Universal Pictures (aka MCA/Universal Pictures)
Producers: David Brown/Richard D. Zanuck
Director: **Steven Spielberg**
Screenplay: Peter Benchley/Carl Gottlieb
Cinematography: Bill Butler
Production Design: Joseph Alves, Jr.
Editing: Verna Fields
Music: John Williams
Cast: Roy Scheider (Martin Brody), Robert Shaw (Quint), Richard Dreyfuss
(Hooper), Lorraine Gary (Ellen Brody), Murray Hamilton (Mayor Vaughan),
Carl Gottlieb (Meadows), Jeffrey Kramer (Hendricks), Susan Backlinie
(Chrissie), Jonathan Filley (Cassidy), Chris Rebello (Michael Brody), Jay
Mello (Sean Brody), Lee Fierro (Mrs. Kintner), Jeffrey Voorhees (Alex Kintner),
Craig Kingsbury (Ben Gardner), Dr. Robert Nevin (Medical Examiner),
Peter Benchley (Interviewer)
Color
124 minutes

1977
CLOSE ENCOUNTERS OF THE THIRD KIND
Columbia Pictures Corporation

Producers: Julia Phillips/Michael Phillips/Clark L. Paylow (associate)
Director: **Steven Spielberg**
Screenplay: **Steven Spielberg**
Cinematography: Vilmos Zsigmond
Production Design: Joe Alves
Editing: Michael Kahn
Music: John Williams
Cast: Richard Dreyfuss (Roy Neary), François Truffaut (Claude Lacombe),
Teri Garr (Ronnie Neary), Melinda Dillon (Jillian Guiler), Bob Balaban
(David Laughlin), J. Patrick McNamara (Project Leader), Warren J. Kemmer-
ling (Wild Bill), Roberts Blossom (Farmer), Philip Dodds (Jean Claude),
Cary Guffey (Barry Guiler), Shawn Bishop (Neary Child), Adrienne Camp-
bell (Neary Child), Justin Dreyfuss (Toby Neary), Lance Henriksen (Robert),
Merrill Connally (Team Leader), George DiCenzo (Major Benchley), Amy
Douglass (Implantee), Alexander Lockwood (Implantee), Gene Dynarski
(Ike), Mary Gafrey (Mrs. Harris), Reverand Michael J. Dyer (Himself), Roger
Ernest (Highway Patrolman), Carl Weathers (Military Police)
Color
132 minutes (special edition)

1979
1941
Columbia Pictures Corporation
Producers: Buzz Feitshans, Janet Healy (associate), Michael Kahn (associ-
ate), John Milius (executive)
Director: **Steven Spielberg**
Screenplay: Robert Zemeckis/Bob Gale
Cinematography: William A. Fraker
Production Design: Dean Edward Mitzner
Editing: Michael Kahn
Music: John Williams
Cast: Dan Aykroyd (Sergeant Tree), Ned Beatty (Ward Douglas), John
Belushi (Wild Bill Kelso), Lorraine Gary (Joan Douglas), Murray Hamilton
(Claude), Christopher Lee (Von Kleinschmidt), Tim Matheson (Birkhead),
Toshirô Mifune (Commander Mitamura), Warren Oates (Maddox), Robert
Stack (General Stilwell), Treat Williams (Sitarski), Nancy Allen (Donna),
Lucille Benson (Gas Mama), Jordan Brian (Macey), John Candy (Foley),

Elisha Cook, Jr. (The Patron), Eddie Deezen (Herbie), Bobby Di Cicco (Wally), Patti LuPone (Lydia Hedberg), Slim Pickens (Hollis Wood), Wendie Jo Sperber (Maxine), Lionel Stander (Scioli), Dub Taylor (Mr. Malcomb), Michael McKean (Willy), Samuel Fuller (Interceptor Commander), Audrey Landers (USO Girl), John Landis (Mizerany), Mickey Rourke (Reese), James Caan (Sailor in Fight-uncredited), Penny Marshall (Miss Fitzroy-uncredited)
Color
118 minutes

1981
RAIDERS OF THE LOST ARK
Lucasfilm Ltd./Paramount Pictures
Producers: Howard G. Kazanjian (executive), George Lucas (executive), Frank Marshall, Robert Watts (associate)
Director: **Steven Spielberg**
Screenplay: Lawrence Kasdan
Cinematography: Douglas Slocombe
Production Design: Norman Reynolds
Editing: Michael Kahn
Music: John Williams
Cast: Harrison Ford (Indiana Jones), Karen Allen (Marion Ravenwood), Paul Freeman (Rene Belloq), Ronald Lacey (Toht), John Rhys-Davies (Sallah), Denholm Elliott (Marcus Brody), Alfred Molina (Sapito), Wolf Kahler (Dietrich), Anthony Higgins (Gobler), Vic Tablian (Barranca/Monkey Man), Don Fellows (Colonel Musgrove), William Hootkins (Major Eaton), Frank Marshall (pilot)
Color
115 minutes

1982
E.T. THE EXTRA-TERRESTRIAL
Universal Pictures (aka MCA/Universal Pictures)/Amblin Entertainment
Producers: Kathleen Kennedy/Melissa Mathison (associate)/**Steven Spielberg**
Director: **Steven Spielberg**
Screenplay: Melissa Mathison
Cinematography: Allen Daviau

Production Design: James D. Bissell
Editing: Carol Littleton
Music: John Williams
Cast: Dee Wallace-Stone (Mary), Henry Thomas (Elliott), Peter Coyote (Keys), Robert MacNaughton (Michael), Drew Barrymore (Gertie), K. C. Martel (Greg), Sean Frye (Steve), C. Thomas Howell (Tyler), Erika Eleniak (Pretty Girl), Richard Swingler (Science Teacher), Pat Walsh/Debra Winger (E.T. voice-uncredited)
Color
115 minutes

1984
INDIANA JONES AND THE TEMPLE OF DOOM
Lucasfilm Ltd./Paramount Pictures
Producers: Kathleen Kennedy (associate)/George Lucas (executive)/Frank Marshall (executive)/Robert Watts
Director: **Steven Spielberg**
Screenplay: Willard Huyck/Gloria Katz
Cinematography: Douglas Slocombe
Production Design: Elliot Scott
Editing: Michael Kahn
Music: John Williams
Cast: Harrison Ford (Indiana Jones), Kate Capshaw (Willie Scott), Jonathan Ke Quan (Short Round), Amrish Puri (Mola Ram), Roshan Seth (Chattar Lal), Philip Stone (Captain Blumburtt), Roy Chiao (Lao Che), David Yip (Rebekkah Sekyi), Clare Smalley (Dancer), Lee Sprintall (Dancer), Jenny Turnock (Dancer), Ruth Welby (Dancer)
Color
118 minutes

1985
THE COLOR PURPLE
Warner Brothers/Amblin Entertainment/Guber-Peters Company
Producers: Peter Guber (executive)/Carole Isenberg (associate)/Quincy Jones/Kathleen Kennedy/Frank Marshall/Jon Peters (executive)/**Steven Spielberg**
Director: **Steven Spielberg**

Screenplay: Alice Walker/Menno Meyjes
Cinematography: Allen Daviau
Production Design: J. Michael Riva
Editing: Michael Kahn
Music: Chris Boardman/Jorge Calandrelli/Andraé Crouch/Jack Hayes/Jerry Hey/Quincy Jones/Randy Kerber/Jeremy Lubbock/Joel Rosenbaum/ Caiphus Semenya/Fred Steiner/Rod Temperton
Cast: Danny Glover (Albert), Whoopi Goldberg (Celie), Margaret Avery (Shug Avery), Oprah Winfrey (Sofia), Willard E. Pugh (Harpo), Akosua Busia (Nettie), Desreta Jackson (Young Celie), Adolph Caesar (Old Mr.), Rae Dawn Chong (Squeak), Dana Ivey (Miss Millie), Leonard Jackson (Pa), Bennet Guillory (Grady), John Patton, Jr. (Preacher), Carl Anderson (Reverend Samuel), Susan Beaubian (Corrine), James Tillis (Buster), Phillip Strong (Mayor), Laurence Fishburne (Swain), Peto Kinsaka (Adam), Lelo Masamba (Olivia), Margaret Freeman (Odessa), Howard Starr (Young Harpo), Daphaine Oliver (Young Olivia), Jadili Johnson (Young Adam), Lillian Nioki Distefano (Young Tashi)
Color
152 minutes

1987
EMPIRE OF THE SUN
Warner Brothers/Amblin Entertainment
Producers: Kathleen Kennedy/Chris Kenny (associate)/Frank Marshall/Robert Shapiro (executive)/**Steven Spielberg**
Director: **Steven Spielberg**
Screenplay: J. G. Ballard/Tom Stoppard
Cinematography: Allen Daviau
Production Design: Fred Hole/Norman Reynolds
Editing: Michael Kahn
Music: John Williams
Cast: Christian Bale (Jim), John Malkovich (Basie), Miranda Richardson (Mrs. Victor), Nigel Havers (Dr. Rawlins), Joe Pantoliano (Frank Demarest), Leslie Phillips (Maxton), Masato Ibu (Sgt. Nagata), Emily Richard (Jim's Mother), Rupert Frazer (Jim's Father), Peter Gale (Mr. Victor), Takatoro Kataoka (Kamikaze Boy Pilot), Ben Stiller (Dainty), David Neidorf (Tiptree), Ralph Seymour (Cohen), Robert Stephens (Mr. Lockwood), Zhai Nai She

(Yang), Guts Ishimatsu (Sergeant Uchida), Emma Piper (Amy Matthews), James Walker (Mr. Radik), Anna Turner (Mrs. Gilmour), Ann Castle (Mrs. Phillips), Yvonne Gilan (Mrs. Lockwood), Ralph Michael (Mr. Partridge), Sybil Maas (Mrs. Hug)
Color
154 minutes

1989
ALWAYS
Universal Pictures (aka MCA/Universal Pictures)/Amblin Entertainment
Remake of *A Guy Named Joe* (1943)
Producers: Kathleen Kennedy/Frank Marshall/**Steven Spielberg**
Director: **Steven Spielberg**
Screenplay: Dalton Trumbo (screenplay *A Guy Named Joe*) Jerry Belson
Cinematography: Mikael Salomon
Production Design: James D. Bissell
Editing: Michael Kahn
Music: John Williams
Cast: Richard Dreyfuss (Pete Sandich), Holly Hunter (Dorinda Durston), Brad Johnson (Ted Baker), John Goodman (Al Yackey), Audrey Hepburn (Hap), Roberts Blossom (Dave), Keith David (Powerhouse), Ed Van Nuys (Nails), Marg Helgenberger (Rachel), Dale Dye (Fire Boss), Brian Haley (Alex), James Lashly (Charlie), Michael Steve Jones (Grey), Kim Robillard (Air Traffic Controller), Jim Sparkman (Dispatcher), Doug McGrath (Bus Driver)
Color
106 minutes

1989
INDIANA JONES AND THE LAST CRUSADE
Lucasfilm Ltd./Paramount Pictures
Producers: George Lucas (executive)/Frank Marshall (executive)/Arthur F. Repola (associate)/Robert Watts
Director: **Steven Spielberg**
Screenplay: Jeffrey Boam
Cinematography: Douglas Slocombe
Production Design: Elliot Scott

Editing: Michael Kahn
Music: John Williams
Cast: Harrison Ford (Indiana Jones), Sean Connery (Professor Henry Jones), Denholm Elliott (Marcus Brody), Alison Doody (Dr. Elsa Schneider), John Rhys-Davies (Sallah), Julian Glover (Walter Donovan), River Phoenix (Young Indy), Michael Byrne (Vogel), Kevork Malikyan (Kazim), Robert Eddison (Grail Knight), Richard Young (Fedora), Alexei Sayle (Sultan), Alex Hyde-White (Young Henry), Paul Maxwell (Panama Hat), Isla Blair (Mrs. Glover), Vernon Dobtcheff (Butler), J. J. Hardy (Herman), Bradley Gregg (Roscoe), Marc Miles (Sheriff), Ted Grossman (Deputy Sheriff), Tim Hiser (Young Panama Hat), Larry Sanders (Scout Master), Jerry Harte (Professor Stanton), Billy J. Mitchell (Dr. Mulbrey)
Color
127 minutes

1991
HOOK
TriStar Pictures/Columbia Pictures Corporation/Amblin Entertainment
Producers: Gary Adelson (co-producer)/Craig Baumgarten (co-producer)/Bruce Cohen (associate)/Dodi Fayed (executive)/James V. Hart (executive)/Kathleen Kennedy/Malia Scotch Marmo (associate)/Frank Marshall
Director: **Steven Spielberg**
Screenplay: James V. Hart/Malia Scotch Marmo
Cinematography: Dean Cundey
Production Design: Norman Garwood
Editing: Michael Kahn
Music: John Williams
Cast: Dustin Hoffman (Captain Hook), Robin Williams (Peter Banning/ Peter Pan), Julia Roberts (Tinkerbell), Bob Hoskins (Smee), Maggie Smith (Granny Wendy), Caroline Goodall (Moira Banning), Charlie Korsmo (Jack), Amber Scott (Maggie), Laurel Cronin (Liza), Phil Collins (Inspector Good), Arthur Malet (Tootles), Isiah Robinson (Pockets), Jasen Fisher (Ace), Dante Basco (Rufio), Raushan Hammond (Thud Butt), James Madio (Don't Ask), Thomas Tulak (Too Small), Alex Zuckerman (Latchboy), Ahmad Stoner (No Nap), Gwyneth Paltrow (Young Wendy), Maxwell Hoffman (5 Year Old

Peter), Kelly Rowan (Peter's Mother), David Crosby (Tickles), Nick Tate
(Noodler), Tony Burton (Bill Jukes), Glenn Close (Gutless)
Color
144 minutes

1993
JURASSIC PARK
Universal Pictures (aka MCA/Universal Pictures)/Amblin Entertainment
Producers: Kathleen Kennedy/Gerald R. Molen/Lata Ryan (associate)/Colin
Wilson (associate)
Director: **Steven Spielberg**
Screenplay: Michael Crichton/David Koepp
Cinematography: Dean Cundey
Production Design: Rick Carter
Editing: Michael Kahn
Music: John Williams
Cast: Sam Neill (Dr. Alan Grant), Laura Dern (Dr. Ellie Sattler), Jeff Gold-
blum (Ian Malcolm), Richard Attenborough (John Hammond), Bob Peck
(Robert Muldoon), Martin Ferrero (Donald Gennaro), B. D. Wong (Dr.
Henry Wu), Joseph Mazzello (Tim Murphy), Ariana Richards (Lex Murphy),
Samuel L. Jackson (Ray Arnold), Wayne Knight (Dennis Nedry), Gerald R.
Molen (Dr. Gerry Harding), Miguel Sandoval (Rostagno), Cameron Thor
(Lewis Dodgson), Richard Kiley (Tour Voice)
Color
127 minutes

1993
SCHINDLER'S LIST
Universal Pictures (aka MCA/Universal Pictures)/Amblin Entertainment
Producers: Irving Glovin (associate)/Kathleen Kennedy (executive)/Branko
Lustig/Gerald R. Molen/Robert Raymond (associate)/Lew Rywin (co-
producer)/**Steven Spielberg**
Director: **Steven Spielberg**
Screenplay: Steven Zaillian
Cinematography: Janusz Kaminski
Production Design: Allan Starski

Editing: Michael Kahn
Music: Johann Sebastian Bach/John Williams
Cast: Liam Neeson (Oskar Schindler), Ben Kingsley (Itzhak Stern), Ralph
Fiennes (Amon Goeth), Caroline Goodall (Emilie Schindler), Jonathan
Sagalle (Poldek Pfefferberg), Embeth Davidtz (Helen Hirsch), Malgoscha
Gebel (Victoria Klonowska), Shmulik Levy (Wilek Chilowicz), Mark Ivanir
(Marcel Goldberg), Béatrice Macola (Ingrid), Andrzej Seweryn (Julian
Scherner), Friedrich von Thun (Rolf Czurda), Krzysztof Luft (Herman Toffel),
Harry Nehring (Leo John), Norbert Weisser (Albert Hujar), Adi Nitzan (Mila
Pfefferberg), Michael Schneider (Juda Dresner), Miri Fabian (Chaja Dresner),
Anna Mucha (Danka Dresner), Albert Misak (Mordecai Wulkan)
Black and White
197 minutes

1997
AMISTAD
DreamWorks SKG/Home Box Office (HBO)
Producers: Debbie Allen/Robert M. Cooper (co-executive)/Bonnie Curtis
(associate)/Paul Deason (associate)/Laurie MacDonald (executive)/Walter
F. Parkes (executive)/Tim Shriver (co-producer)/**Steven Spielberg**/Colin
Wilson
Director: **Steven Spielberg**
Screenplay: David H. Franzoni
Cinematography: Janusz Kaminski
Production Design: Rick Carter
Editing: Michael Kahn
Music: John Williams
Cast: Morgan Freeman (Theodore Joadson), Nigel Hawthorne (Martin
Van Buren), Anthony Hopkins (John Quincy Adams), Djimon Hounsou
(Cinqué), Matthew McConaughey (Baldwin), David Paymer (Secretary
Forsyth), Pete Postlethwaite (Holabird), Stellan Skarsgård (Tappan), Razaaq
Adoti (Yamba), Abu Bakaar Fofanah (Fala), Anna Paquin (Queen Isabella),
Tomás Milián (Calderon), Chjwetel Ejiofor (Ensign Covey), Derrick N.
Ashong (Bukei), Geno Silva (Ruiz), John Ortiz (Montes), Ralph Brown
(Lieutenant Gedney), Darren E. Burrows (Lieutenant Meade), Allan Rich
(Judge Juttson), Paul Guilfoyle (Attorney), Peter Firth (Captain Fitzgerald),

Xander Berkeley (Hammond), Jeremy Northam (Judge Coglin), Arliss
Howard (John C. Calhoun), Willie Amakye (Folowa)
Color
152 minutes

1997
THE LOST WORLD: JURASSIC PARK
Universal Pictures (aka MCA/Universal Pictures)/Amblin Entertainment
Producers: Bonnie Curtis (associate)/Kathleen Kennedy (executive)/Gerald
R. Molen/Colin Wilson
Director: **Steven Spielberg**
Screenplay: Michael Crichton/David Koepp
Cinematography: Janusz Kaminski
Production Design: Rick Carter
Editing: Michael Kahn
Music: John Williams
Cast: Jeff Goldblum (Dr. Ian Malcolm), Julianne Moore (Dr. Sarah Harding),
Pete Postlethwaite (Roland Tembo), Arliss Howard (Peter Ludlow), Richard
Attenborough (John Hammond), Vince Vaughn (Nick Van Owen), Vanessa
Lee Chester (Kelly Malcolm), Peter Stormare (Dieter Stark), Harvey Jason
(Ajay Sidhu), Richard Schiff (Eddie Carr), Thomas F. Duffy (Dr. Robert
Burke), Joseph Mazzello (Tim Murphy), Ariana Richards (Lex Murphy),
Thomas Rosales (Carter), Camilla Belle (Cathy Bowman), Cyndi Strittmatter
(Mrs. Bowman), Robin Sachs (Mr. Bowman), Elliot Goldwag (Senior Board
Member), J. Patrick McCormack (Board Member), Ross Partridge (Curious
Man)
Color
129 minutes

1998
SAVING PRIVATE RYAN
DreamWorks SKG/Amblin Entertainment/Paramount Pictures
Producers: Ian Bryce/Bonnie Curtis (co-producer)/Mark Gordon/Gary
Levinsohn/Allison Lyon Segan (co-producer)/**Steven Spielberg**
Director: **Steven Spielberg**
Screenplay: Robert Rodat

Cinematography: Janusz Kaminski
Production Design: Thomas E. Sanders
Editing: Michael Kahn
Music: John Williams
Cast: Tom Hanks (Captain John Miller), Tom Sizemore (Sargeant Mike Horvath), Edward J. Burns (Private Robert Reiben), Matt Damon (Private James Ryan), Jeremy Davies (Corporal Timothy Upham), Vin Diesel (Private Adrian Caparzo), Adam Goldberg (Private Stanley Mellish), Barry Pepper (Private Daniel Jackson), Giovanni Ribisi (Medic Harlan Wade), Ted Danson (Captain Brian Hamill), Paul Giamatti (Sergeant Hill), Dennis Farina (Lieutenant Colonel Anderson), Joerg Stadler (Steamboat Willie), Max Martini (Corporal Henderson), Dylan Bruno (Toynbe), Daniel Cerqueira (Weller), Demetri Goritsas (Parker), Ian Porter (Trask), Gary Sefton (Rice), Julian Spencer (Garrity), Harve Presnell (General George C. Marshall)
Color
168 minutes

As Producer

Band of Brothers (1999) TV miniseries (executive)
Gladiator (1999)
Saving Private Ryan (1998)
Mask of Zorro, The (1998) (executive)
Pinky, Elmyra & the Brain (1998) TV Series (executive)
Toonsylvania (1998) TV Series (executive) (aka *Steven Spielberg Presents Toonsylvania*)
Deep Impact (1998) (executive)
Invasion America (1998)
Last Days, The (1998) (executive)
Men in Black (1997) (executive)
Amistad (1997)
Twister (1996) (executive)
High Incident (1996) TV Series (executive)
Survivors of the Holocaust (1996) TV
Balto (1995) (executive)
Freakazoid! (1995) TV Series (executive)
Casper (1995) (executive)
Pinky and the Brain (1995) TV Series (executive)

ER (1994) TV Series (executive)
Flintstones, The (1994) (executive)
I'm Mad (1994) (executive)
Schindler's List (1993)
SeaQuest DSV (1993) TV Series (executive)
Family Dog (1993) TV Series (executive)
Animaniacs (1993) TV Series (executive)
Class of '61 (1993) TV (executive)
Trail Mix-Up (1993) (executive)
We're Back! A Dinosaur's Story (1993) (executive)
Habitation of Dragons, The (1992) TV
Water Engine, The (1992) TV (executive)
Tiny Toon Adventures: How I Spent My Vacation (1992) TV (executive)
American Tail: Fievel Goes West, An (1991)
Wish for Wings That Work, A (1991) TV (executive)
Arachnophobia (1990) (executive)
Gremlins 2: The New Batch (1990) (executive)
Back to the Future Part III (1990) (executive)
Akira Kurosawa's Dreams (1990) (executive)
Joe Versus the Volcano (1990) (executive)
Roller Coaster Rabbit (1990) (executive)
Always (1989)
Back to the Future Part II (1989) (executive)
Dad (1989) (executive)
Tummy Trouble (1989) (executive)
Who Framed Roger Rabbit (1988) (executive)
Land Before Time, The (1988) (executive)
*batteries not included (1987) (executive)
Empire of the Sun (1987)
Innerspace (1987) (executive)
American Tail, An (1986) (executive)
Money Pit, The (1986) (executive)
Color Purple, The (1985)
Amazing Stories (1985) TV Series (executive)
Back to the Future (1985) (executive)
Goonies, The (1985) (executive)
Young Sherlock Holmes (1985) (executive)

Gremlins (1984) (executive)
Twilight Zone: The Movie (1983)
E.T. The Extra-Terrestrial (1982)
Poltergeist (1982)
Continental Divide (1981) (executive)
Used Cars (1980) (executive)
I Wanna Hold Your Hand (1978) (executive)

As Writer

Dig, The (1995) (VG)
Goonies, The (1985) (story)
Poltergeist (1982) (story)
Close Encounters of the Third Kind (1977)
Sugarland Express, The (1974) (story)

As Televison Director

Amazing Stories (1985) (episodes "Mission, The" (1985), and "Ghost Train" (1985))
Savage (1973)
Something Evil (1972)
Duel (1971)
Owen Marshall: Counselor at Law (1971) (episode "Eulogy for a Wide Receiver" (1971))
Columbo: Murder by the Book (1971)
Psychiatrist, The (1971) (episodes "Private World of Martin Dalton, The" (1971), and "Par For the Course" (1971))
Night Gallery (1970) (episode "Make Me Laugh" (1970))
Marcus Welby, M.D. (1969) (episode "Daredevil Gesture, The" (1970))

STEVEN SPIELBERG

INTERVIEWS

At Sea with Steven Spielberg

DAVID HELPERN/1974

How did you get started in filmmaking?

SPIELBERG: Making my own films, home movies, 8mm, 16mm, 35mm —
you know — $10, $100, $1000 over a period of ten, eleven years. And then I
made a short in 35mm; I found a backer, he gave me $10,000 and I made a
short film and Sid Sheinberg saw it (he's president of Universal Studios), he
saw the short and put me under a term contract to direct television.

How long a contract?

SPIELBERG: That was a seven year contract.

Are you still under that contract?

SPIELBERG: No. But I signed that contract about five years ago.

And your first picture was Night Gallery?

SPIELBERG: My first professional film was *Night Gallery*, with Joan Crawford. It was the pilot, the trilogy. She played a blind dowager in Manhattan
during the New York blackout. It was a clever Rod Serling piece which was
very hard for Joan to memorize. She couldn't remember words like tran-
scendental and esophagus.

*What was it like being 21 and working with established stars like Joan Crawford
and Barry Sullivan? Was that very difficult for you?*

From *Take One*, March/April 1974. Reprinted by permission of the author.

SPIELBERG: Yeah, it was, it was. It's funny—I blocked, really blocked, most of that first experience because it was so traumatic, because it happened literally within four weeks of signing my Universal contract. See, I thought I'd sign the contract and then I'd kick around the studio for a while, before I ever got a show, and I signed the contract and within four weeks I was on the stage with Joan Crawford, so it was massive culture shock—hemorrhaging, you know, my first day—and I had the show so well planned, you know. I was so in shock that I realized I better plan the show out front, because I'm not going to be much use to anybody on the set. And it was very strange working with a professional crew for the first time, men in their 50s and 60s. But they were very helpful. I asked a lot of questions and they gave me a lot of answers. One thing I was very careful about was not to know it all on that first show. I tried to keep a very open mind and I planned every shot and it was a television show, right—a seven day schedule—and I showed up with 35 shots I wanted to get that day—ridiculous—and we wound up doing 15. But the script wasn't suited to me. It was a lousy way to start, it was a real meller. It was almost an a.m. soap.

Any special problems with Joan or Barry?
SPIELBERG: No, none. Barry and I became the closest of friends because of that show. Barry sort of took me under his wing after that show.

What were the other TV shows you did?
SPIELBERG: Well, I began with *Night Gallery*—the pilot—and then I did two of the episodes of the series and then I did the first *Colombo* that was ever on the air and I did one *Name of the Game*, did one *Marcus Welby*— tried everything—did one *Owen Marshall*. I did two shows from a series that I really liked called *The Psychiatrist* with Roy Thinnes. I did the first show and the last show, out of six shows. I did three TV movies, *Duel* and *Something Evil* and *Savage*, and then I did *Sugarland Express*.

Do you have any explanation for the tremendous success of Duel *in Europe theatrically?*
SPIELBERG: No. I really don't know why it caught on like that. I know how it caught on, I know what first brought it around: Dylis Powell saw the picture and she flipped out for it and she gathered all the London critics

together in one room and showed it to them one night, and the criticism got Universal and the C.I.C. to release the picture in Europe. But Dylis really began it, much like Pauline Kael did with *Last Tango in Paris.*

How do you feel about the picture. Do you like it?
SPIELBERG: Oh, I love it.

Would you like to see it released theatrically in the United States?
SPIELBERG: I wouldn't, for only one reason. It's been seen—I figured it out—it's been seen by about 15 million Americans. I just don't think it would be so successful here.

Was it difficult to make the transition from television to theatrical movies?
SPIELBERG: Not at all, but the problem was my not wanting to get into movies right away. You see, I waited. I had a chance to make four or five different movies and I just didn't. You can do five bad television shows, but you cannot do five bad motion pictures. "Bad," meaning films that aren't received critically, or commercially. And so I just waited and waited and waited. I had a little bet with myself that the first movie I ever directed would be from my own story and it was really sort of a mental deterrent for other projects that came along. I'd say to myself, well, I could direct this, but I couldn't film this and then *Sugarland Express.* I had read a story in the *Citizen News* that was about the Texas hijacking and I wrote the original story and worked on the screenplay with the writers. So I sort of considered that, it was—for me, anyway—it was worth waiting for.

Do you consider Sugarland *a political film?*
SPIELBERG: Yeah, highly political. It's a terrible indictment of the media, more than anything else. It was a circus on wheels.

Is that what attracted you to the story, the whole idea of the media?
SPIELBERG: Yeah, I liked the whole idea of the media. Also, I liked the idea of here is the American condition of today, that people want to be a part of the Walter Cronkite *7:00 News.* They don't want to just watch it, they want to be in it; and I like the idea that today any one of us can create a major news story by doing the smallest, most simple, neurotic act—which is sort of what this picture's about. It's really an act of the heart. It's an

errand of mercy, but it's so simplistic that it had to develop, it had to mushroom into something that fucked up.

Are there heroes and villains in that picture?
SPIELBERG: Yeah, sure. I think the heroes of the picture are really the police. For me, anyway—nobody else sees it that way—but I think the heroes are the police, and I think the villains are the well-wishers that wished a little too much for these people. I didn't see it as a folk, I didn't see Clovis and Slide as folk heroes. A lot of the critics saw them as folk heroes, but I didn't see that at all.

What about Goldie Hawn? She's a very manipulative character.
SPIELBERG: Yes, she is, she is. Which is really contrary to the real-life story, because in real life it was the Clovis character played by Bill Atherton who was the manipulator. And in our story (we didn't have to, but we chose dramatically, and because of the structure, because of how the true story fell into place and our imaginations contradicted it), we tried to see the picture through Goldie Hawn's eyes and through the eyes of Ben Johnson— you know, the captain. Oh, yes, she's highly manipulative. You see, to me the real villain's Hawn; she's the heavy for me—I mean, I intended it to be that way. But everybody has a different interpretation of who their villains are and who their heroes are. She was so motivated to get her child back. What made her a villain was the lapses in her memory about the child when she began looking for herself and not for the mission. She began eating the chicken and she began getting the gold stamps, and she began to tell her husband what to do, and her idea of the American dream was the Indian Chief mobile home.

Why do you think Sugarland *failed commercially, or had a tough time commercially, despite such good reviews?*
SPIELBERG: Well, for one thing, we've pulled the picture, so we don't consider that the picture has failed in its openings. We're waiting for a release time, because I think that the main failing of *The Sugarland Express* was the fact that we came out with two other films thematically similar— *Badlands* and *Thieves Like Us*—and that the audiences were wrapping all three films into one bundle. And I really think, in talking with other people, that they got the reviews—the good reviews of Terry Malick's film *Badlands*, which analyzed the film and were really a turn-off commercially

because the theme of Terry's picture is a great downer—they mixed up my reviews with his and his reviews with mine. I just don't think that the general public was aware at that time that these were essentially different motion pictures. The other big feeling was the release time. Nothing really made it during that spring, especially when six hits had come out from September to January, including *Serpico, The Exorcist, The Sting, Papillon,* and (my god, there were so many pictures making it) *American Graffiti;* so many pictures making a lot of money, that just when we came out all those pictures had left their exclusive or flagship runs and were going wide to the theatres and drive-ins near you, and that really spoiled it for the movie-goer who, today, more than any other time in the history of movies, is so selective about what they go to see. And a third factor I feel was the advertising and publicity: In Universal's efforts to sell the picture, I think they did a milk-sop job on *Sugarland Express.* They just dropped it on the country. With no preparation, with a trailer that I didn't like at all, and with a campaign based not so much on it being an event film, a true story based on something that happened in Texas in '69, but based on the fact that Goldie Hawn was in it and was the star and was all smiles.

Then you have no control over that?
SPIELBERG: No, none. So what you have, you have Goldie smiling— she's smiling next to a teddy bear and *Sugarland* is like *Willie Wonka and the Chocolate Factory*—and I think the campaign was so sweet, you know, people got a little overdose of glucose, or sucrose, and they didn't go.

One of the few criticisms that I have heard is that some people thought it was very condescending to middle America.
SPIELBERG: I don't feel that way at all. No. It wasn't even so much my vision of middle America. I didn't twist the story or the locales, you know, to fit my vision of middle America. I went there, I saw it and I shot it. What you saw in the picture is actually what happened and is happening in Texas. Aside from the phenomena of all those police cars lined up, which in fact happened twofold in the real-life story, we used something like 65 locals in speaking parts, and we let most of them make up their own dialogue.

Are there plans now to re-release the picture?
SPIELBERG: Yeah. They're re-evaluating the campaign, they're working on more of a true-life action campaign, and they're planning to re-release the picture in the summer.

Have you been given any opportunity to put any input into the new campaign?
SPIELBERG: Yeah, I have, and I sat down with the graphic artist just
before I came on this show and we, together, drew seven or eight new
sketches that will be the basis for the new graphic campaign.

Was the critical reception of Sugarland Express *a big boost for you after the
problems you had had in this country?*
SPIELBERG: Yeah, it was a great boost for me, except I wasn't there to
really get off on it. I was here working. I asked them if they would shut
down this picture for three days and they said no. I was very upset that I
didn't go to the Cannes Festival. Rick is missing—what festival are you
missing?—he's missing the Berlin Festival.

What attracted you to the Jaws *project?*
SPIELBERG: I can tell the truth?

Go ahead, tell the truth.
SPIELBERG: I could get in trouble if I tell the truth. Actually, what really
attracted me to the *Jaws* project was in the novel; the last 120 pages, when
they go on a hunt, a sea hunt for the great white shark, and that extended
drama. The extended drama between these three people who are against
each other, and then finally join forces to fight the shark. And that got me
off when I initially read the book. I hated the first two acts, the first 200
and some pages of the novel and I told Zanuck that I—because I volun-
teered to do the picture—I said I'd like to do the picture if I could change
the first two acts and base the first two acts on original screenplay material
and then be very true to the book for the last third. And he agreed and
that's how I became involved.

Do you feel a lot of pressure on this picture because of the problems of Sugarland
commercially?
SPIELBERG: I feel I have more freedom on this picture than I had on
Sugarland. I have at least twice the freedom that I had on *Sugarland.*

*Was it difficult to work with a well-known novel, in that people have certain
expectations?*
SPIELBERG: Yeah, they do and that's always a danger when you start
futzing with a bestseller, that people are going to be very disappointed

when they walk into the motion picture theatre and see favorite scenes from the book deleted in their entirety. That's a problem. But I really think—and this is my ego speaking—that the involvement of three actors and myself and a writer (a new writer), and a producer, that the six, seven of us have gotten together and we've really, I think, made a better movie than *Jaws* is a book. I hope we have, and if we haven't we'll hear about it next spring. In the dollars of the American Revolution. Have you read the script?

No, I haven't, but I'd like to see it before I . . .
SPIELBERG: We would too, because we have been making it up as we go along. Actually, Hooper and even the parts of Quint and Brody are hugely likeable characters, but they have to evolve into that likeability. Like Quint evolved rather late in the picture. The scenes we're shooting right now—after the sequence there's an understanding, the two men have more of an understanding of Quint and so does the audience, than we ever had before. And this leaves the whole staging area open to fight the shark rather than each other. Because there really is no time to bicker and quarrel when the 25-foot great white is chewing holes in the boat. In sitting around, we were trying to find a way to side the three characters together, and the idea came up to have them singing a song—to let the song join the three in some kind of unity. These are the magical things that are coming out of three very loose actors working together and discovering new relationships as we beat the shark.

What are some of the special problems with this picture?
SPIELBERG: This picture? Well, you're sitting on one. It's anchoring the boats in the morning, the time it takes to anchor. And really, you're so limited in your composition at sea, you're so limited being on a boat that I find myself running out of shots; I found myself out of shots really the third day at sea. This picture is being very simply shot. The idea is put the cameras on the actors and let them work.

Why did you shoot it on location, knowing there would be these problems?
SPIELBERG: Well, I wouldn't want to do it in a tank, because it wouldn't be believable, especially today when pictures like *The French Connection* and *Midnight Cowboy* are shot documentary style, on location. The audience looks at *Poseidon* or *The Sting* and they say, "That was shot in a studio." I

think you can tell; *The Sting* looks like it was shot in a studio backlot and *Poseidon Adventure* looks like it was shot on a sound stage; it's really, you know, the look of your movie, and I think we underestimate the intelligence of the public. They can tell.

Sugarland was in Cinemascope wasn't it?
SPIELBERG: Yeah, it was in Panavision.

And why did you choose to use that?
SPIELBERG: Because of the highway. Because the highways are horizontal, and to show more cars. The same way I chose to shoot Panavision: the shark is so long.

The camera placement, the movements, do you leave those pretty much up to Bill Butler, or do you make those decisions yourself? How far in advance were those kinds of decisions made?
SPIELBERG: I pretty much set the camera, except when Bill comes up with terrific ideas, which he does—a lot of good ideas—and I let him put the camera where the idea is better. Whoever has the best idea is where the camera should go, really, I haven't got much of an ego about that. But there's no camera movement.
DREYFUSS: Whoever puts the most ideas in there wins the shark at the end of the shooting.
SPIELBERG: The shark dictates all the shots.
DREYFUSS: The real one.
SPIELBERG: There's only one shark in this picture, and he is real.

When you're improvising with the actors, and since you haven't made decisions beforehand about a lot of the camera setups, what do you do to make it as easy as possible for the cameraman and the actors? If there are too many variables in a scene it makes it very difficult, especially when you're improvising.
SPIELBERG: The way I like to work—we've only done this some of the time—is to rehearse the actors first, and then once I see where the actor's going to move in, I put the camera down to accommodate that. Sometimes, it just happens the opposite way, because of a closed situation; they can't really move around in this scene, the camera goes in first and the actors work around the camera. I think in this picture it's been 50/50. I

think some of the time I've waited to see what they do and then I choreograph around ideas I find from their movements, and then other times I have a shot in mind or a visual idea for the scene itself. Like the beginning of the drunk scene; I wanted to begin on a single of Robert in a scar-comparing contest and as he reaches over to compare a scar, it moves into a two-shot, and as Rick leans back to reconnoiter his body for a scar, it's into a single, and when he presents his scar it's back into a two-shot again. I like that idea and the actors accommodated to the camera in that case. It's dicey on this picture, because I have done virtually no preparation. It's the first movie that I have not prepared. Because I had no time. The studio wanted to begin this picture quickly because of the intended Actors Guild strike. And they got the film going at least two months prematurely. And suddenly I found myself in Martha's Vineyard looking at locations and rewriting the script every night with Howard Sackler and then Carl Gottlieb, and I found no time to do any visual planning. So visually, this will be the simplest picture I've ever attempted. Except the third act will be incredibly visual and *very* exciting and *very* horrifying. With horrific aspects. It's funny how in the middle of an action sequence you can get a lot of character relationships in, I mean — no joke — in the middle of a shark attacking a boat, a look from Robert, a look to Roy, a look to Rick really says a lot of things. It's all looks in the third act. I want a cut on the head turn, on the turning of the head!

The affair between Brody's wife and Hooper has been removed from the film. Was that your decision?

SPIELBERG: I made that personally. I guess I'm personally responsible for removing that, but I felt that it had absolutely nothing to do with the crisis. It was almost an ingredient in an already well-publicized formula of the making of a best seller. The Mafia, the sex, it's just one more ingredient that I felt should be removed. I took the Mafia out of it, I took, not the sex out, but the affair out, because there really is no time for a romantic icthyologist to show up in this town, and rather than do his job, cuckold the sheriff, thereby making the icthyologist unsympathetic, the sheriff unsympathetic for being an unreasonable Ahab character in the book. The first change I made when I read the book was that that affair would have to go, although some women are really attracted to the verbal seduction scene in the book.

Have you added any scenes that weren't in the book?

SPIELBERG: About 27. The whole first two acts are additions. It's brand new.

Peter Benchley did the first screenplay.

SPIELBERG: The first three. So Peter was in on, Peter actually condoned, the removal of the affair. So he was the first writer to remove the affair from the screenplay, and then Peter and I invented three major scenes that did not exist in the book. And then Peter, by himself, constructed two other scenes that are in the movie that he never thought of for the book. And then when the next writer came in, he added a scene or two, and when the third writer came on the project, he added two or three scenes that worked very well.

One of the problems that you talked about in this picture was the lack of preparation time that you had.

SPIELBERG: Lack of preparation time, right, it was a major problem. Because I couldn't rehearse with the actors and we had to make these performances come together virtually 24 hours before we began shooting; or during Take Three an idea would pop into my head, so we'd get into a huddle, break, and re-shoot it. I didn't have Robert Shaw until we were almost shooting. I didn't have my, I have so many small parts that still aren't cast. We're casting as we go along. Roy was the first person cast in the picture and Roy only had a three week headstart. And when Roy got me on the telephone to talk about ideas, I was right in the middle of getting the script ready, and so Roy and I couldn't really communicate that much by telephone. We tried, we had a lot of meetings in L.A., I mean New York. We went to Joe Allens' every day I was in New York, Roy spent every day with me. But Rick had no preparation except one day at the Boston 57 Hotel where we twisted his arm to make this movie. We made him 17 promises; we've kept 13 of them.

Are you going to keep the other four?

SPIELBERG: No.

Are you afraid of all the pre-production publicity around this picture? Are you afraid of something like Great Gatsby?

SPIELBERG: Yes, and I've been very careful about interviews. I mean, this picture is certainly not going to set a wardrobe trend, and people are not going to go out and buy dungarees and old army jackets and baseball caps when it's over. The pre-publicity, I think, is because this movie is somewhat of a novelty. Seeing as how it's a movie about a great killer shark, a man-eater, and fear of the water, and paranoia about the water—it's never been done before. So I think there's that kind of excitement. I don't think we're getting, thank goodness, any of the *Gatsby* pre-publicity that tends to make people walk into the motion picture expecting to see *Gone with the Wind* and walking out very disappointed.

Is there a direct influence of any director on your work? Or even an indirect influence?
SPIELBERG: Yeah. Sure. I mean, I'm influenced by everybody I'm supposed to be influenced by because I'm a filmmaker. The question you asked me, I'm asked that question a lot, and the answer I give is usually (I don't want to give you a bunch of stock interview answers except that it's true), that I really like my contemporaries and can get more out of George Lucas, who's a good friend of mine, than I can by sitting in a screening room and screening eight Preston Sturges films. I mean, I really can; because at least these people are alive and living and there's a rapid exchange back and forth of scripts and ideas. I watch hundreds of old movies, so don't get me wrong, but I haven't learned that much from watching old pictures. I've learned economy from John Ford. But I haven't learned economy—I'm really self-indulgent in so many ways. But John Ford, if he's taught me anything at all, he's taught me how to hold back for an overhead shot, you know, when to go wide, when to go close—don't shoot close-ups every scene or every shot, they don't mean anything. When a close-up is good. I mean, Ford was so judicious about his close-ups and his wide shots. Ford, technically, was, for me, the perfect filmmaker and Orson Welles was second. I only put Ford in front of Welles as a technician, as a great technician, although I've been yelled and laughed at for that.

You mentioned George Lucas. Who others of your contemporaries do you put in that group?
SPIELBERG: There's a friend of mine, he's not directing yet, but he'll be a very good director some day. His name is Willard Hike. Gloria and

Willard Hike are a writing team that wrote *American Graffiti*. And they've done a picture of their own now, George Lucas' third movie, called *Movieland Murders*. And I consider Brian DePalma a close friend and a contemporary, and I consider John Milius a close friend. And I consider other people. I mean, I like a lot of Bill Friedkin's work—I love *The Birthday Party*. People don't know that film exists. I love Friedkin's work on *The Birthday Party*. One of the reasons I cast Robert Shaw in this film is because of *The Birthday Party*. And *The French Connection*. I didn't like *The Exorcist* very much. It's interesting, it's not so much that I get a lot of information from these filmmakers because they're young, it's just because they're the people that I most easily fall into contact with. I see them all the time. It just so happens that when you get into a bull session about directing with other directors, sparks fly a lot of the time. I can get off on that much more than I can from screening ten pictures with the six great American directors of the last sixty years. That's the way I operate. I haven't got any style yet, I haven't found my style. I mean, you know, it's funny; I've made two films so far and I still feel very out of touch with filmmaking, you know, I'm still feeling my way along.

What do you mean by out of touch with filmmaking?
SPIELBERG: I mean, I have all the tools, but I don't have the command of the language yet. It's like learning French. It's like I'm in my third year of French and I've got about three to go before I can even go over there and talk to people without them saying, "You're an American, let me speak English to you. I can speak better English to you than you can speak French to me." I still feel that I have a ways to go. I mean, *Jaws* to me is an exercise in filmmaking, but it's an exercise, it's not something that comes that easily, that instinctively to me. It takes a lot of thought, a lot of walking in circles, wondering why I'm doing this and analyzing it—and then I discover, the minute I analyze, the minute I get very analytical about something, it doesn't work. But when I feel it should be right, but maybe cannot provide a reason for Rick when he says "Why are you doing this?," usually everybody agrees that it's the right way to do it.

Do you think you have a view of the world that comes through in your film work?
SPIELBERG: No. Not yet. Ask me that question in ten years.

But do you think that's a problem in developing an approach to material . . .
SPIELBERG: No, that's just called maturing, you don't stop when you're thirty, you keep going. *Sugarland Express,* for instance, would have been a very different picture had I made it six months ago. Began shooting it six months ago with an eye to releasing it next December. It would have been a wholly different film.

In what way?
SPIELBERG: I would have made it just like a documentary with the whole thing hand-held, the whole thing in 35mm hand-held. Colour, but the whole picture would have been done behind the police cars, shooting over them to the fugitives, the way we see it on television. It would have been from Ben Johnson's point of view; Ben Johnson would have been the star and you would've gotten to know these people through binoculars, monoculars, police radios, rear-view mirror glimpses on the horizon, long shots, small figures standing by the car, and I would have told the whole story from behind the police lines.

So, everything once removed from their reality.
SPIELBERG: I would've taken everything away from its reality. I would've taken a very specific point of view. Because in *Sugarland* I took a broad point of view. I told everything from three different points of view. The media, the police and the trio.

Are you attracted to things that actually happened as subjects for films?
SPIELBERG: Yeah, I'm much more attracted to news stories than I am, you know, by a dream or a fancy idea. I love current events, I love Costa-Gavras. I'd love to do a picture like *Z* someday, a political thriller. But the picture I'm doing next is a political thriller.

What is that?
SPIELBERG: I can't really discuss it in depth, but it's a science fiction film.

And who are you doing it for?
SPIELBERG: I'm doing it for Columbia, for Michael and Julia Phillips, who produced *The Sting.* I'm doing that next.

Do you think it's become easier for a young filmmaker to make a first film than it used to be?

SPIELBERG: Yeah, much easier. It's so easy to make a picture in 16mm today without a lot of bread, and get a lot of help, because the major studios are looking for new people. And one thing that you'll get, you'll finish a picture and screen it, and you'll get the studio heads storming the projection room to hear if it's good. I mean studios today are really into a policy of "you make it, we buy it. You make it, we distribute it." So you have a great chance of getting good distribution on your films. If you can somehow get $200,000 to make a film; independently or someone like Ed Pressman, who's a good angel to have in your corner. He made *Dealing,* he made *Sisters,* and *Badlands.* I mean, he's a very good guy to have in your corner.

What's your biggest problem this moment in filmmaking?

SPIELBERG: Finding a story that interests me, and finding a story that will hold my interest for the nine months it takes to make a motion picture from start to finish. That's my biggest problem.

What's the most exciting part of making a picture for you?

SPIELBERG: The conception of the story is the most exciting part about making a picture for me. The second most exciting part is assembling the film. The most nerve-wracking part of the movie, the process that I most dislike is the actual shooting and directing of the picture. It's true.

Yeah, it's sort of an anti-climax. You don't get quite what you want.

SPIELBERG: You know exactly what you want, it's like painting by the numbers. And that's why in this picture, I'm more excited in making this picture than I was in *Sugarland,* because *Sugarland* was all planned out. But in this one there are surprises every day. Every day something new happens, every day something gets fucked up, but it's exciting.

What have you learned about making pictures on your first two pictures that will make it easier for you to make a third picture?

SPIELBERG: If I get this question right, they'll get Paul Lynde next?

No, but they could bring out a surprise guest.

SPIELBERG: How is it easier? Well, here's how I would evade the question: By saying that each picture is different, and you never learn enough to make one film perfect. You never can gather so much data that you go into a picture and cruise through it like it's warm butter. That's the way to evade the question. I don't know how to really answer the question. I really don't yet. Stick around today, ask me that in about two hours. I want to give it some thought. It's a good question. It's the best question that anyone's asked me in the picture so far.

Filming *The Sugarland Express:*
An Interview with Steven Spielberg

ANDREW C. BOBROW/1974

ANDREW C. BOBROW: *In doing* The Sugarland Express, *did you work initially from a conceptual idea or from the characters? That is, did you first have the idea of cars chasing all over the landscape and sort of find a story to fit it, or vice versa?*

STEVEN SPIELBERG: The human drama of Lou Jean and Clovis Poplin, which was based on a 1969 Texas-sized true-life event, inspired me long before I was visually wooed by the thought of all those cars.

The Sugarland Express is partly based on truth and partly on the wonderful cartoon imaginations of two genius writers, Hal Barwood and Matthew Robbins, with whom I collaborated. In the true story, about 90 police cars from 11 counties and God knows how many tank towns and four-way stops fell into this ragtag formation. Our budget only allowed us 40 police cars, but I had to make it look like 100.

One of the things that interested me most was the idea of showing the American condition represented by the state of Texas, which is a microcosm for any state in this country.

And I loved the *Ace in the Hole* similarity of *The Sugarland Express*: I liked the idea of people rallying behind a media event, not knowing who the characters are or what they're about but just supporting them because they are on an errand of mercy to get their baby back—and that sparks a good deal of good old American sentimentality.

From *Filmmakers Newsletter*, Summer 1974. Reprinted by permission of the author.

A B : *Was your screenplay highly detailed, or did you work out the mechanics of the shot breakdowns after the master scene was written out?*

S S : Because it was such a monumental logistical problem, everything in *The Sugarland Express* was worked out beforehand based on a highly detailed master screenplay. In fact, it was worked out to the point where the prose was so metaphorical that it inspired a lot of shots in the movie.

You have to know Barwood and Robbins' work to understand what I mean, but for instance, they described in one shot 5 police cars zooming past the camera like the Daytona 500—which immediately brings to mind the tilted camera image that you're so used to seeing on the "Wide World of Sports at the Daytona 500." That kind of metaphor, that kind of imagery contained in a simple sentence helped trigger half of the shots to mind.

A B : *How tightly did you work out things beforehand on the set—a la Hitchcock with every shot pre-planned, or did you play it by ear?*

S S : I had a graphic artist come into my office and sketch the entire movie on what you could call a Shell Oil map which I was able to tape to one wall of my hotel room in Texas. So I could see exactly what the film would look like from a bird's eye view as it progressed from 1 police car followed by 2, then 10, then 50; plus all the exciting pit-stops throughout the movie— the chicken-stand scene, the portable potty scene. So I always had a visual overview in terms of day-to-day scheduling.

We shot the entire picture in continuity because we had to: it's very hard to put out a *Cleopatra* call sheet: 200 cars for Tuesday, 7 for Wednesday, 1 for Thursday, then 150 for Friday. And of course doing the film in continuity helped the actors understand their roles much better.

But there's a danger in being so thoroughly prepared that when you come on the set the next day your thinking is not spontaneous because it doesn't fit into the homework pattern of the night before. Marvelous accidents happen on the set—actors have suggestions, technicians have suggestions, a passing stranger might have a suggestion—and I think a director should keep his mind open everyday and not get trapped by the kind of homework he falls in love with on the eve of shooting the actual scene.

A B : *You staged quite a few major accidents in this film, and one in particular—a major night collision between the Georgia State Police and the Texas State Police. Yet I understand no one was injured. I imagine this was a combina-*

tion of extremely careful preparation and probably some good luck as well.
Would you discuss this?

SS: Carey Loftin is the single personality responsible for the lack of injuries during the stunt work. Carey takes every precaution imaginable to protect his people, and he hires the best stunt men. Although he was our stunt co-ordinator and physically involved in driving some of the cars, naturally he couldn't drive all of the cars in all of the stunts, so he sent to Hollywood for some great personnel.

The most difficult crash sequence to stage was the night collision at the crossroads that we called Schooner Four Corners, and it was difficult because it entailed a local police car sideswiping our principal car 2311. But it was a sideswipe that could only cave in the left hindquarters of the principal car because if it hit the door or the engine it could put the car out of commission. Carey told me he would drive the sideswiping car because that was the most delicate of all the stunts. And sure enough, he hit 2311 exactly where we told him he could. Also tied into that same stunt and covered by four cameras was Ben Johnson's car slamming into the local police car that had just sideswiped 2311, and that in turn is followed by 10 Department of Public Safety cars rear-ending each other in true Rube Goldberg fashion.

Vilmos lit the Schooner Four Corners set with overhead source lighting (we had to create our own source because the area was pitch black), and the art director at Vilmos' suggestion built a tractor rental station across the street from where the wrecks would take place and strung 50-watt light bulbs, 200 of them from one side of the lot to the other. The neon gas station sign was the second point of source light, and the third was the interior of the gas station and the gas island light.

Vilmos spent 4 hours lighting the set: he began at 4 p.m., and as it got dark we were ready to shoot. But I had to shoot my coverage before I got my master. Once the cars hit and wrecked, that was the end. So I shot the coverage of the cars almost hitting, spinning out and not quite coming to blows, and after that was resolved it was 1:30 a.m. and I found myself with another four and a half hours of night light to shoot the actual wrecks.

But the stunt I'm proudest of is the KION-TV van capsizing in a mud puddle and sending six reporters flailing into the sky. I'm proud of that stunt because it was a perfect combination of stunt timing by Carey, who was driving the news van, and the camera placement, which was ground-level at 6 inches away from the edge of the mud puddle with a wide-angle lens. And I'm also very proud of one stunt man, Ted Grossman, who did the highest jump of anybody: as it began to turn over, he threw himself straight into the air, pancaked and spread-eagled, and came down head first into a mud puddle only 2 feet deep—his head stuck right in the mud just like a Road Runner cartoon!

There is an individual, personal excitement on the part of every stunt man to best the other stunt guy. And when you get six highly competitive stunt drivers in one scene, wonderful things can happen before the camera. An example of this is the scramble of cars from the football stadium when Captain Tanner gets word that there's a shoot-out in progress at a used car lot only a mile away. We had 11 stunt drivers that day from Hollywood and Chicago, and we had over 45 actual police officers from Texas. A directive had come down from the Department of Public Safety to all their drivers saying that they must not scramble their cars; they must all drive their cars in a sane, orderly fashion out of that lot.

Well, it was very interesting to see what happened. I felt the whole day was ruined when I envisioned 11 cars peeling out and 45 other cars in single file padding gently from the parking lot. But I explained the situation to the assistant director and he went around to get the Texans riled up by saying that Hollywood drivers were better than Texans. When the assistant director, Jim Fargo, waved the white flag, 48 of those 50 cars made dirt bike trails where none had been! And if you've seen the picture, it's one of the more spectacular scramble scenes in the movie.

A B : *What was your shooting ratio—particularly on those car scenes?*
s s : It really varied. The action ratio was pretty much 2 to 1; but the acting ratio was more like 6 to 1. In stunt work you pretty much have to get it on take 1 or take 2. But the acting is more arduous and improvisational at times. For instance, Goldie is wonderful on take 1 and take 2, gets her second wind on take 7, and is marvelous again on take 12 or 13. On the other hand, Bill Atherton is a New York actor who is very serious and very demanding; and he gets better with takes. So as Goldie was wearing thin as the takes were wearing on, Bill was getting better and better.

That's one of the reasons I had to cover the interior dialogue scenes by giving Goldie her close-up in takes 1 and 2 and then have her remain in the over-the-shoulder until take 11 or 12 when Bill was hitting his peak.

AB: *Did you use any locals in the cast?*

SS: It was primarily cast from local actors walking the streets of San Antonio, Houston, and Dallas. Mike Fenton and Sherry Rhodes were the two casting people, and the three of us looked around those cities for local talent and we found plenty of it.

I think it's a crying shame to shoot a movie on location and then import California or New York actors to play the indigenous parts. In *The Sugarland Express,* I cast Goldie Hawn, William Atherton, Michael Sacks, Ben Johnson, and Steven Canally—all consummate professionals from New York and California. But for the 65 speaking roles throughout the movie I felt it would be a crime not to go after the real people.

AB: *In what way did you work with your cinematographer, Vilmos Zsigmond? Did you work closely with him? Did he have any free rein?*

SS: Vilmos and I were almost brothers on our movie. Vilmos is a very interesting man: when you employ his great camera eye, you also get gratis his thoughts. He would offer ideas beyond the definition of the American cinematographer.

As for having free rein, I have never worked with a cinematographer who has had free rein: when a cameraman does have free rein, he becomes the director and the director becomes the apprentice. Vilmos is a very strong cameraman and he is opinionated (only for the good of the picture, that is), and sometimes his "Ah-hahs!" will conflict with your own ideas and that's when you have to be strong and really be the director and say, "I appreciate the idea and it works from your point of view, but I want to do it my way." And Vilmos is enough of a professional to immediately do it any way you wish. Vilmos never said no to a shot, and although we had our share of arguments, in the long run if Vilmos was right the movie would score two points, and if I was right, that would total four. I'm looking forward to working with him on my next 6 or 7 films.

To give you an example of how he works: We were setting up a love scene between Goldie Hawn and Bill Atherton in bed, and there was a critical focus problem. Vilmos, speaking with his ingratiating Hungarian accent, would say, "OK, Goldie, half an inch forward. Now stop." Then, "OK, Bill, a quarter-inch back. All right. Now stop." Then, "Now you, Goldie. Half an inch forward. OK. Now on one elbow. Can you support yourself that way? OK? Fine." Then, "Now, Bill, half an inch that way. Now stop." Then, "OK, Goldie, we're ready now. You can scream."

A B :   *Would you describe in detail how you directed those long, long shots of those tremendous lines of police cars?*
s s :   It's like being accused of directing traffic. There is very little to directing automobiles; it's harder trying to direct Texas itself. For one thing, the landscape is flat as a pancake, and unless you're up very high, you lose everything after the 4th car and can't see the other 45. Many shots were made from a cherry picker, and in other shots I employed long lenses to compact the line of vehicles in one tight plane of action. There's a lot of wasted production value in having 45 patrol cars when you can only see the first 7 or 8 and the rest taper into the horizon line and vanish. So the long lens was an invaluable aid in making 45 cars look like 100.

Our two biggest helpers on *The Sugarland Express* were the 5-watt walkie-talkie and the Department of Public Safety. The Highway Patrol had to literally reroute traffic in some cases; at other times they had to block traffic 2 miles to the north and 2 miles to the south, leaving a mile clear for the shooting area. This meant that after take 1, in order to prepare for take 2, all 45 police cars had to turn around, go back a mile, turn around again, and then regroup. Then we had to sit on our rear-ends and wait while the Department of Public Safety (which is the Highway Patrol in Texas) and the officer in charge released the accumulated traffic which went anywhere from 10 pick-up trucks to 100 cars from the north and the same amount from the south—all angrily honking their horns because they had been sitting there twiddling their thumbs for 15 minutes. To sum up: per set-up, figure an hour and a half.

A B :   *Much of the dialogue in the film was by 2-way police radio. Did you choose this method because of the logistical problems or because you felt it would serve the story better than cross-cutting and the other techniques traditionally used to show parallel action?*
s s :   John Carter, who was the soundman on *The Sugarland Express,* rigged the non-working microphones in the police cars to a 5-watt walkie-talkie which enabled the actor to depress the button and talk into his microphone. Then under the floorboards and out of sight of the camera was the

actual speaker with Ben Johnson's response from a paralleling car. We had a 5-watt walkie-talkie in Johnson's car, another in car 2311 (the principal police car), and another in Mashburn's car. And this actually enabled us to transfer 2-, 3-, and 4-way conversations, which gave it a documentary feeling and a very natural, realistic look.

This also let you hear that great burst of squelch when you key a mike or take your thumb off a mike which you can't get when you artificially mix it on a dubbing stage. Had we not used the 2-way police radio method in dubbing, we would have had to filter the sound. If we were in 2311, you would have heard the questions unfiltered and the response from Ben Johnson in the paralleling car unfiltered through the pretend speaker. But this way I could sit in the dailies and see it as it really was.

AB: *There is a lot of night material in the film. What techniques did you use, and were any of those scenes particularly difficult?*
SS: All night-for-night sequences are difficult because of the time it takes to light the scene. We chose to go night-for-night because day-for-night is not convincing unless you're in the desert or on the ocean.

In order to shoot day-for-night in *The Sugarland Express,* we would have had to hot-light all the windows in neighboring structures with arcs, which would have been too costly. Besides, Vilmos doesn't carry big lights with him: he carries a few Xenons and inkies and uses the sun or the soft diffused light from overcast skies. Vilmos is a source artist, and he doesn't believe in using heavy conventional lighting apparatus.

At night, inside the police car, I came up with a crazy thought that Vilmos at first balked at because he thought it was too theatrical, but then he warmed to it and so we did it. That was the idea of putting a red and a green inkie under the dashboard pointed up at the face of Officer Slide, so every time he keys the microphone his face is bathed in red from an off-screen red light on the transmitter, and when he takes his finger off the microphone and receives, his face is bathed in green from the receiving signal light on the transmitter. This also worked for the two Louisiana hot jocks in the car-to-car sequence just before they go off into a John Ford sunset. And it worked again when the three principal characters were lounging at night and Clovis was playing with a flashlight, Lou Jean was sitting in a funny yoga position chewing bubblegum, and Slide was tired and trying to keep his eyes open.

A B : *The special effects in the used car lot sequence were very impressive. How did you plan the scene to get the most out of your effects?*

S S : I had the art department build a miniature used car lot from cardboard and match toys, and believe me, it's a hell of a lot simpler to shuffle around toys in a 6-foot layout than to try to move the real thing. Then from this mock-up I chose all of my angles, determined all of the squib hits, and choreographed the crossfire.

In the course of all of this, I decided to paint certain cars green on one side and red on the other, so two shot-up automobiles were actually one and the same. This also saved us a lot of money, because you saw 20 cars being punctured by gunfire when actually we only shot up 10.

Also, John Milius has had a great effect on me. I am a fan of his special effects, more particularly the unique Milius "ricochet shot." So I was determined to have a great show of force in the used car lot shoot-out and to make all of the squib hits much larger than they are in most movies. When a bullet punctures glass in *The Sugarland Express,* not only does the glass spiderweb, but the entire windshield is torn loose from its nuts and holders and goes flying across the lot. And when a tire is hit by a bullet, the whole tire blows up, the hubcap flies off, and the entire car settles in a plume of dust. I really wanted to make this scene among the most violent pyrotechnically; I wanted you to feel that the flying glass could do just as much harm to the characters as the actual velocity of the screaming bullets.

A B : *Was the close physical resemblance between Michael Sacks (Slide) and William Atherton (Clovis) intentional?*

S S : Yes, they were deliberately cast to resemble one another — if not closely in body, then at least in spirit and attitude. We wanted two actors cut from the same cloth, two characters who could have lived in the same neighborhood, grown up together, and then gone their separate ways — one into the police force and the other into holy wedlock with an irresponsible blonde bombshell.

A B : *What was the budget for* The Sugarland Express?

S S : $2 million 5 hundred thousand — which includes a Universal Studio overhead of 25%. The film was scheduled for 55 shooting days, and I went 60. I happily take blame for 3 of those 5 days, and the other 2 I'll pin on the weather, which was unpredictable and for the most part intractable.

AB: *Are there any techniques in particular which you feel contributed to the success of* The Sugarland Express?

SS: If there are, I don't want to be too conscious of them. I don't want to fall back and have to rely on old techniques that worked once so why not again. I don't want all of my movies to look the same. That's why I'm divorcing the automobile from my life. In *Jaws,* the picture I'm working on now, I've cut out virtually all of the automobiles. The local constable rides to work each morning on a bicycle.

AB: *Well, do you feel that the work you have done for television and the rigors of that medium—tight budgets and shooting schedules—have influenced your style with regard to composition or your frequent use of the moving camera?*

SS: If anything, it has expanded them. I've always resented the television medium even though it was through TV that I found an inroad to theatrical films. I've tried to play against the standard recipe of television techniques by shooting master scenes with little or no cut in the camera coverage and by rediscovering the tracking shot, a technique foreign to most veterans of the post-*Playhouse 90* years. I've tried to compose shots for the television screen.

And I shoot wider than most TV directors. I call a close-up any shot where the camera cuts the subject at the waist; TV calls a close-up anything where you can just see above the neck. On the other hand, I call it a choker when you can just see above the neck, but TV calls it a choker when all you can see is between the nose and the forehead line.

As for the tight schedules, they have enabled me to get away with a lot of murder. The executives are just happy that you made your 10 pages that day. Whether it's a broken-up sequence with heavy coverage or one wide tracking master angle—10 pages all in one shot.

AB: *You mentioned John Milius awhile ago. In interviewing him for the* News-letter *about* Dillinger *last year [Vol. 6, No. 12], he said that he sees directing as being somewhat like a general in charge of a battle: a matter of perfect strategy, logistics, timing, etc., and then being able to "wing it" successfully. What do you feel about that?*

SS: I agree that making a movie is like a scene of battle, but I like to think of it as more of a contest of personal physical endurance.

For me, principle photography is the loneliest part of the process. It's sort of like solving a mathematical equation: you go into a neutral corner and sweat it out until the divine revelation comes. Sometimes that never happens and you sit alone with five mediocre alternatives. That's when the production manager tells me to get off my ass. So directing is not like being a general at all; it's like being a first lieutenant: the general is the money man who's barking at you long distance from Puerto Vallarta.

A B : *Would it be accurate to say that you see yourself as an action director, in the same school as William Wellman, for example?*
s s : I'm not interested in being any one type of director. I love action; I love to grip an audience and watch them lean forward in their seats or flinch at a wreck or at something frightening. I like involving the audience on a level of total participation. But I think that can be done without bending fenders or blowing engines.

I'd love to do science fiction or a love story; I'd like to make a woman's picture because the motion picture industry has systematically shied away from the women's movie and there are few major roles in the works for the self-realized woman. Yet it's the women who shove their men into the movie theaters each weekend.

In the long run, action is sensational and I think one of the reasons a lot of directors fall back on the action motif is because they don't want to be bored during the three months of location filming. A laugh a minute or a stunt a minute is always very exciting. You know, controlling 100 cars, or Mike Nichols controlling 20 B-25's, or Stanley Kubrick sending thousands of French soldiers up the Anthill—it's a great feeling. There's something funny about the supercharged ego-drive of the action director. He wants to move mountains, not people.

A B : *What about the picture you are currently working on,* Jaws?
s s : *Jaws* is a horror story about the great white shark. Unlike the dolphin, it doesn't speak; it just chows down. But it's really a movie about our fear of the water. When you're out swimming and you turn to tread water, half of your body is under the surface and you can't keep tabs on what's happening down there around your feet. *Jaws* will scare the hell out of anyone who's ever swum in the ocean!

I wasn't involved in writing the initial four drafts. Peter Benchley, the author of the book, wrote the first three drafts and Howard Sackler wrote the fourth draft, and I've worked on the 5th, and Carl Gottlieb is now working with me on a day-to-day basis as we shoot. Here I don't have as stable a script as I had on *The Sugarland Express*. Right now I have a lot of good scenes strung together by a slender thread, four or five set pieces, and a sea-hunt that's a great third act topper and what originally attracted me to the book.

A B :   *There are several stories going around about how you got your first job. Would you care to tell us how it happened?*

S S :   Well, the story that's been circulating around town for the last 5 years is mostly true, even though it sounds mythological. It's the one about my crashing the gates at Universal, carrying a briefcase and wearing a suit and tie, finding an empty office, finding a vacant parking lot, and spending the next four or five months standing around on sets observing and taking notes, meeting directors and writers, making contacts and trying to find a toehold in the business.

But my first job had nothing to do with crashing the gates at Universal Studios. The first job came when Sid Sheinberg, who was president of television production at Universal at the time, saw a 24-minute short I had made called *Amblin'*. I made the short while I was a student at Cal State, Long Beach, but not as part of a film program at Cal State; it was done on my own with $15,000 from Dennis Hoffman, an independent producer.

When Sid Sheinberg saw it, he just said, very simply, "I'd like you to spend the next 7 years of your life here at Universal Studios. Along with that, you will be directing, writing, and producing. How would you like that? How does that sound?" Well, it sounded fine to me. There were no other jobs in the offing, and I had just turned twenty-one. It was a dream come true.

He immediately put me into a TV movie, a pilot trilogy called *Night Gallery*. I shot the second section with Joan Crawford, a 43-minute story written by Rod Serling. I didn't work for a year after the show came out.

A B :   *What advice would you give others attempting to get ahead in the commercial film industry?*

S S :   Do a lot of writing, try to make a short film or two, cut it yourself, also do the photography, and if you're a ham, star in it. But it's almost impossible to get work with none of your abilities showing. Studios aren't buying qualities like eagerness and enthusiasm and a willingness to learn. They want material evidence that you're a movie-maker who's going to turn a profit. They want to see and feel how good you are before they're going to give you $300,000 to make a movie.

I began by making 8 and 16mm films, some for $15 apiece and some for $200. You can't excuse yourself by saying, "Well, I can't raise the money to make the short film to get into the front door and show my work." It's not expensive to make little movies, even if they're in Super-8 and done with a Kodak Ektasound camera you've borrowed from a friend.

A B : *What, in your opinion, has been the major factor which helped you get where you are now?*
s s : Wanting it more than anything else.

Primal Scream:
An Interview with Steven Spielberg

RICHARD COMBS/1977

'PEOPLE ARE ALWAYS LOOKING for—I don't know what you'd call it—I guess, the cosmic entertainment. More than the meteorological explanation. From the behavioural science point of view, I was just as interested in finding out why people looked to the skies, and want to believe, as I was in looking to the skies myself, to try to understand what's happening up there, that the Air Force and the Government don't want to tell us about.'

After his tussle with the deep in *Jaws*, Steven Spielberg has turned his eyes heavenward, and the result, *Close Encounters of the Third Kind*, a contemporary story of 'science speculation' dealing with the UFO phenomenon, will be seen later this year. At the time this interview was recorded, one important scene remained to be shot, in Bombay, with François Truffaut (appearing for the first time in a film not directed by himself). 'The Indian scene is his, in a central plot twist. Without that scene, the Truffaut character doesn't make much sense.' About the scene or the character, however, Spielberg would say no more; security is still being maintained as tightly about the actual content of the movie, and the nature of its speculations, as it was during shooting around the unit's main base in Mobile, Alabama.

STEVEN SPIELBERG: We have quite a large set. The production designer showed me that the model he had built, and that I had subse-

From *Sight and Sound*, Spring 1977. Reprinted by permission.

quently fallen in love with, was four times larger than the largest sound stage at MGM or Cinecitta. And the only alternatives were to shoot it outside, where I'd have no control over the weather, and shoot at night which is very costly, or to find a dirigible hangar somewhere. I wanted to use Kubrick's hangar, until I found it has a lot of main beams running down the centre; and the only two available hangars were in Oregon and the one in Mobile. It's at a defunct and demilitarised Air Force base — there are weeds growing out of the tarmac. The entire base was cordoned off. We hired security police and built a small kiosk. And the two hangars that we used began to resemble motion picture studios. We had to administer picture IDs that were coded, so you couldn't go down to the local newspaper, fake one and try to get in that way. The *Washington Post* tried everything to get on to our set. Their reporter, who likened himself to Bob Woodward, decided that the best way to break our security was to interview some of the extras at night in bars, when they're loose and fancy-free, and then write his story in the first person, as though he had been there reporting the whole thing himself. It was printed, and it was the most erroneous, far-fetched encounter of the fifth kind I had ever read. But he made it sound even more intriguing to the general reader, because by not knowing what he was talking about, he wrote a very interesting story.

But despite the secrecy, your film is not dealing with the futuristic paraphernalia of 2001, for example?
It covers in spirit the thirty years of the UFO controversy, but in actual screen time it's a contemporary film. If you believe, it's science fact; if you don't believe, it's science fiction. I'm an agnostic between the two beliefs, so for me it's science speculation. It's not ten light years away, it's right in the heart of American suburbia.

Did the story come from any particular incident?
Nothing that ever happened to me. It was a compendium of research I had done. I read everything on the market, including the clippings from the *National Inquirer* and the wire services, and even tried to get into the Blue Book archives, long before the project was declassified, to no avail. I was mainly inspired when I began to meet people who had had experiences, and I realised that just about every fifth person I talked to had looked up at the sky at some point in their lives, and seen something that was not easy to explain. And then I began meeting people who had had close

encounters of the second kind, where undeniably something quite phenomenal was happening right before their eyes. It was this direct contact,
the interviews, that got me interested in making the movie. I interviewed
enough people to know that all of them could not possibly be lying. A lot
of the sightings people have at night are because they never look and are
just discovering the sky; so many reports are easy to explain astronomi-
cally, conventionally. There are other reports that are impossible to describe
conventionally, but the basic scientific community isn't ready to change
Einstein's rules.

And close encounters of the third kind?
That's when you meet them. It's much more outspoken in Europe than
it is in America, where there's a sort of hush-hush about these things that
go bump in the night. Somehow, in Brazil, in France, in Italy, throughout
South America, there's much more open-mindedness and a general acceptance—there's less scientific scepticism. In America, how can UFOs exist
over the sky when *Phyllis* and *Maud* and *All in the Family* are on television
at the same time? When do people go outside and look up any more?

Are there many reported instances of the third kind?
There have been hundreds. Betty and Barney Hill, the interracial couple
from New Hampshire, had that experience when they were taken aboard
a space craft. They were allegedly both given thorough physical examina-
tions, Betty communicated with some of the entities in the vehicle, and
then they forgot the entire episode completely. They spent two years having
a horrendous time with each other and their marriage, persistent nightmares. Then they went to a psychiatrist, and separately they were put
under hypnosis and were able to piece together what happened during
those three missing hours, when they suddenly noticed they were ninety
miles further down the road. There's a book on it by John C. Fuller called
The Interrupted Journey; it was also the basis of a television movie.

The contact was that Betty was shown a star map with a configuration
of broken lines and solid lines, and different points which she didn't attempt
to memorise but which she looked at very carefully. 'They' explained to
her that the broken lines were trade routes and the solid lines were expedi-
tionary routes, and under hypnosis she reproduced the map. When it was
published in this book in the mid-60s, no one could figure out what the
hell the map meant. And then three or four years later, four crucial stars

were discovered by our most advanced telescopes, and those stars completed Betty's map. They were able to find the exact duplicate of her map existing up there.

You mentioned the secretiveness of the government and the Air Force about UFOs. Does the film make any connection between the growing incidence of UFO sightings and feelings of political paranoia, a sort of science fiction version of The Parallax View?

It does and it doesn't. In a way, it shows the kind of Swiss precision of covert operations in the U.S. today, as they deal with campus unrest, and the Red menace, and also UFOs. It's all really part of the same thing. The government's position on UFOs has been covert and just very secretive over the last thirty years. They could have saved a lot of money by simply telling the public that they were experimenting with the SR 71, let's say, before it was put in the skies as our new supersonic spy plane. It would have been easy for the government to come right out and tell the public that the things you see in the night sky over your back yards are super-secret terrestrial vehicles being tested. But the government isn't saying things like that, and it's not willing to say things like that. The U.S. is a policy-ridden country, and in 1947, after Kenneth Arnold sees those twelve silvery discs—Arnold coined the term 'flying saucer'—the government sets a policy that this is not to be discussed among the scientific community or professional officers of the U.S. Air Force, and for thirty years, unless there's a directive from the White House that rescinds that order, people are going to follow it to the letter. It's just the nature, the structure of the U.S.

The Parallax View was the most paranoid movie I've ever seen, next to *Mickey One*. This movie's more like *The French Connection,* as brutally realistic within a dramatic story-telling structure. I think our film does to UFOs what *The French Connection* said about crime in the streets and narcotics and New York City. It's more of a movie than it is a film, really. It's quite entertaining and it's about people and not about events, but it's about people who are innocent until they are ensnared by the event, and then have to rise above it.

How did you work with Truffaut? Was language a problem?
He speaks English well enough to communicate, though he feels that he doesn't speak English as well as he'd like. He'd been taking some lessons

with his private instructor at the Berlitz School. So in our movie there are actually scenes where, while he sleeps in different motels across the country, he plays a tape-recording of this Berlitz lesson.

Truffaut was my first choice all along, but I didn't have the courage to phone him up and ask the great French director if he would be in this newcomer's movie. I put it off. I had a meeting with Lino Ventura; I didn't contact Trintignant but I expressed interest in him; I expressed interest in Philippe Noiret. After a while I decided that I really wanted François Truffaut, and the best thing to do was to call him up at home. He said yes for various reasons. I don't think particularly because he enjoyed or understood the script that well, but because the timing is right. He's preparing a book called *The Actor*, and he wanted to experience the hardships of waking up at six o'clock in the morning to stand around seven hours, to work under pressure the last hour and a half, for another director. And, my God, he sure learned fast.

Is a film like this completely preplanned?
In that respect it was exactly like *Jaws*. Every set-piece was sketched, I had hundreds of little drawings, I pre-cut the entire film and then shot it to cut later. There are moments with the people when they improvise and go beyond the script. Essentially I'm not a writer and I don't enjoy writing. I'd much rather collaborate. I need fresh ideas coming to me, because I can't send ideas out into space and expect them to return, I need them to bounce off something. So I locked myself away to write *Close Encounters of the Third Kind*, and when I came out I had a pretty good structure but I wasn't crazy about some of the characters. The actors helped me shake out the fat and get right down to what the scene was about—essentially the same thing I did on *Jaws*. We would find the theme of each scene, we would do improvisations about that theme (I had a tape-recorder running), then I'd quickly run to the typewriter, find the best lines, and rewrite the scene so that the next morning the actors had a written script based on some loose improvisations the night before.

Does that method create any problems with the producers of such expensive films?
For some strange reason I got away with murder on *Jaws*. They just left me alone. I changed the script every day, but I never received a telephone call from any of the powerful executives on the West Coast. I don't think any-

body was ever in love with any of the screenplays, and felt that the story and script could only be improved.

I chose to make a movie that would reach audiences really on two levels. The first level was a blow to the solar plexus, and the second was an uppercut, just under the nose; it was really a one-two you're out combination. I never intended anything deeper than that, because when I read the book I had a lot of fun, and when I began reworking the screenplay I had even more fun. And I really said, I'm going to make a primal scream movie.

One of the most interesting analyses of the movie was 'The Last Bastion of the Ecological Sergeant-at-Arms.' You've got man controlling the environment inland, building artificial lakes by blocking off natural dams, and suddenly you've got this sentry out in the ocean saying, stop, Mr. Cousteau, go no further. It's our turn to fight you. When I first got involved in the project, the thing that terrified me most was the idea that there's something else out there, that has a digestive system with intake; and the whole idea of being on somebody else's menu was just utterly horrifying. It was a horrifying thought to be part of a food chain. *Jaws* is a raw nerve movie, it's just baring your nerves and saying this is about the birth sac, you swim around in yourself.

That's why I like parts of *Duel* much better than I like parts of *Jaws*, because *Duel* was more daring. It was about a very unnatural occurrence, whereas *Jaws* is as natural as the evolution of mankind. *Duel* was much more of a challenge, because trying to create that kind of fear out of a truck is a lot harder than the established fear of a man-eating fish underwater. But *Duel* had a whole new set of rules.

Do you have a strong sense of the similarities between your films, of any kind of stylistic continuity?
I can certainly see a pattern and a similarity between *Duel* and *Jaws*, a similarity between *The Sugarland Express* and a film I'm about to begin. But as far as style within a body of work is concerned, I'm a little too subjective to have feelings about that. What I'm fighting is believing my own journalism, and just trying to form my own opinions about myself. I don't think I've made enough films to do that yet, and most of my films haven't been as personal as I think I am to myself.

The film-maker who really influenced me more than any other is John Frankenheimer. Not visually but as an editor. His editing often has more energy than the content of the story. When I saw *The Manchurian Candidate*, I realised for the first time what film editing was all about. After that, I made a number of 8mm films at home and began to experiment with cutting and juxtaposing scenes and tricks in the cutting room. I learned all the negative things, the things I try not to do in movies, from television. One thing I learned from TV was that there was nothing worse than a close-up that's from the chin to the forehead. I remember watching *Paths of Glory* and realising how few tight close-ups there were, but when Kubrick used a close-up it meant something.

I think *Badlands* and *Barry Lyndon* are very similar films in terms of starring the period and mood of the film, the way the film feels between your fingers, over what you tell your friends it's about. I like *Barry Lyndon*, but for me it was like going through the Prado without lunch. And when Terrence Malick's film was over, I really felt as though I was covered with dust and my hair was greasy and I felt like taking a shower. I'm just the opposite, I think, in terms of the films I'm making. Sometimes I'll completely forfeit style for content. That's why I feel that *Jaws* does not have a style. *Jaws* is all content, experiment. *Jaws* is almost like I'm directing the audience with an electric cattle prod. I have very mixed feelings about my work on that picture, and two or three pictures from now I'm going to be able to look back on it and see what I've done. I saw it again and realised it was the simplest movie I had ever seen in my life. It was just the essential moving, working parts of suspense and terror, with just enough character development that at one point in the movie you hate Scheider and you hate Shaw and you hate Dreyfuss, within the roles they're playing, and then you like them again.

We would get into these very deep conversations about everyone's motivation, and why they were born to fight the shark, and go out next morning and kiss their wives goodbye and duel with the deep. And then I saw the movie last week and realised that what we were talking about were the basic primitive instincts man has about things that he doesn't understand and is afraid of. We were talking about things that go bump in the night.

I could have made that a very subtle movie if I wanted to. I could have done a lot of things to make it much more appealing to the way I think at night as opposed to the way I think on a sound stage. I think in a way I'm two different people; my instincts always commandeer my sensibilities, or my intellect is always beaten down by my instincts.

Close Encounter with Steven Spielberg

MITCH TUCHMAN/1978

"THERE WERE SEVERAL WOMEN in—I believe it was—
Georgia," Steven Spielberg recounts, "who had a UFO encounter of the
first kind, where they saw a lighted vehicle passing low over their heads,
and written in lights along the starboard side were the letters *U, F, O.*

"Now 99.9 percent of the people who hear this story are going to say
here are two very misinformed individuals, who obviously made it up.
They were so naive about the phenomena, that that's what they thought,
that's what they reported seeing. In fact, an other-worldly intelligence has
come all this way perhaps to observe growing up in the twentieth century.
If they would like to deceive people as to their being here, then what better deception is it than to embrace the fantasy and kind of make an absurd
comment about how we view them by allowing us to see them in the same
way as we imagine. If they're smart enough to come all this way, they're
certainly smart enough to psych us out.

"I've heard encounter reports that I wouldn't give any credence to at all.
You can't take any report on face value. You have to consider who the person is who is telling you the story and their background and other stories
they might have told other people about other strange phenomena. But
there have been so many people that have come forward with stunning
encounter experiences that I just can't brush them aside.

"The ones I find convincing are not the third-kind encounters but the
second kind, the ones where physical evidence is left behind.

From *Film Comment,* January-February 1978. Reprinted by permission of the author.

"I've never had a close encounter of any kind—except with a $19,000,000 movie."

What is the kernel of truth in the legend of the boy sneaking onto the studio lot?
That is now the great popcorn yarn. Actually it's not apochryphal at all. I did sneak on the Universal lot—it was 1967—and I spent three unauthorized months looking at other directors working in television.

How did you do that?
I just walked on the lot. There was all sorts of pedestrian traffic going to and from the main gate during lunch hours and early morning. I would get up at the crack of dawn, wear a suit, and carry a briefcase, and for some reason Scotty at the gate waved me through each day. I just assumed that people assumed I was somebody's son, one of the executives in the Black Tower. So that's a true story: I found an office and moved in.
   But actually it was a cul-de-sac experiment for me, because, once in, I discovered nobody really wanted anything I had to offer, that it was still a middle-aged man's profession. The only young people on the lot were actors. It was just the beginning of the youth renaissance.

Do you think you're one cause of that renaissance?
I'm not a cause, but I think I'm among the maybe five or ten individuals that helped prime the engine.

Is there any kind of community among those individuals?
There is now; there wasn't then. I didn't know anybody then except George Lucas—and I only met George at a USC retrospective of all the student projects of that year. I knew John Milius very early, because John was in that USC group. Just a year down the line from them I met Hal Barwood and Matthew Robbins. Matthew was AFI, and Barwood was USC. Coppola at that time was my shining star, because here was a student from UCLA, who was writing professionally, who was making a living from his writing, and just starting out as a director with Roger Corman, I think about '67 or '68. So, in a way Francis was the first inspiration to a lot of young filmmakers, because he broke through before many others.

What's the nature of the community? Do you see each other? Do you talk about your films?

We see each other when it's convenient and we exchange screenplays, make comments on each other's rough cuts. Hal Barwood and Matthew Robbins just did their first feature. I think we probably saw it before the MGM people saw it. I've seen it twice now. There's Hal, Matthew, and Rob Cohen—he's a producer, probably the only young generation producing successfully working today—and there's John Milius and George Lucas and Brian De Palma and Bill Huyck, Phil Kaufman, Mike Ritchie, and Marcia Lucas. We spent a lot of time gossiping, speculating what the business is going to be like twenty years from now: will there *be* a business twenty years from now?

Will there be a business twenty years from now?
I think there will be, yes.

You have been quoted as doubting the influence of particular filmmakers on your career. If not filmmakers, what were some of the resources upon which you could draw? I have no sense of your being one of those kids who haunted Saturday matinees.
Not at all. As a matter of fact, I was one of those kids whose parents said stay away from movies. My parents rationed television and motion pictures. I could only see films in their presence and usually pictures that appealed more to them, which today you would call of the General Audience nature, like Danny Kaye pictures, like musicals, like *The Court Jester, Funny Face* with Audrey Hepburn, and Disney films. I remember the first film I ever saw was *The Greatest Show on Earth* by C. B. DeMille, and everything after that happened to be a Disney cartoon or a Disney adventure. Television to me was Imogene Coca, Sid Caesar, Soupy Sales and *The Honeymooners*. In Phoenix, Arizona, television never really carried very good movies. They kept showing *The Atomic Kid* with Mickey Rooney four times a week. So that probably was the only way I was influenced in that sense. We didn't have a good art house where I could see a Preston Sturges retrospective or Frank Capra films. TV stopped at 10:30 at night, and the test pattern wasn't that compelling.

So your notion of movies was not imitation of idols.
No, no, not at all. It wasn't until I was professionally making films that I began to see some of the old pictures and have my own renaissance in film appreciation.

Were you the kid who really wanted "to practice his violin," who wanted to be making his movies instead of doing the other things kids do?
Some kids get involved in a Little League team or in music, in band—or watching TV. I was always drowning in little home movies. That's all I did when I was growing up. That was my escape.

How many little home movies were there?
About fifteen or twenty 8mm films before I ever did a 16mm film, and long before I ever shot *Amblin'* in 35.

Do you still have all those little films?
I have most of them. I looked at a few of them not too long ago.

And what was your feeling about them? Were they recognizably Spielberg films?
They were recognizably home movies with youngsters in cowboy hats and German combat helmets. It was a joke to see them today. What surprised me was there was technique in some of the earliest films, the fast cutting.

Did you play all the parts behind the camera?
I did everything, including act.

Is it too soon for a retrospective look at your career?
Oh, sure it is, unless you take into consideration eleven television shows, including three TV movies. It's hard to discuss somebody's who's only made three feature films. I'm always asked to talk about myself, and it's hard to do that, because my perspective is I'm only 100 yards from the starting line. It's like I'm running the 880, and I've just gotten out of the blocks.

It's very hard for me to comment about my own style, because I don't see it yet. I read so many conflicting things about it. Nobody seems to agree. Nobody has seen the same thing, least of all myself.

There's an existential style that people comment about, but it's not a technical style.

What does that mean?
Just that people have drawn the conclusion that because most of my films are about concepts, I make concept movies—as opposed to films where

the story starts with the individual's emotional problems and blossoms from there. The story starts with a broader concept, and the people join the concept. The concept is the engine, and the people are the coal tender. Because most of my pictures aren't concept-oriented it isn't necessarily the case that they haven't grown out of personal dilemmas or my own personal center.

I thought of the concept as the menace—although the mothership in Close Encounters *isn't menacing. Your characters play against something that has no motivation, or, at least, we have no way of figuring it out. Why it is doing it is not the important point.*
I think it's like life. A lot of things happen to you during your lifetime that simply offer no logical explanations. Television has certainly always taught us easy answers, easy solutions, everything has a *raison d'être*—and, you know, life isn't like that. I love movies where there are no rules.

Have there been concepts you've toyed with and rejected as subjects for films?
Yes, certainly. (But not really.) Invasion has always been a favorite subject. I'm talking about homeland invasion, total occupation. It's the oldest subject in the world. Steinbeck's *The Moon Is Down*. Actually I'm not really that preoccupied with being the spokesman for the paranoid Seventies, because I'm not really that paranoid in real life.

I designed the graphic for *Close Encounters:* the idea of a highway tapering off to the vanishing point with something waiting on the other side. I think that most of the movies I've made have been movies where a journey is involved. The goal is always in sight in the first act. A lot of my films are question-answer pictures leading up to an inevitable conclusion that the audience is waiting for, and hopefully they won't be disappointed. I think every movie I've made promises an arrival zone, and it's just a kind of drama that intrigues me.

Could you summarize over your career to what degree you have initiated projects, or, in cases where things were assigned to you, to what degree you have been able to make them your own?
Amblin' I initiated entirely. That was an original story. I wrote the script, cut it myself, and did just about everything except the music and photography.

Amblin' was an attack of crass commercialism. I had made a lot of little films in 16mm that were getting me nowhere. They were very esoteric. I wanted to shoot something that could prove to people who finance movies that I could certainly look like a professional moviemaker. *Amblin'* was a conscious effort to break into the business and become successful by proving to people I could move a camera and compose nicely and deal with lighting and performances.

The only challenge that's close to my heart about *Amblin'* is I was able to tell a story about a boy and a girl with no dialogue. That was something I set out to do before I found out I couldn't afford sound even if I wanted it.

How do you feel about the picture now?
Oh, I can't look at it now. It really proved how apathetic I was during the Sixties. When I look back at that film, I can easily say, "No wonder I didn't go to Kent State," or "No wonder I didn't go to Vietnam or I wasn't protesting when all my friends were carrying signs and getting clubbed in Century City." I was off making movies, and *Amblin'* is the slick by-product of a kid immersed up to his nose in film.

What is the correct order of your TV credits?
Night Gallery, Marcus Welby, The Psychiatrists, Name of the Game, Owen Marshall, Columbo, then the TV movies *Duel, Something Evil,* and *Savage.*

How much do you want to talk about those?
The *Night Gallery* episode was something that was assigned to me. I didn't initiate that at all. It was assigned on the basis of "You've just turned twenty-one. You want to be a professional director? Here's a show. Go, direct it."

Do you feel that any of the episodes you did can say this is characteristically a Spielberg film?
Maybe *Columbo* and *The Psychiatrists.* I did my best work with actors in *The Psychiatrists.* It was very interesting. What I liked about that was I was able to cause input in the writing of it. Jerry Friedman was the producer. He had his own longhair film society right in the heart of Universal Studios. He employed a number of writers, directors, people dealing with esoterica, and he hired people from his college and people he knew from the East.

I was just a young person, whom he liked at the time, and to whom he said, "Here, do two *Psychiatrists* for me."

Jerry, in a way, really gave me my best material. I did a show about death, and I did a show about a little six-year-old boy lost in a world of fantasy and comic books. They were so opposite to each other, and I did them back to back, and I was able to really have a lot of input into the writing of the shows. So it was a real challenge.

Actually I think my best work in television was the second *Psychiatrists* I did. It was the first time since my 8mm days when I could have an idea at nine o'clock in the morning and incorporate that idea into the show at two o'clock in the afternoon. In the show Clu Gulager is dying of duodenal cancer. He was on the PGA circuit as one of the top golf pros. He's lying in his hospital bed, and two of his golf partners come to visit him. As it was written, they're so uncomfortable: Gulager has faced his death many times, but these two men can't face it along with him. They can't share his acceptance, and eventually they have to leave.

I thought it would be very moving—it was just an idea I had in the morning—if these two golf partners went out to the eighteenth hole with a shovel and dug out the entire eighteenth hole, put it in a shoe box, stuck in the flag, brought it to the hospital room, and laid this thing on him. So in the scene he gets the gift, opens it up, and here's the dirt and the grass and the flag. It was wonderful. Clu began to cry—as a person and as an actor. His immediate response when the camera was rolling was to burst into tears. He tore the grass out of the hole and he squeezed the dirt all over himself and he thanked them for bringing him this gift, the greatest gift he had ever received. It was just a very moving moment that came out of being loose with an idea. Everything didn't have to be locked down because of so many hours in the day and so much film in the camera and so much money in the budget. You could do more things like that and make a film grow and make characters come to life more.

It's easy to be overwhelmed by sequences in your films, with you as an orchestrator of enormous effects.
Each of my movies has showed enough humanity to allow the audience to identify with the person who is having the experience. I haven't made my *It's a Wonderful Life*. I haven't done that yet. I will some day. But in the meantime I wouldn't be satisfied with my films if there weren't

human beings functioning as your guide through this world of mechanized madness.

How do you accomplish that?
Just by placing myself, Steve Spielberg, in the situation and saying, "What would I do?" One day I was thinking of a way to get at Quint, the Robert Shaw character in *Jaws:* if I were Hooper, how would I get back at Quint? And I made up the gag where Richard Dreyfuss squeezes the styrofoam cup in response to Robert Shaw's drinking the Naragansatt Beer and squeezing the tin and throwing it overboard.

Or just projecting how I felt and improvising a scene that wasn't in the script between Roy Scheider and his son, where Roy is wallowing in self-pity, and the little boy is imitating his every move, his every expression. Roy notices his son imitating him, and they exchange with each other a soft moment. It's little things like that that I'm able to interject in terms of humanizing my movies.

Those things happen as improvisations as opposed to things you write out?
Those are improvisations within the rigid structure of how the film must work and behave. I'm almost at my most improvisatory when I've planned most thoroughly, when my story-boards are in continuity. That gives me confidence to ad lib. I sort of lose my confidence when I haven't done my homework, and I haven't planned ahead a number of weeks. I'm basically very loose when it comes to working with actors in a nonlogistical setting. But within an action sequence or within a climactic arrangement of scenes, I pretty much stick to what I've visualized months before. Then when I improvise, I improvise around the planned stuff.

With *Close Encounters,* believe it or not, a lot of the human stuff was on the paper. All the paper does for me is it shows me that I'm going to be wide here for an emotional reason; I'm going to be tight in this angle for an emotional reason. Everything is for an emotional reason; it's not really a mechanical reason at all. I mean that's what all film is: all the prismatic images in a motion picture are solicitous of a visceral response from people who are looking at the overall movie.

Before moving on to the TV features, are there other things to be said about Name of the Game or...

My segment of *Name of the Game* I didn't originate, but I came in very early when Philip Wylie had just written his screenplay. I became involved in the project with Dean Hargrove. Dean actually did most of the writing on it.

How about Columbo?
The *Columbo* was fun, because *Columbo* was an experience in helping, but mostly watching Peter Falk find this terrific character. They had made two TV movies about Columbo before this, but mine was the first episode of the series, and Peter was still finding things. I was able to discover "Columbo-isms" along with Peter that he's kept in his repertoire.

And Owen Marshall?
The *Owen Marshall* was just an assignment.

I understand at the time Duel *was made, the production board was quite extra-ordinary.*
It was really neat. It was huge. It was forty yards long, and it was five feet tall. It was a mural of the movie.

Till then TV movies were shot like one-hour episodes of series. An assistant direc-tor ordinarily would have done the truck shots. Was this board more a studio tactic than an artistic necessity?
I don't think so. I did it at first as a kind of visual overview for myself, because the script was so verbose—well-written—verbose in terms of descriptions. I finally had to break the script down and visualize the entire movie on a road stretched all around the production office. I divided up each key moment and gave it a nickname and was able to walk the net-work people through the entire story, so they could more easily see what *Duel* was about.

Had they ever seen anything like it before?
Never.

How did they react?
I think quite well. It was certainly unique. They had never seen a map of a movie.

Is there any chance that without having done that, you would not have been able to shoot the way you wanted to?
No. It helped me also to plan my two- and three-camera set-ups. I think without that overview I would be a little confused about where to put the cameras, and I shot it in sixteen days. It was really a movie that should have been done in fifty days, and the only reason I did it in sixteen days was I could look at a sequence where the car passes the truck, the truck passes the car, and the car passes a truck, and I grabbed that entire scene like a documentary with three cameras all in one.

After *Duel* came out on television, that first week, my agent received ten or fifteen feature film offers.

All through Universal?
No, various studios. Warner Brothers and United Artists and Fox.

Could you work only for Universal?
Unless they'd loan me out. It was when I was still under an exclusive, seven-year contract, and the time had not expired on my time clock.

Now, *Something Evil* was something I wanted to do.

But that was not Universal.
No, that was CBS. They let me out for that. Universal had nothing for me and rather than watch me sit in my office and kill time, they said, "Go ahead."

Savage was an assignment bordering on *force majeur*. *Savage* was the first and last time the studio ordered me to do something.

The one thing that came to me that I almost made was *White Lightning*, the Burt Reynolds' picture. I spent two-and-a-half months on the film, met Burt once, found most of the locations and began to cast the movie, until I realized it wasn't something that I wanted to do for a first film. I didn't want to start my career as a hard-hat, journeyman director. I wanted to do something that was a little more personal. So I "ankled"—to use a Hollywood term—I ankled *White Lightning* and went to *Sugarland Express*. I had done *Duel, Something Evil,* and *Savage,* and then decided I would direct *White Lightning* that same year. Three months later I decided against directing *White Lightning* and found the *Sugarland Express* story and developed that instead.

It seemed there were three challenges in Sugarland Express: *the changing rela-tionships among the trio in the car, the nature of "the chase," and how to handle the digressions.*

That's the one film that I can honestly say, if I had to do all over again I'd make *Sugarland Express* in a completely different fashion. The first half of the movie I would have played out the hand of Captain Tanner [Ben Johnson]. I would have drawn the whole first half of the film from his vantage point: from behind the police barricades, from inside his patrol cruiser. I would never see the fugitive kids, only hear their voices over the police radio, maybe see three heads in the distance through binoculars.

Why is that?

Because I don't think the authorities got a fair shake in *Sugarland* to know really why they were . . . why the posse formed, why there was an over-whelming amount of vigilante activity and freestyle heroism, and why Capt. Tanner finally had to make the decision to put an end to this by destroying the characters in the car through force and violence. Capt. Tanner's decision is for me much too weak and unmotivated right now. I would spend the whole first half of the movie getting to know this man, his history, how he became a Texas Ranger, why he valued human life so.

Why didn't you do it that way?

I don't know. I'm just telling you in 20-20 hindsight. Probably, through the other police, I would have given a very biased vivisection of the people in that car. We would have seen them as petty criminals with loose morals and no motivation, and we would have sort of seen through Capt. Tanner's eyes, as far as he was concerned, these kids weren't just kids, but had a gun and had a law officer in the car with both hands in the air.

Then the second half of the movie I would have told the entire story inside the car and how really naive and backwoodsy these people are and how frivolous and really stupid their goals were, how naive their goals were. I would have then, in the second half of the movie, created an under-standing of this camaraderie, this triumvirate relationship inside the automobile with the cop becoming nothing less than an accomplice.

I would have spent the second half of the movie doing that, and then for the last ten minutes nothing would change.

The baby is irrelevant.

The baby *is* irrelevant. It really becomes a story of any rock 'n roll group who achieves overnight success and can't handle it.

Two themes seem consistently present in your movies: spectacle and exploitation. They are there in Sugarland, Jaws, *and in* Close Encounters. *The microphone and the cameraman and the crowd.*

I'm always interested in the way the media can determine the outcome of a public event. Ever since I began following the seven-o'clock evening news, I've watched the complete commercialization of news programming all across the country. I think it began in media centers and then branched out successfully into the smaller towns. *Network* certainly makes the point better than I ever could.

You say there's a kind of "arrival zone" in your pictures. I wonder how much of some of your stories actually pay off there? For instance, the class antagonism between Quint and Hooper, how does that pay off in the actual killing of the shark?

Basically it pays off in teaching Hooper a lesson, because Quint is right. Hooper was wrong. The greatest product of man's technology could not kill the shark. What killed the shark was cunning and resourcefulness on the part of the least qualified in that trio.

You've surely heard the Fidel Castro comment that Jaws *shows just how far capitalists will go — to the point of killing — in order to protect an investment.*

Wonderful! That's the whole "enemy of the people" question.

But that question of closing the beach is finished before you get on the boat. It has no payoff in the climax of the film.

When I was constructing a screen version of the book, I felt I needed more than the embattled class position among these three guys to sustain a movie, to keep your interest up the entire way. So, in a way, it was sort of like cooking an omelet: I wanted a little bit of ham, a little bit of cheese, and I wanted some onion.

But when you get to the end, the ham, cheese, and onions are gone, and you end up with scrambled eggs.

That's terrific.

You want it that way?

What I think I wound up with was exactly what I went for. There were certain questions about *Jaws* that had to be answered before the final blows. There was that whole opening and closing of the beach issue, which became academic once the shark attacked on the Fourth of July. So that paid off. There was more than one climax in *Jaws*. There were several payoffs. The first act proved it was indeed a shark out there. The second act proved the mayor wrong, the beleaguered police chief right. And the third act was basically a man-against-beast tale. It could be called a celebration of man's constant triumph over nature—not necessarily for the good.

Jaws wasn't the story of the mayor, and I didn't want to spend one more minute on the mayor's problem. The mayor was a device to shore up the movie's mid-section. When he said we must open the beaches, the audience tenses—it's shark time! (I never liked the mayor's story from the original, Peter Benchley novel.)

How about in Close Encounters, *the question of the Army's control of knowledge?*

I think the Army's knowledge and the ensuing coverup is so subterranean that it would take an entire screen story, perhaps a sequel or perhaps a "prequel" or perhaps somebody else making a picture and giving it the equal time it deserves. I was just torn between suggesting a wide-spread coverup and concentrating most of my efforts on this meeting of the minds.

Maybe the end isn't the place where all things have to be concluded.

I don't think in any of my films the end answers all the questions. I think in everything I've done, including *Sugarland,* each act has a climax, so that the final act probably answers the most cosmic question but not everything.

Why? Why spoonfeed? Why set out a buffet? So the audience can walk out of the theater knowing more than they did coming in—especially when you're dealing with an enigma like UFOs? I don't have all the answers, and I didn't want to pretend that I knew the answers. There were questions that needed answering. How does the music translate into English? During the musical exchange, what are they saying to each other? What does it mean in basic "Dick, Jane, and Sally"? I didn't want to preach. I didn't want to stand there at the end of *Close Encounters* and say, "Here's what they said to each other." I'm happy to know they said, "Hello." It's a movie for people who like to use their imaginations. It's not a film for people who will fold their arms and say, "Prove it." I can't prove it. Nobody can prove it. I really don't know if anybody wants to prove it today, but we all want to know that we're not alone.

Would you comment on "the Spielberg blonde"?
That's funny, because I've never really had a blonde in my life. Most of my girlfriends have had dark hair.

It's not the Jewish boy and the Gentile girl?
Maybe that has a lot to do with it. Maybe I've been searching for the ultimate *shiksa*.

Richard Dreyfuss. Why Richard Dreyfuss?
Richard's so wound up in a kind of kinetic energy. He's as close an actor to Spencer Tracy as exists today. I also think he represents the underdog in all of us.

Why is that good for the central character in your films?
Because he is a lot like Everyman at the same time. Richard's easier to identify with than, let's say, Robert Redford. Most of us are like Richard Dreyfuss. Few of us are like Bob Redford or Steve McQueen. I've always believed in the movies I've made, my central protagonist has always been—and probably always will be—Mr. Everyday Regular Fella.

I want to ask you about the quality of particular collaborations, especially John Williams and Verna Fields.
All the editors I work with are just sort of completing my vision. I'm stopping the moviola on a signal frame and saying, "Mark here." Sometimes they rework a sequence that I've carefully planned, and it's better than the plan. But I'm a real stickler for having things my way. Johnny Williams I have very little control over, except we listen to music together and I'll show him my film and try to talk it through and give him a sense of my taste in musical atmospheres. But once Johnny sits down at the piano, it's his movie, it's his score. It's his original overdraft, a super-imposition.

The "sky tones" are part of the story in Close Encounters.
Yes, they're part of the story. That was in collaboration with Johnny.
Johnny was involved in this project two-and-a-half years ago. Even before
he wrote the score for *Jaws,* we were having meetings about *Close Encounters.*
We're very close friends, and I'm so involved with music anyway. I wanted
more of a mathematical, musical communication than a "Take Me to Your
Leader."

His motif makes it possible to use music in place of the shark, too.
Had it not been french horns, it would have been something else, but
there was going to be a shark theme. That was something we determined
a long time ago, with an "out to sea" theme, a Quint theme, a "preparing
for battle" motif, and a victory march.

*Were you saving the shark? That bit of wharf that goes out into the water, then
turns around and comes back is terrific.*
I think a) it's more challenging and more fun to disguise the menace, and
b) I think that the collective audience has a better, broader imagination
than I do. They fill in the spaces between the lines. They saw a much more
horrific shark in their heads when I suggested an occurrence below the surface than I provided with the rubber shark when my commercial
sensibilities told me I had to make it visible.

   Johnny is an asset, and so is Joe Alves. Joe Alves, who was the art director
on *Encounters* and *Jaws* and also *Sugarland,* has made major contributions,
not only to the look of the picture, but to the story. He's been a real ally
and sounding board.

How about the writers? Do you now have any preference for writing yourself?
No, the only reason I wrote *Close Encounters* was I couldn't find anybody
who would write it the way I wanted it. Everybody wanted to make it
much more of a James Bond adventure. Either that or the other side: too
personal, too cloistered, with nothing really ever happening, getting into
why a man's life comes apart. It was either all family or all UFOs. Nobody
wanted to do both. I prefer working with other writers, because I get my
best ideas when I'm talking out loud. It's nice to have a collaborator.
Johnny Williams was my collaborator for *Close Encounters,* as was Michael
Kahn, the film editor. Hal Barwood and Matthew Robbins have been the
collaborators on every movie I've made including *Close Encounters.*

I wonder to what degree you see yourself being shaped into a businessman if that's something apart from being a filmmaker.

I find myself having to fight for my own ideas nowadays, not so much with a creative collaborator but with boards of directors, bankers.

Are you able to hold your own as well?

I'm able to hold my own in that, because it's the coming thing. It's things to come. Banks, individual businessmen, whole countries are backing motion pictures today. It's more Madison Avenue conferences than Brown Derby luncheons.

Have you less freedom and power or more?

I think certainly there's much more freedom and power today. The people who are financing movies aren't necessarily creative, nor do they want to be. They're happy with their oil wells and their Wall Street dealings, and they just want to make sure that you're going to be responsible with the money they give you and that you're not going to come back for more every three or four months—which you invariably do anyway.

When it comes down to what you put in front of the camera, do they care much?

No, hardly at all. What they care about is the finished product. But still there is a board of directors, and on *Close Encounters* I had to meet with the treasurer of Columbia many times. I had to meet with each member of the board individually on occasion. We had them down on the set in Mobile, Alabama, looking at our supersets. The financiers still want to hear it right from the director's mouth, not from the producer's.

I think of the powerful filmmaker as a metaphor for freedom. In the days of Dr. Zhivago and Ryan's Daughter, people looked at David Lean with respect out of all proportion to his talent. What you've got is not increasing freedom but a slightly different kind of bondage.

There's still a great measure of diplomacy. I hope I'll always be diplomatic. I hope I'll never have a temper tantrum on the set, throw things down, and say, "I can't work in this setting," or walk out of a meeting because a banker won't put up and wants me to shut up. I hope I can still deal with people as people and not as slot machines. Anybody who's had as much responsibility as I've had the last two films *has* to be a businessman. He can't avoid it.

Marcia Seligson's profile of you in New West *noted that the responsibility connected with* Close Encounters *had left you with no fingernails. I remember you when you were making* Sugarland Express. *You've* never *had any fingernails.*
Marcia's wrong. I've been biting my fingernails since I was four. I don't drink. I don't smoke, I don't take drugs. All I do is bite my fingernails. It's my only vice. Journalists go for effects just like filmmakers.

Are you ready to begin another project?
I just don't have the energy or the resolve to jump right into another movie. I don't have the heart for it.

Do you have *another project?*
I do. I have several, but I just don't have the heart for it this year, '77, or part of '78, because I'm really tired. Executive producing a film like *I Want to Hold Your Hand* is kind of like backing your car into a tow truck and getting your battery recharged. I feel when this is over I'm going to be so restless, I'm going to want to jump right back on a sound stage. But right now I'm basically exhausted.

Is it true you're working with George Lucas on a project?
Lucas and I are planning to do a movie together that he'll produce and I'll direct, and we'll both probably wind up rewriting whoever we hire. But that's in the future.

Let me ask you about I Want to Hold Your Hand. *It's almost a remake of the Steven Spielberg story with your giving Bob Zemekis the break you had.*
That's really the truth. It's not that I'm being philanthropic about it. I've known Bob for several years, and I've liked his films for several years. He's made some shorts that I really admire. It was just a matter of time that Bob would write a script that could be done for a reasonable price where I would want to step in and produce it so he could direct it. It's that simple.

Do you aspire to being a producer?

No, not at all. This is an exception. What I hope won't come from this are another twenty scripts a week from people who want to be Bob Zemekis and want me to be the godfather.

Is that happening?

It happened the last four years without my giving the break to Bob. It happened when Sid Sheinberg gave me my first start. I got scripts saying, "Don't you feel it's your turn to share some of the wealth?"

And what is your response?

My response is that I'm not in the studio executive business. I'm still trying to make a career for myself. I'm still fighting so I can be good in my eyes. When I'm good in my eyes I might even quit. I don't see that happening for years. I haven't satisfied myself with a film yet. I haven't made a film that I think is great.

Jaws, Sugarland Express, and *Close Encounters of the Third Kind* are not the films I could have made five years from now and hopefully as you get deeper in life and deeper in values . . . as I find myself caring more for people, the people around me, the people whom I love, my family, I find my films get much more personal, much more emotional, and I think that I'll be a good filmmaker when I eventually can make that turn and deal with that material and start with a personal problem and let the personal problem create the excitement.

The Mind Behind *Close Encounters* *of the Third Kind*

STEVE POSTER/1978

POSTER: *We both grew up in the television age. How did this influence you specifically?*

SPIELBERG: It really didn't have any influence on me at all, as far as cinematic junk food was concerned. My parents wouldn't let me watch television until embarrassingly late in life. (I won't mention how late in life because I wouldn't want you to know how long I was at home with my mother and father.) But my parents censored all television. To get to watch *The Honeymooners* meant that the kids—my three sisters and myself—had been good all week. So we were given an hour or so—a kind of recess—to watch TV. The TV set was always this big taboo piece of furniture in the living room that I would sneak down and watch when the babysitter was there and my parents had gone out to a party. I really can't say that the video medium stimulated me to copy or emulate or become involved in it. I had no idea that I would eventually get started in TV—but I got started in a whole different way.

POSTER: *Then how did your interest in movies first develop?*

SPIELBERG: It developed because my father would take a lot of home movies on our camping trips. I had an outdoorsy family and we would spend three-day weekends on outings in sleeping bags in the middle of the wilderness up in the White Mountains of Arizona. My dad would take the camera along and film the trips and we'd sit down and watch the footage a week later. It would put me right to sleep.

From *American Cinematographer*, February 1978. Reprinted by permission.

POSTER: *But how did you actually get started making films?*

SPIELBERG: Well, I'd take the camera and kind of heighten the reality of the field trip. I'd make my parents let me out of the car so I could run up ahead 200 yards. Then I'd wave them forward and they'd pull up and get out of the car and start unpacking. I began to actually stage the camping trips and later cut the bad footage out. Sometimes I would just have fun and shoot two frames of this and three frames of that and ten frames of something else, and it got to the point where the documentaries were more surrealistic than factual.

POSTER: *You're now an avid film fan. When did you first get that avid?*

SPIELBERG: I became a film fan after I became involved in the movie business. It was only after I began making films myself that I'd go to the Nuart Theater in Los Angeles and rediscover movies that friends of mine who had been into film history for a much longer time knew all about. I was 17 or 18 years old—which is relatively late, because nowadays kids 13 and 14 years old know all about Fellini and Antonioni.

POSTER: *So your first experience was really just playing with home movies of the family?*

SPIELBERG: That and the fact that I was a Boy Scout who wanted to get a merit badge in photography. The prerequisite was that you had to tell a story with still photos. Rather than shoot stills, I took my movie camera and made a little Western three minutes long, using friends of mine from the same Boy Scout troop. I cut the film in the camera (didn't do any splicing when I got home) and showed it to the Boy Scouts about a week later. Not only did I get my merit badge, but I got whoops and screams and applause and everything else that made me want it more and more. That was sort of the raw beginning.

POSTER: *Then that first success inspired you to make more films?*

SPIELBERG: It influenced me enough to want to go off and make another Western seven minutes long—using two rolls of film. It was a little more sophisticated. I discovered the editing tool. I discovered the wet and dry splice. My F&B/Ceco, my Birns & Sawyer were all the local camera store in Scottsdale, Arizona.

POSTER: *When you first got started, where did your ideas for scripts come from?*

SPIELBERG: They came right out of my ears, really. I mean, I wasn't a movie recluse. I had seen a number of films that my parents would take me to—mostly Walt Disney—so I had some idea of what a movie was. The first one I ever saw was C.B. DeMille's *The Greatest Show on Earth,* and I guess, in a way, I tried to emulate at that stage some of the techniques I'd come to appreciate. But really, it was more gut instinct that anything else. I made a war film next called *Fighter Squadron,* because I was inspired by those 8mm Castle Films capsule documentaries of the Forties. They were in black-and-white and they had great gun camera shots of tracer bullets flying out and Messerschmidts catching fire and plunging to earth and tanks and trains exploding. I'd buy seven or eight of those films and pull out all the exciting shots and write a movie around them. The film stocks didn't match, so you could always tell when I was cutting to an actual stock shot. The overall tint would change radically.

POSTER: *Where did you get your actors from?*
SPIELBERG: I used young people in the neighborhood, friends of mine from school. If I needed a shot of a young flyer pulling back on the stick of a P-51, we'd go out to the Skyharbor Airport in Phoenix, climb into a P-51 (after our parents got us permission), and I'd shoot a closeup of the stick being pulled back. Then I'd cut to a piece of stock footage of the airplane going into a climb. Then I'd cut back to a closeup of this 14-year-old friend of mine grinning sadistically. Then another closeup of his thumb hitting the button. Then another stock shot of the gun mounts firing. I'd put the whole thing together that way.

POSTER: *So you really created a lot of your own footage.*
SPIELBERG: And a lot of my own technique, also. I remember doing things at 16 that I was later surprised to see being done in 35mm in the movie theater. I don't believe anything to be original. I didn't really invent anything, but I remember doing flash cuts long before *A Man and a Woman* came out.

POSTER: *Did you actually write your scripts out or just make them up as you went along?*
SPIELBERG: Most of my scripts were written on the backs of graded arithmetic papers, in loose-leaf notebooks, anywhere I could find something to write on. Most of the time I would write the scripts, commit them

to memory and then tell the people what to do. It wasn't until much, much later that I would sit down at a typewriter, write a shooting script, make Xerox copies and hand them out. But it was one of the best lessons I ever learned. I learned to keep a film in my head, then dole out what was needed to be told to the people who were performing and who were the technicians.

POSTER: *At that point, who were your cast and crew?*
SPIELBERG: Just youngsters my own age who went to the same school and had nothing to do on Saturdays—just like me. All the guys who discovered girls early never had anything to do with my movies. The guys who were dating at 12 and 13 thought making movies was kid stuff, and so most of the friends I had helping me on those films were the late-starters in life. Someday I'll have a late-starters reunion to see how happily married they are, as compared to the jocks and others who had no time for us. I just had lunch with two of my old high school friends who were late-starters and they were telling me that all the jocks and heavy-hitters in high school are now divorced and miserable... and cops.

POSTER: *What kind of movie equipment did you use when you were just starting?*
SPIELBERG: My father began by buying himself a regular 8mm Kodak movie camera. There was no through-the-lens viewfinder. You looked through two plexiglass flip-up finders. Later, when he bought a triple-turret model, there were three rectangular outlines on the plexiglass—red for the telephoto lens, yellow for the medium lens, and blue for the wide-angle lens. Those cameras were the wind-up toys. You had about 35 seconds of wind and then you'd have to crank it up again. Then later one of my films won first prize in an amateur film festival—the Canyon Film Festival in Arizona—and the prize was a 16mm camera.

POSTER: *How old were you?*
SPIELBERG: I was 15. But I knew that I couldn't afford 16mm film processing and I knew that the camera would just sit on the shelf until I could afford it, so I traded the camera in on a Bolex-H8 8mm movie camera. It was very fancy equipment at the time. At the same time, with a little help from my dad, I got a Bolex Sonerizer, which was the first piece of technol-

ogy capable of recording sound directly onto 8mm film with a magnetic coating down the side. Now I was able to make pictures, send the cut footage to Eastman Kodak and have them put the magnetic stripe on and send it back to me. Then I would post-sync all the dialogue, sound effects and music in my living room.

POSTER: *This more sophisticated equipment must have made it possible for you to make much more ambitious films.*
SPIELBERG: Yes. I did science-fiction movies and, with the Bolex, I was able to shoot a sequence, rewind the film and then shoot double-exposures—people disappearing, beautiful young women turning into ghoulish nightmares. I'd use the old Lon Chaney dissolve trick—applying a little more makeup every few feet and dissolving from one stage of malignant facial growth to the next until I had Vampira. A lot of the technique was dictated by what the camera could do. I bought a little double polarizer so that I could fade in and fade out. These are antique now, just as Lionel trains are now antiques, but I was able to use the state-of-the-art such as it existed in 1961–62 and still make films that were pretty sophisticated.

POSTER: *To what extent did you get involved in editing at the time?*
SPIELBERG: I edited everything myself. Once I discovered how important the cut was, I never cut in the camera again. I would shoot all the master shots on one roll, all the closeups on another roll and all the action and trick shots on a third roll. Then I would break the film down and hang the separate shots on pins on a little makeshift cutting rack in my bedroom at home. I'd label each one with a piece of tape, identifying it by number, what was in the scene and where it was to go. Then I would pull each one off its pin and cut the way they cut today. So I really assembled the film. I became a film editor before I became a professional director.

POSTER: *Your techniques were pretty sophisticated. Where did you learn the methodology that you used?*
SPIELBERG: I don't know, Steve. I've thought about that a lot, because I really can't say that I went to movies and would come out so excited by a technique that I would come home and try it myself, because I actually didn't. When somebody in a scene walked, I'd walk the camera with him

because it seemed natural to move with the person who was walking, as opposed to putting the camera in cement, letting the person walk over to it, say his line and walk away. So certain things were, I think, more natural than learned.

POSTER: *Did you read about film technique?*
SPIELBERG: No, I didn't, because in 1961–62 in Phoenix, Arizona, film literature wasn't what it is today. They were writing books called "How to Make a Movie," which told you what cloudy-bright meant, as opposed to open-shade. It was only later really, when I was in college, that I belatedly started to read up on the things that were available at the time—but not in a small city like Phoenix.

POSTER: *How did you exhibit your first films and who made up your audiences?*
SPIELBERG: The audience was usually composed of children under 12. I sold tickets for a dime (later raising it to a quarter) and they'd come over to my house. We'd use the family room and they'd sit on card-table chairs. That was my first audience—youngsters. I made a film at 16 called *Firelight,* which was a very ambitious science-fiction film that ran 2½ hours. It was made with a sound stripe and had sync dialogue, music and special effects created in the camera involving four, five and sometimes ten passes on a single piece of film. I showed that film at a buck-a-head to 500 people. The film cost $400 and I made $100 profit the first night it showed. With that, my father was transferred and we moved the next day to San Francisco— actually 24 hours after the premiere of my first sophisticated full-length movie. After that my life changed and I went without film for about two years while I was trying to get out of high school, get some decent grades and find a college. I got serious about studying.

POSTER: *In your first projects you had to do most of the things yourself that it takes to make a movie. What parts of the process did you enjoy the most?*
SPIELBERG: I guess I enjoyed setting up the shot, placing the camera so that what took place in front of it would be more interesting. I found that making set-up choices was much more interesting than anything else. I was very much into angles, tricks, subjective points of view, and I'd always let the camera tell the story. Later I learned how to let the story tell the camera, but it took a while before I learned that lesson.

Secondly, I enjoyed editing, because I would be able to see my mistakes, fix my mistakes and make it better. Also, there was much less pressure involved in sitting by myself in front of a tiny wet splicer and viewer than there was in trying to beat the sun—all the things I find haven't changed even today.

POSTER: *When you began to get more involved, what responsibilities did you begin to delegate to other people?*
SPIELBERG: I didn't. My problem was that the more involved I got, the more I did everything. (I'm still talking about making amateur films.) But the more films I made, the more I wanted to do myself—short of acting. I did about everything else. I was my own gaffer, my own key grip. I built the sets myself. I did everybody's makeup. I wrote all the scripts. I used the high school band to score a movie. I played clarinet and wrote a score on my clarinet and then had my mother (who played piano) transpose it to her key. We made sheet music, the band recorded it, and I had my first original sound track. So the more I got involved, the more I wanted to do, and the first time I realized it was impossible to do everything was when I started to work professionally and found that there were certain limitations dictated by certain unions that wouldn't let me run the camera, cut the film, and compose the music—all on my DGA card.

POSTER: *After watching you work last summer, it's obvious that you influence almost every aspect of production, but in working professionally what are the areas of responsibility that you still like to control and what areas do you delegate?*
SPIELBERG: Now I delegate happily the functions that I feel there are people much better equipped to execute than I am—functions like makeup and set construction and composing music. These are things I used to do myself, but now I delegate them to people with whom I feel very secure—and I never look back. But there are other functions that I continue to get involved in—where the person is either my surrogate or my sounding board, and I pretty much work directly with these functions through the person that I hire. For instance, cinematography. Although I can't set the lights, I feel that I'm very influential in deciding how a scene should look photographically. I like to set the mood by talking to the cameraman and spending as much time as it takes to get my vision across to him. And setting up the camera I still do myself. I feel that part of my

function is to interpret the movie visually, in terms of where the camera goes, what lens is used and how the actor is viewed. I feel that this is my responsibility to the story. The other function that I'm autocratic about is editing. I consider myself the editor of my own movie and I collaborate with the person there. If that person has anything to offer and it's a good idea, I'll use it without question, but for the most part, I feel that editing is my thing, as well as cinematography. The other thing that I'm getting into now is exhibition—how a film should be distributed, what the ad art should look like, what the campaign should be like and what the marketing should be like. These are things I'm getting more and more involved in now that I know how easy it is to injure a film after it's made and before the audience sees it. After *Sugarland Express* I learned how important marketing is. I think it's as important as making the picture.

POSTER: *Your films show that you have an amazing ability to strongly affect an audience. What did you learn from your early films that helped you develop this ability?*

SPIELBERG: Well, the first thing I realized is that the audience is the key. I've been making films through myself and for an audience, rather than for myself and the next of kin who understand me. I guess I might be called an "entertainment" director—or, to be more crass, a "commercial" director. I don't pretend to understand how an audience changes every two or three years—which they do—but I know what I like and I hope there are enough people out there to share that. So I kind of use myself. I'm kind of my own audience.

POSTER: *You're a storyteller.*

SPIELBERG: Yes, I like to spin yarns. I thought *Jaws* was a big fish story and I had fun spinning that one, as opposed to *Close Encounters*, which was much more of an inspiration for me than a methodical attempt to manipulate an audience, as *Jaws* was on my part.

POSTER: *What do you mean by "inspiration"?*

SPIELBERG: *Close Encounters* was an original screenplay from an original idea, so it was a much more organic involvement. *Jaws* was based on a novel, so the idea came from elsewhere. The basic structure of the film is related to you through the novel, so what I did was adapt the novel into a movie that I thought was more me than Peter Benchley, and that made me happy. But what I'm saying is that it wasn't 100% my film. It's a film that I'm going to share with a lot of people for a long time, as opposed to *Close Encounters,* which is much closer to me.

POSTER: *How do you determine what an actor needs from you in order to give you the performance you're looking for?*

SPIELBERG: Basically by how insecure he is as an individual. I think a more secure actor is much more of an experimental actor. He doesn't fall back onto himself. He'll fall back on a strange idea that he can't really relate to. He'll try just about anything. The other kind of actor who is, I guess, a lot more neurotic and concerned about how he comes off, how he's going to sell, how he's going to look, is the toughest kind of person to work with, because he's just the person who won't take a chance, won't experiment, but falls back on the things he knows how to do. I've worked with both kinds of actors. There's a certain type of actor who can do only one thing, and because he has been successful at it, he doesn't give himself the chance to explore any deeper than what is saleable. Richard Dreyfuss isn't that kind of actor. Richard is the kind of actor who will go out on a limb, even to the point of embarrassing himself — to be different, to do something unusual, to not be Richard Dreyfuss, but to be the person that the writer intended him to be.

POSTER: *How much of that do you decide beforehand?*

SPIELBERG: It's all in the casting, Steve. I feel that 40% of my creative effort has been realized once the people have been cast in the film. I use actors to service me in what I'm doing. I try to make it a collaborative effort, because if an actor has a good idea and it's going to make the picture better, I'm not going to ignore it because of an ego thing. It's something that I'm going to put into the movie as fast as the idea sounds appropriate. But I know when I first cast a film that it's going to be pretty much a typecast film. I hired Robert Shaw for Clint, but possibly Robert Duvall would have been more interesting — although not as powerful or as theatrical as the character should have been played. I could have gone many different ways with *Jaws.* The book suggested somebody like Robert Redford to play Matt Hooper, but I felt there would be more sympathy for the character — that he would seem less of a dilettante — if someone like Richard Dreyfuss played him. So, in that instance, I went against the grain of what was written. It really depends on the story. I feel that the story dictates everything.

POSTER: *This sort of leads us to the subject of previsualization. You seem to preplan most of your shooting (the sketchbook of scenes we used last summer was a good indication of that), but when you get on the set I've seen you throw out the original ideas and completely redesign a scene. Just how important is previsualization to you?*

SPIELBERG: Well, it's important perhaps in the sense that it makes me feel secure in knowing that no matter what new ideas may come, if I'm bone dry one day and nothing new hits me, I can fall back on a good idea that already works on paper. It's important that I get up in the morning knowing that if worse comes to worst, I have the "A" Plan that worked in preproduction, worked on paper, and will work on film. But I always try to fight the rote method of filmmaking. I try to work from my imagination day-to-day, slightly veering off from that methodology of sketches and the Hitchcock-Disney syndrome—but the preplanning has really helped me in action sequences. I'm lost unless I've preplanned an action sequence—first in my head, then on paper, then finally, over a period of weeks, on film. But in other instances, I'll preplan scenes basically, but would rather let the actors inspire me. If there's an emotional scene to be played, I'd much rather stage it with the actors, tell the cameraman, gaffer and crew to wait outside, and then begin making visual choices after I've watched a rehearsal. After I've let the actors move where they feel they should move, I come in and somewhat choreograph the action. Then the third phase is to introduce the camera and film to it. So I actually have two different methods of working.

POSTER: *When did you first begin to develop these two different methods?*
SPIELBERG: When I first began doing TV and I realized that they really wanted me to make a one-hour television show in six days, I knew that everything had to be pretty well planned, because there's no time in television to improvise. Fancy footwork isn't smiled upon in TV. It's a producer's medium; whereas, movies are a director's medium. In television the producer is very strong and very concerned about schedule. When you go over schedule one day in TV, that's the equivalent of going over schedule 10 days on a feature film, unfortunately. So I kind of had to swallow my

pride and start paying my dues. I did 11 or 12 television shows over a three-year period. That doesn't seem like many; some directors make 50 shows a year. But for me that was a lot, because I would put so much of myself into each show. I considered each show a mini-feature and I would shoot it as I would shoot a feature. The one thing I refused to conform to was the television formula of closeup, two-shot, over-the-shoulders and master shot. I kept hoping that every time I'd make a TV show, enough people would see it and like my work and give me a feature to do, but it took a number of years before they began knocking on my door.

POSTER: *In production there's constant compromise and that always creates a certain amount of pressure. I've seen you in such situations and you always appear completely together.*

SPIELBERG: I'm not. Inside I'm asking myself, "Is this the right way to go? Am I painting myself into a corner? If I shoot a closeup of François Truffaut, does it mean that I'm going to have to cover him in a sequence I shot yesterday without any closeups?" I mean, I'm always stewing about something. I don't know how I appear outside, because I'm inside, but I just know that even with the best laid plan, I'm always worried that it's not working. I've had too many experiences where my best planned sequence was cut together and was a workable idea, but had no spontaneity, no energy. The planning took over and you could see the girders; you could see the superstructure sticking out of the surface cover. So scenes that I would plan and cut together would sometimes be very disappointing. At other times I would pat myself on the back and say, "Planning is the best way to go." It depends on several things, but I'm always worrying inside about whether I'm making the right move.

POSTER: *What kinds of things happened in your earlier films that may have taught you to handle the pressures?*

SPIELBERG: Only that the worst they can do is fire you; they can't kill you. I've always taken movies seriously, but I've always sort of had my tongue in my cheek at the same time. When you stand back and get those sudden precious moments of total objectivity and you see 100 people running around, doing their jobs, trying to impress their partner, dropping things, making mistakes, crying over their mistakes, losing their tempers, locking themselves in their dressing rooms, spilling their coffee, losing their money—you just sit back and laugh and tell yourself that the movie business is a wonderful, intoxicating carnival, but that if you take it too seriously, it'll kill you. But if you can always laugh about it when the pressure is really on—if you can stand back and find something funny to laugh at—it's a way of saving your presence of mind, and this is what I do when things get really bad, like on *Close Encounters*. I'd go up on a scaffold, look down at this 400 x 200-foot concept, and remember how it was designed in papier mache and plaster—12 x 18 inches. I'd laugh. It was a big erector set.

POSTER: *How else do you feel you've progressed in terms of being able to back off from the pressures?*

SPIELBERG: I used to lose my temper when I was a kid. I don't lose it as much anymore, although I lost it a few times on *Close Encounters*. But I used to have a real bad temper when I was 12 or 13 years old and I didn't like myself very much as a result, because I could see how people reacted to it. I don't like to lose control in any situation, emotionally or as a filmmaker, and I think that's one of the things that helped me put the brakes on.

POSTER: *As a result of what you've learned during your last 15 years of making films, do you ever think about the earlier ones and what you might have done to make them better?*

SPIELBERG: I never look back like that. In a way, it's just the reverse. My earlier films taught me how to prepare myself for my later films, and I've never really been able to look back and ask myself how I could have made *The Last Gun* (my first 8mm three-minute Western) better with what I know now. The whole creative process is a growing process, and to look back and sort of speculate on how things could have been is a little scary.

POSTER: *But aren't there elements of the filmmaking process that you've learned to pay more attention to, as a result of what went before?*

SPIELBERG: Yes—mainly acting, the actors. I've learned that one explosively dramatic scene between two people with the right chemistry is so much more exciting than a thousand people on the steps in *Potemkin*. It dawned on me that one good performance by an actor like Richard Dreyfuss is worth a couple of big action sequences—Custer's Last Stand, car chases, King Kong, whatever.

POSTER: *After* Jaws *and* Close Encounters *you have the freedom to make almost any kind of movie you want to make. How do you approach finding your next project?*

SPIELBERG: I don't know. I don't really worry about it that much. I'm usually lucky in having things come to me when I'm not looking. I become interested in a project, not because of the pressure of having to work again, but because I read something or I had an idea that was exciting and I put it down on paper and eventually planned to make it. There's a comedy I'm going to make next which came to me at the beginning of *Close Encounters*—just at the time when I shouldn't have been looking ahead. I found something that I put in the back of my mind and I said to myself, "Maybe I'll make this film someday." And, as it turns out, that will be my next picture. What is difficult for me is when the offers start coming in and I have to read the books and I have to read the scripts. But on the other hand, if I hadn't read the galleys of *Jaws* before it was published as a book, I never would have become involved. So I'm a little nervous about not reading, not searching constantly for new ideas.

POSTER: *Can you tell me a little more about how you did become involved in* Jaws?

SPIELBERG: It was somewhat accidental. I was cutting *Sugarland Express* and Zanuck and Brown, who were the producers of that picture, were offering me everything under the sun that they had and I wasn't really liking very much of what they had to offer at the time. But I had a meeting with them on the first or second cut of *Sugarland* and I noticed in the outer office an unpublished book manuscript called *Jaws*. I don't know what seized me, but I thought the title was so fascinating—I thought it was about a credit dentist—that I picked up the book (actually swiped the damned thing), took it home, read it over the weekend, and knew that that was what I wanted to do next. So I went to them on Monday and said, "We've been looking for a film to do together and I've found it in your office." They said, "Well, we'd love to have you on this, but the agent who sold it to us also sold us a director. He's part of the package deal." And I said, "Well, if anything happens in the future and he falls out of the project, give me a call." And that's exactly what happened. About two weeks later they called up and said, "You've got the job, if you still want it."

POSTER: *You told me that you'd like to do a musical at some point. What other kinds of things are you interested in doing?*

SPIELBERG: Oh, your garden variety love story, a Western, a musical, a war film, an erotic fantasy, a comedy...a little bit of everything.

POSTER: *So you'd really kind of like to play the field?*

SPIELBERG: Yes...whatever strikes my fancy that year. The one thing I don't want to do is have a 10-year game plan, where I have my next five projects already lined up—one through five. I think that'd be an awful way to go through life—knowing what your next five films are going to be over the next 10 years. It's not only boring, but you also change. Nobody stays the same for more than a couple of years. Some people change every week. What I liked in 1971 I probably wouldn't have made now. I probably wouldn't make *Duel* now. Looking back, I probably wouldn't make *Jaws* three years from now. So it's important not to plan too far ahead, because each project is a reflection of what you were that year.

POSTER: *One of the main objectives of this interview is to encourage people just starting out in film to take advantage of the technology available to them today. What advice can you give those people?*

SPIELBERG: Get one of the Super-8 sound cameras that are on the market. Get it for Christmas. The equipment available today is so sophisticated — which is both an advantage and a disadvantage. For example, if I'd had in 1961 what teenagers and even preteenagers have available today, I wouldn't have had to spend so much time on each project—but I wouldn't have learned as much. The problem with the new-fangled equipment today is that it obviates the necessity for post-dubbing, working with tape recorders, balancing and mixing music to sound. Everything is so "instant" that it goes right onto the film. Back then it was fun, because I learned about recording sound, I learned about music, I made my own sound effects. But today, making sound movies is as easy as getting out of bed in the morning—if that happens to be what you think is easy.

POSTER: *Does that mean that you feel that the very sophistication of present-day Super-8 equipment is a limiting factor?*

SPIELBERG: Not if you want to make quick and painless home movies. But the people who aspire to becoming professional filmmakers will learn

what they really need to learn only when they get into working with
16mm and 35mm. From Super-8 they'll learn nothing about laboratory
work, color correcting, lap dissolves, opticals. They'll learn nothing about
mixing sound and very, very little about lighting, because the new film is
so fast that all you have to do is turn your lamp on and you have a very
nice Gordon Willis cross-light. If your subject sits near a window, you've
got natural light coming in and the camera adjusts itself. So you don't
become skilled at lighting, at changing your aperture, at under-exposing,
over-exposing, flashing, shooting through filters. It's all a little too pat
with the equipment they have today. But on the other hand, the results
are instantaneous. I had to wait a week and a half for dailies, because that's
how long it took to send the thing out and get it back. Today you see your
film with sound on it the next day, 24 hours later—just like the real
pros—and when you sit back and watch those dailies, you're going to
know right away whether you want to make movies for the rest of your
life.

POSTER: *What advice do you have for those people who decide they want to
make movies for the rest of their lives?*
SPIELBERG: For people who are interested in directing movies, I'd say:
start as young as you possibly can and make your own films, rather than
reading about other people who have made their own films. There is no
substitute for getting out there and shooting, cutting and then showing—
especially showing, especially listening to the audience and seeing how
tuned in you are to their needs. At the same time, what young people—
even those who are dedicated to a career in filmmaking—are finding out
is how hard it is to get more established types to look at their work. But
that's just part of the footwork—the tired feet, the suffering, the disappointments. I get a lot of letters from young people who say, "I've finished
four films. Who can I show them to? Nobody seems very responsive." And
they're not. They're not responsive; they're not receptive. I had a hell of a
time showing any of my films. A lot of it is luck, and a lot of it is wanting
it so much that you're going to take the hinges off the door to get it open.
There are people out there who are sympathetic to young filmmakers and
there are those who are not. But that's where the hard work comes in...
selling yourself. Selling yourself is the hardest thing in the world to do—
even harder than making movies, when you're first starting out.

1941: Bombs Away!

CHRIS HODENFIELD/1980

"You never know what is enough unless you know what is more than
enough."

—William Blake

ARE THEY LAUGHING? THAT anxious question has, since the
beginning of time, transformed young comedians into old comedians. It
has been working on director Steven Spielberg's mind since at least the
beginning of last year. His latest picture, *1941*, concerning war panic in Los
Angeles after the attack on Pearl Harbor, was being touted as the most
expensive comedy in all of chuckledom. "It's a multi-million-dollar Three
Stooges movie," said his old pal John Milius, *1941*'s executive producer.
Spielberg had to start explaining the dollars-per-laugh ratio. That is, if
indeed there were laughs.

The kid had proved his Midas touch with *Jaws* and *Close Encounters of
the Third Kind.* As one Hollywood insider said, "If he wanted to make a
film about toilet paper, they'd give him the money." But Spielberg knew,
by last August, that he'd miscalculated. His conversation was diddled with
phrases like "utter horror" and "total conceptual disaster." This just seemed
a modesty act.

Much later, I understood Spielberg's grim countenance.

From *Rolling Stone*, 24 January 1980, © 1980 by Straight Arrow Publishers, Inc. All Rights
Reserved. Reprinted by Permission.

An off-kilter, or *modern*, sense of humor was needed to dream up *1941*. *Mad Magazine* logic had been applied to a time of "ennobling sacrifice," as veterans remember the days following Pearl Harbor. The very real jitters led to the rounding up of Japanese-Americans, who spent the war years in California desert internment camps. But none of these people will be sucking on reefers in the Bijoux balcony.

Screenwriter Robert Zemeckis: "This is a picture that could only be conceived, written, and made by guys who know World War II by seeing it in the movies. None of us were even born when the Japanese attacked Pearl Harbor." (Only forty percent of the country's current population was alive at the time.) Zemeckis and his partner, Bob Gale, both now twenty-eight, dreamed up the story four years ago and took it to their mentor, director John Milius, who was teaching a film course at the University of Southern California. Milius had them develop it, and he put on the name *The Night the Japs Attacked*. The very title brought *him* under attack. Milius, who rose to directorhood by writing scripts about larger-than-life men in *The Life and Times of Judge Roy Bean, Dillinger,* and *Wind and the Lion,* recalled that trying to sell the idea to the Hollywood Bosses was a suicide mission.

Milius is a large, bearded fellow with a jovial yet sinister growl; he'd have you believe that we'll all soon be staring down Soviet bayonets. *The Night the Japs Attacked* was rejected because, figuring on a cost of $6 million, it was too expensive and, some said, it just didn't sound funny. While Milius was proceeding toward dubious reward with his surf movie, *Big Wednesday* ("I was practically accused of being a war criminal because of it"), he handed Zemeckis and Gale's screenplay to Spielberg. Suddenly the Hollywood Bosses thought the idea sounded funny as hell. And what's a few million dollars between friends? T-shirts were printed up for the production crew: "I WILL NOT MAKE THIS FILM IF IT COSTS ONE PENNY OVER $11 MILLION." JULY 1978. STEVEN SPIELBERG. Six weeks later, Universal Pictures (which grossed $400 million on *Jaws*) and Columbia Pictures ($200 million from *Close Encounters*) pooled their resources and agreed to a $21.5 million budget.

Spielberg didn't relish explaining *1941*'s eventual $26.5 million price tag, having seen the terrible press awarded two other directors, Francis Coppola with *Apocalypse Now* and Michael Cimino with the forthcoming *Heaven's Gate,* both of whom invested thirty-something million dollars apiece on moving pictures. Next up will be director John Landis, who is currently making *The Blues Brothers* and finding that nobody trusts a budget over $30 million.

Dan Aykroyd, who plays a stern-talking commander, compared the structure of *1941* to *American Graffiti*—the events of one cataclysmic night. The movie is billed as a "comedy spectacular," and spectacle has indeed been Spielberg's forte. "Barnum & Bailey" is what Bob Gale calls him. And the epic visual stunts performed on a vast miniature city built by Gregory Jein set a new standard in special-effects work. The last comedy spectacle I can remember is *It's a Mad, Mad, Mad, Mad World*, which proved in 1963 that pratfalls and slapstick do not necessarily grow funnier when the format grows huge. Surely Spielberg must have spent a few lonely nights wishing he was cranking out Charlie Chase two-reelers instead.

Spielberg's training was five years of television dramas (a directing job won on the merits of a student film), then he was lost to the take-no-prisoners world of movies. His features, starting with *Sugarland Express* in 1974, have been about crowds in motion, Americans going nuts, middle-class life as it's lived—all strung up to the snapping point. I think he likes to see a crowd reacting in unison to some big wazoo. Years ago in the Universal commissary he would have Richard Nixon paged on the public-address system, just so he could watch a roomful of studio executives rise up from their tables and crane their necks.

For *1941*, he left his strong suit—the art of creating suspense—hanging in the closet; the movie races by too fast. Even with great character actors like Slim Pickens, Robert Stack, Warren Oates, Christopher Lee, Toshiro Mifune, Dan Aykroyd, and John Belushi, the audience barely has a character to hold onto or identify with. Bodies are continually being hurtled into unwieldy situations. An audience can be surprised only so many times. Chuck Jones, the animation genius behind Bugs Bunny and Road Runner, was consulted in the early design stages. Paying homage to cartoons and the old silent comedians in vivid color and pugnacious six-track sound transformed socko high jinks into something brutal. Spielberg learned about comedy on the most gargantuan canvas affordable.

The old comedic components—the slow burn, the double take, the dreadful anticipation, the witty rejoinder—were abandoned for the continuous slam-bang. For instance, if you knew beforehand that a paint factory was waiting behind closed doors, and that a careening army tank was heading straight for it, well, you'd be waiting. As it stands, the viewer is suddenly aware that a paint factory has materialized and this army tank is crashing through it. Or, in a café, a man's face pitching toward the counter suddenly meets a birthday cake. The mind registers these various happenings moments after the eye perceives them.

A few test previews of the film in Dallas and Denver caused some early nervousness (*Are They Laughing?*), which led Spielberg to trim several minutes from the early reels. He might have cut too close to the bone. With the explanatory subplots cleaved away, we are left with a movie full of strangers. Later, he tried to find some consolation in John Williams's thunderous score. "Johnny's been overwriting over my overdirection over Zemeckis and Gale's overwritten script," Spielberg said.

Dan Aykroyd groped for lessons in this movie: "There were so many elements that had to be chopped out because the movie was so big, and he had to get down to a manageable time. That's the big lesson, I think. Before you even start to walk onto a set or think about production, you've got to have a solid story that is so clear and vivid that there isn't much room to deviate and improvise, and therefore you don't have the selective process of cutting once it's all over. You have what you need in the can, and it enables the director to build on what was in the original script."

He came home from work one day last summer and parked the green Porsche. He entered his Beverly Hills aerie through the kitchen and stuck his nose into the icebox. Bertha, the respectable-looking housekeeper, said she'd make tea.

Spielberg's face was chiseled into a very serious structure. Gone was the youthful, cross-eyed goofiness. All of thirty-one years old, he looked a little more contemplative, a little more rugged. The lips were set. Decisions had left their mark. The jeans and the heavy dark blue shirt were built for comfort, but he's lately replaced the striped jogging shoes with handsome brown boots.

It was a cavernous house in tasteful browns, high wooden beams above. It was something that might have been erected by a discreet, wealthy rancher. There was an antique billiard table, and outer-space sharpshooter game, a screening room under construction in the living room. He led the way to the den. It seemed to be the one cozy, overstuffed room in the mansion. Navaho rugs hung on the wall. A neat fan of Japanese architecture magazines lay on the table.

Dropping into a pillowy brown sofa, he chewed over a host of agonies. Maybe, he figured, it was time to get out of the dead spiritual air of Los Angeles. Get away from The Business. Maybe he should buy a ranch in Montana, like his business manager said. Standing on a Beverly Hills street corner, he couldn't hear Aaron Copland in his head. Slaving over a typewriter was much better in New York.

(When later I mentioned these hard lines of doubt to John Milius, he burst out laughing. "What it is, is he's getting *married*. He has to grow up and become a real *adult* now.")

The workday had been one long bout of the self-examination that a director gets in the sound-dubbing laboratories. To fine-tune the soundtrack, he had to watch the same ten-minute reel of film over and over again, and it's while doing just this job that the worry explodes and he sees what he did wrong and calls out the camera boys for another shot.

"I can't correct the overall conceptual disasters in *1941*," he said, putting his ankle on his knee, "but I can get little pieces here and there that I think will help speed the pace. If you can't do anything about it, then you're at the mercy of what comics call 'the death silence.' You expected a laugh and all there is is a hole."

This made me laugh. It was not the kind of boosterism a director usually serves before a picture's release. His eyes lifted a little, ready for any understanding. He has, finally, an affable face. You find yourself agreeing with it.

I reminded him about his vow to laugh all the way to the final print.

"Yeah?" He smiled grimly. "Well, surprise, I didn't. A comedy is an elusive, chameleonlike beast. It's really an area of film . . ." (his voice fell to a halt; he groped, then returned in an almost-bark) " . . . that I'm not going to make a habit of. It's too fucking tough, panhandling for your supper. Reaching for laughs. Sometimes stretching the credibility of the story line beyond all recognizable shape for a simple yuk." He might have been talking about his best friend's divorce.

"I could have made two kinds of comedy. I could have made a drawing-room comedy that would have cost $3 to $4 million. Or I could . . . *did* make a comedy spectacle of action-adventure-visual madness. Those words have dollar signs and decimal points attached to them. There's no getting away with it in this town anymore. If you have more than twenty extras in the background every shot, and you've got more than four or five people in the cast, and if you crash a car or two, or detour a tank through a paint factory, you're no longer talking $4 or $5 million, you're talking $24 to $25 million. We're pricing ourselves out of work."

He slurped his tea. He made it all sound so simple. Of course, nothing he shoots is simple.

"If Mack Sennett, Harold Lloyd, Charlie Chaplin, Buster Keaton . . . if they were alive, making movies today, not changing a single beat, except possibly adding color instead of black and white, the average Mack Sennett film would run between $20 and $25 million, instead of $5000. Put it this way: ten years ago, *1941* would have cost $12 million."

So, I asked, it weighs on your mind?

"Not really. What counts is, is the same film worth four bucks at the box office."

Your difficulty with comedy was unexpected, since even *Jaws* resounded with comic moments, particularly in the portrayals of small-town life.

"I'm . . . I'm comically courageous when comedy isn't home plate. You see what I'm saying? I'm much better when I'm playing shortstop and I can add comedy, for instance, to *Jaws*, which I thought needed a lot of laughs because of the amount of intensive storytelling. It was sort of like the potion and the antidote. In *1941*, there better not be a serious moment in the entire film or I'm in big trouble. Hello, Amy!"

Suddenly, there was Amy Irving standing there in yellow pants and turquoise top. His bride-to-be is an actress (the nice friend in *Carrie* and the star of *The Fury*), olive-tanned and sunny. "Carry on," she said. She slipped away like an autumn breeze.

"For the most part, it's a picture made by people who aren't dealing with a full deck. This is why, I think, it was important for me to get it out of my system. On Columbia-Universal's tab."

(Spielberg often jokes about sticking companies with the check for lunch. Richard Dreyfuss recalled that just before starting *Close Encounters,* he and Spielberg went to Disneyland. During the drive home, Spielberg reeled in the back seat, hollering that Columbia was giving them $11 million to have fun. He eventually rolled them for nineteen.)

"The script came to me in a funny way. I was shooting skeet with John Milius at the Oak Tree Gun Club and these two young protégés of mine and John's, Robert Zemeckis and Bob Gale, brought me this first draft to read for an opinion. I don't think there was one comic line in the entire first draft, but there were some wonderful visionary set pieces.

"It wasn't a film from my heart. It wasn't a project that I initiated, dreamed about for ten years, although I have shed blood over it as if it were my own. Rather than a bastard adoption, I like to think of it at times as if it were a project I was forced to take because of my own state of mind."

Now *this* was anxiety. A couple of years ago, seeking a change of pace, he planned a picture about children, his own suburbs-of-Phoenix Our Gang comedy called *Growing Up.* What happened to that?

Spielberg sank back into the cushions.

"Problem was, I hadn't grown up enough to make *Growing Up.* Hopefully, *1941* is the last movie I make that celebrates the boy in me. And then hopefully I can go on from here and do something more adultlike and perhaps more boring."

That's an interesting concept, I said, *celebrating your boyhood.*

"Yeah," he grinned. "And how many people get $30 million to do it?" He picked up a sandwich.

And next, you're going to direct a movie from George (*Star Wars*) Lucas's *Raiders of the Lost Ark.* Another adventure?

"It's an adventure story of high intensity and..." (glancing up from the sandwich) "...high secrecy. We don't want to get ripped off. I talked openly about *After School,* a.k.a. *Growing Up.* And a year later six kid pictures hit the theatres."

Is *Raiders,* shall we say, more grown-up?

"Yeah,...I mean, it's certainly more grown-up than *1941.* A six-year-old is more grown-up than *1941.* If movies weren't fun, I'd stop making them. I'd go into design research. I'd go into R&D with computer games. Video electronics. That'd be fun."

Do you design games?

"Yeah, as a hobby, I think of them, run them around in my head. I'm strategically oriented. I'm not dexterous. I...I really couldn't unscrew a light bulb without breaking it. But I can design the lamp. Someday I'll design the penultimate video game."

It's been a long time, I said, since anyone has attempted the highly choreographed, Keystone Kops kind of action that's in *1941.*

"It's difficult to find people to step into their shoes. The Chaplins, the Harold Lloyds, the Fatty Arbuckles, the Snub Pollards of yesterday have become the more coifed and slick Steve Martin, Albert Brooks, Robin

Williams, and John Belushi. There's more verbal wit in comedy today, with
the exception of Belushi, who I think is the most visually prone actor-
comedian working in film and theatre. I think he's amazing. There isn't
anyone like him. Or who comes close.

"Comedy has become glib. And current. Almost too current. The comics
today are faddish, and audiences grow weary of today's comics the way we
used to with Marvel and D.C. and the Green Lantern and Batman. It's . . .
there's a lot of brief infatuations between audiences and comedians. And
film styles. There are very few comedians who I believe will survive into
the next fad. Right now I think we're into a punk fad, a punk comic fad.
And who knows who the next one will be? Probably dinner-jacket chic."
He rubbed his chin and laughed as if he'd like to make himself believe it.

"Dan Aykroyd is interesting. He's a contemporary soldier of our time. As
far as I was concerned, working with Danny, he was the comic sergeant-at-
arms on *1941*. He has one of the fastest minds for situation comedy and
funny storytelling, and at the same time he's very technical. He can tell
you all of the byproducts of gypsum . . . and have you roaring with laughter!

"There are other people who I think will be around for a while, Jon
Candy and Joe Flaherty. There's nobody to touch Gilda.

"With this current five-year fad, comedy is appealing to younger and
younger kids more than before. It used to be comedy was a college-level
humor. But six-, seven-year-olds know every one of Steve Martin's routines
and repeat them at school, on the playground.

"It was that way when I was in school. Things started in the school-
yard . . ." (he snapped his fingers rapidly) " . . . and then went into the
home. Remember when Davy Crockett hit the theaters in 1955? I guess I
was in third grade at the time. Suddenly the next day, everybody in my
class but me was Davy Crockett. And because I didn't have my coonskin
cap and my powder horn, or Old Betsy, my rifle, and the chaps, I was
deemed the Mexican leader, Santa Anna. And everybody came after me
with the butt ends of their flintlock rifles. And they chased me home from
school until I got my parents to buy me a coonskin cap."

You and Aykroyd are working on a project?

"We're talking about it. But Danny's essentially into comedy—adult-
precision comedy—and I'm not going to do comedy for a while, having
experienced the utter horror of *1941*."

At what stage did you perceive the "utter horror"?

He slipped into a glassy gaze. "It was sorta . . . like going in for x-ray treatments each day and you realize the cure is worse than the disease. Every day I'd go onto the set, it would just get worse and worse. The utter pressure of having to deliver funny material. We had to come up with it privately, or in a great crazo outcry of '*Make me laugh, asshole!*'

"The film does cater to the lowest moral character in all of us . . ." (he raised a forefinger) ". . . without licking the sewer. It's just a tongue's reach away from good sewer humor. But falls short of classic comedy."

The Japanese didn't come off too badly in this picture.

"I was personally drawn in sympathy to the Japanese story when I first read the script. I said, 'Here's my chance to work with the greatest samurai of them all, Toshiro Mifune.' He came into my house when we first met. He walked in wearing a business suit, with his thinning hair and great big smile, with very little English to his credit, but he had a wonderful interpreter with him. And we exchanged gifts. He opened up the book and he said, 'Now here is where the script is wrong.' Our submarine was wrong, according to Toshiro, and we made corrections. So in that sense, Toshiro cleaned up the Japanese act and made them professional and worthy of our great fear and respect."

Mifune even had the Japanese extras running drills on the set, during lulls in filming. However, the Americans were not portrayed as fightworthy.

"All the actors seemed to get caught up in that kind of civic madness. No one wanted to be normal — as much as I tried to normalize certain relationships . . . because realism is the cement floor of comedy. Without it you're floating in a fantasy netherland. But everybody watching John Belushi and Dan Akyroyd perform . . . some of our other characters wanted to be just as crazy. They all wanted to be bigger than the war. Bigger than history."

So you had to tone them down.

"I failed." His voice fell into a graveyard shift. "I failed at toning them down. They don't teach you that in acting school. It was sort of like trying to stop a herd of kids at your local Toys R Us."

Tell me one scene.

"A lot of the cast asked the writers to let them wind up inside the tank that was commandeered by Dan Aykroyd and his maintenance crew. And to be taken up to Hollywood Boulevard to quell a riot because Dan Aykroyd can't stand the notion of Americans fighting Americans. But because in the movie Dan Aykroyd is hit severely over the head and suffers a kind of amnesia that allows him to be four or five characters all within ten or fifteen minutes, everybody wanted to be like Danny. And with everybody talking at once, trying to get their dialogue out—with my stopwatch method, which is to get all the information out in half the time that's indicated on the written page. If the script girl says that this scene will run sixty seconds, because it's one page long, I'll do it in thirty. That was my philosophy on *1941*. It's sort of called 'cut time.'

"So having to get all this priceless story information out all at once, it was like a nightmare Bob Altman. Something I'm sure Bob only dreams about, and then casts out of his head as just having eaten too many pimentos the night before."

Could be. In viewing *Jaws* the other day, I saw scenes done in a rhythm usually considered Altman's province.

"Sorta. Howard Hawks did it first. Hawks didn't invent it either. But Hawks was certainly one of the first to do a movie in cut time."

Capra said he started that technique on *American Madness* in 1932.

"Of course, the real actors on the film would come over to me and complain bitterly, because they're used to playing the moment. They're used to playing the beats *between* the measures. *Between* the written words. My philosophy on *1941* was, there's no dead air."

Been keeping in touch with Francis Coppola lately?

"No." Silence.

"I don't know what happened to Francis." Longer silence.

"Making a movie, any movie, is like fighting hand-to-hand war. I don't care if it's a film the size of *Apocalypse,* or a small film the size of *Animal House.* There's a discipline that...ah, can sometimes turn brave men's minds to poison. And ruin a strong personality and collapse an ego. Bring a man down to his knees in tears. Just because he goes out to tell a story on film. It's never easy. It's too bad only a handful of people know how true what I'm saying really is."

Then the moviemaking process would suppress the maker's reflective side, and bring out the general, the commanding officer. Eventually, most movies are made from the general's point of view.

"*Every* filmmaker is a commanding officer," he replied sharply. "Even the director' most noteworthy for their rapport and expertise with the actor. I mean, don't kid yourself. Kazan was just as much a general on the set of *On the Waterfront* as Coppola was in the Philippines. It's a war. The only real winners are the public. The only real losers, often, are the film-makers. It's an unnatural act to make a movie."

Movies today often reflect the attitudes of con men; it often takes a con man's abilities to get a picture made.

"Con men?" He started up. "You mean people who are not writing from their hearts but rather to get the film studios to make it? Do you know how many scripts are written each year that are contrary to popular demand? And they're never made. Half of them are never read because the idea isn't commercial. So a writer backtracks and says, 'I'm going to break into this business.' So he writes . . . ah, a movie called *It Came from the Rings of Saturn to Devour Cleveland.* And he sells it to a small independent. And of course he becomes very successful, so he writes one more biggie, *The Creature from the Bermuda Triangle,* and sells that. And then of course he's in a position to write and sell his *Grapes of Wrath.* But he's been so stung by success that the initial human impulse to write *The Grapes of Wrath* is quenched by the easier commercial sellout, and so be it. He remains a commercial screen-writer and keeps turning out films he *thinks* will be popular. And that becomes his *raison d'être.* And the noble impulse to make that personal work of true beauty and satisfaction is dormant forever. I've seen that hap-pen. And . . . I've seen that start inside me. And . . . there's a way to protect yourself from that kind of . . . pothole. I think."

Hearing a director dissect a movie can be as illuminating as, say, hearing Shakespeare recited by someone who understands the bard's pictures. So I asked Spielberg to pick out a favorite movie and analyze it.

He sat with his elbows on his knees. "I don't know what film I would pick or if I could do it justice. I admire a film like [Stanley Kubrick's] *Dr. Strangelove or: How I Stopped Worrying and Learned to Love the Bomb.* This is one of the few films I've ever seen that is nearly a perfect motion picture. Because what Kubrick set out to do, he accomplished. And that's always my first, my major, criterion for perfection.

"I'm not a critic, I'm not an analyst of film. I subconsciously analyze pictures, and some of it stays with me and goes into my own films, and other elements just stay with me and make me happy when I think of it."

Spielberg pulled himself forward and warmed to it. "But it's fun to think about, gee, why did Kubrick photograph that sequence where George C. Scott gets the phone call to report to the War Room and he's on the crapper and his secretary-girlfriend is lying under a sunlamp, for some reason, at four in the morning. He picks up the telephone in the mirrored boudoir, and it's about a six-minute sequence, all shot from one angle, with a very slight push-in to a tighter two-shot when George Scott climbs over the bed and says, 'I'll be home sooner than you can say bombs away.'"

We laughed, and he went on to marvel over the brilliance of the parallel storytelling. Spielberg knew every frame.

"He's a master of concept lighting, and composition and bravura subject matter. There are things in that film that are 100 percent technically perfect. The sequence where the minute-man missile tracks the B-52 and explodes a mile away, and the shock wave sets the 52 on fire, and sparks and smoke and fire erupt inside the cockpit and fuselage. Kubrick personally operated the camera. It was handheld. It was just the way you experience a *60 Minutes* report. As the missile detonates, the sound of the radar engineer's voice speeds up and statics out to pure white noise. And there's maybe a beat of total silence before the whole thing explodes. Little things like that. The eye Kubrick has for minute detail. That makes the movie different.

"The brilliance of *Dr. Strangelove,* and in my humble opinion one of the failings of *1941,* is the fact that in *Strangelove,* the broad, baroque comedy was extra funny, because the reality of the situation was so true to life. In the way he shot it, and the performances were so underplayed—with the slight exception of George C. Scott's—and the reality of where the camera was and how the scenes were lit, it all made the broad comedy acceptable. And believable. The juxtaposition of docu-drama and crazo-comedy has never worked better in any movie."

He slipped into remembering.

"It was a mistake, a happy accident, that during *Strangelove's* final tirade, when he's beating his Master Race arm senseless, Peter Bull starts to lose it. And he breaks twice, bites his lower lip, but doesn't break. Want to see it?" He picked himself up. "Come here."

He led the way down the hall to his bedroom. It was a green-curtained affair, dim with a dark aquarium light. There, connected to a television the size of a deep freeze, was a video unit. Conveniently, a cassette of *Dr. Strangelove* was reeled up.

We watched Slim Pickens sitting astride an atomic bomb and freeing the B-52's hatch door. Then riding the bomb like a bronco horse into Russia.

Then in the War Room, the Kissinger-like Dr. Strangelove explaining to the President that, after all, Doomsday Device or no, we can go on reproducing in radiation-free salt mines. But he's plagued by his uncontrollable black-gloved hand and, sure enough, the Russian ambassador is trying hard not to break up. Then mushroom-shaped clouds explode the world over while Vera Lynn sings "We'll Meet Again."

The ending always gets me.

We staggered back down the hallway.

"One of the reasons I remember *Strangelove* so well is that I was standing in line to see it in San Jose, California. I was in high school at Los Gatos High. And my sister came running up with a letter and said, 'Look, it's from the Selective Service.' In line for *Strangelove,* I opened up the letter and it said, 'Report for your physical.' It was very apropos at the time, when you're about to spend an hour and thirty-three minutes with *Dr. Strangelove.* The Cuban blockade was still fresh in everyone's memory. And that was the year *Fail Safe* came out.

"At least for my generation, that's a film that will live as a nearly perfect example of moviemaking. And storytelling. I mean, Hollywood is cranking out a lot of films these days, but few of those films are truly visionary. The only truly visionary film to come out this year is *Apocalypse Now.* It's such a staple business. No longer a hatching ground for real bizarre originality. There aren't that many brave souls with movie cameras out there grinding away. Which there were. Everybody plays it safe, plays it for the big bucks."

Being a visionary can't be taught.

"Yeah, but also, people must allow you to do it. You must be *permitted* to be a visionary today. In other words, you gotta get your budget approved.

"I admired Kubrick for the sheer variety in his films. I'm sure *The Shining* will be the best haunted-house movie ever put on film. *Paths of Glory* was the best antiwar film ever made, including *Apocalypse Now. Lolita* was, for me, the best picture about the social mores in America. It was way ahead of its time. It was the best film about kids and adults ever made."

Well, when you met Kubrick, were you the perfect fan and ask him how he did it?

"Yeah, I pumped him a little, as a fan would. But he's such a ... *mensch.* He threw me off guard. Through school, studying Kubrick, seeing all of his movies many times ... this image I conjured in my mind—what a Stanley

Kubrick was—was nothing like the man with his sleeves rolled up, with wrinkled clothes like Columbo's."

Spielberg gazed fondly at the carpet. "His beard. His probing, questioning eyes, always looking at you to see if you're true or false. To see what you're made of, to see what you've got upstairs. His chess player's eyes. Real surgeon's eyes.

He looked up.

"I was happy to find that he was a nice guy, that he laughed and *liked* movies. He talked about the films he liked, as opposed to so many of my other contemporaries who are haughty, supercilious about films, critical of them, and don't give that much credit to other people.

"A lot of students think that people like Hitchcock, Kubrick, Welles, and Truffaut, the surviving greats, are squeaky clean, basking in a kind of unattainable royalty, an ineffable royalty. Where you must say 'Mister' or 'Sir' or 'Lord' before speaking. And that's nonsense."

Do you have to ease people from their preordained conceptions of you?

"Yeah." He scratched his neck and mulled over a while. "When people call me *Mr. Spielberg,* in my head I'll yell, 'Don't call me Mister! I'm not a grown-up yet!' "

We laughed about that one for a good long time.

Steven Spielberg in His Adventures on Earth

SUSAN ROYAL/1982

FROM THE MURKY DEPTHS of *Jaws* to the stellar
heights of *E.T.*, director Steven Spielberg has led film audiences
around the world on a field trip to adventure. In an industry
where commerciality and artistic quality have often been called
antithetical, Spielberg has repeatedly proven himself the master
of their combination. In this interview with *American Premiere*,
Spielberg offers personal and professional insights into a career
which has generated new film classics, box office records and a
public awareness and popularity equalled by few directors in the
history of motion pictures.

PREMIERE: *Why did you decide to release* Poltergeist *and* E.T. *at the same time?*

SPIELBERG: I just did it that way, since I'd made both movies at the
same time. In the motion picture industry, there's no such thing as "air
traffic control." You just throw movies out on the marketplace like some
colorful mid-Eastern bazaar, and they go out and they do whatever they
can. And sometimes it's predictable and sometimes it's destiny, and sometimes it's just real surprising. I stopped guessing. I never predict what my
movies will do. You never know. That's what's exciting about Christmas
and summer... the big guns come out and sleepers emerge. Often, the best

time to release a film is in the in-between months, the so-called "Death Valley days" between Halloween and Christmas, or that infertile period when people prefer not to release big films: from January up 'til Easter or Memorial Day. Sometimes there are big surprises, like *Graffiti* and *Animal House,* which opened during "Death Valley days." No one expects anything to make very much money at that time, but the audience will see a good movie any time of the year. All of these demographics and all the research the studios do about prime playing times, and who goes to the movies when, on what day, really don't amount to a hill of beans. Statistically, the summer is the best moviegoing time, but if there's a movie that everybody wants to see, it doesn't matter when you release it, although it is true that *Jaws* would have made a little less money Christmas of '74 as opposed to summer of '75. You just can't tell anymore. Sometimes big films fall down and little sleeper films like *Arthur* emerge. Nobody expected *Arthur* to make a hundred million dollars. That film just came out of nowhere and went to the top.

PREMIERE: *There is a substantial number of sequels coming out this summer:* Rocky III, Grease II, Star Trek II, Friday the 13th Part III.
SPIELBERG: And *Halloween 3* in the fall. Yeah, there are a lot of "two's" and "three's" coming out.

PREMIERE: *You once said that doing sequels reduces filmmaking from an art to a science. Do you still feel that way?*
SPIELBERG: I still feel that way, depending on the sequel. The *Jaws* I designed was a one-time shot. And the Sequel, *Jaws II,* proves only that you can make a few dollars just by applying mechanical science to a successful formula. But there are other films which make a wonderful continuing story. There's nothing wrong with making ten *Rockys,* nothing wrong with making twenty *James Bonds,* there's nothing wrong with making twenty *Star Wars*; those are continuing anthological adventures. Each movie is really a separate story. The only thing that continues through it are the basic characters. There's nothing wrong with that. I'm sure *Grease II* is going to be good, but *Grease II* is not a natural sequel; it's a forced sequel. *Star Trek II* is more of a natural sequel. *Raiders II* will be another adventure; that's more like *James Bond* or *Star Wars.* But if I made a sequel to *Close Encounters,* it would be a forced sequel. The movie essentially

ended in the best way it could possibly end, with Richard going away, never to return. If I made a sequel and Richard returned, it would be undermining the uniqueness of the first story in the same preposterous fashion in which a similar shark, some thirty feet long, attacked the very same island in *Jaws II*. *Close Encounters* wouldn't make a good sequel, as *Jaws II* didn't.

PREMIERE: *You've been pretty verbal on the subject of studios cheating directors out of profits. After reading the details of the deal you and George Lucas made with Paramount for* Raiders, *it's clear that won't happen to you.*

SPIELBERG: George and I, well, "We make money the old-fashioned way...we earn it." For many years the studios have been making four dollars in overhead, distribution fee, interest and profit for every one dollar that the creative individual, say the director or director/writer, makes for coming up with the idea in the first place. We structured the *Raiders* deal based on our past histories. George had the number-one picture at Fox, and I had the number-one picture at Universal and Columbia. (Together, they share the number-one picture at Paramount now with *Raiders*.) We just thought it was about time we stopped making money for the studios, and the studios made a few bucks with us. And we wanted to come first. So with George flailing *The Empire Strikes Back* and *Star Wars* in one hand, and me with *Jaws* and *Close Encounters* on the other hand, we went to Paramount and said, "George is going to control the copyright and the negative, we're going to own this movie, and we're going to give you a share of our action for your distribution services." And a lot of studios turned us down. Universal said they wouldn't touch the deal with a ten-foot pole. Fox, Disney and Warner Bros. said "no" to us. Paramount said, "Okay, we'll take a chance," knowing that it would have to do over sixty million dollars before they would begin to see substantial money. Paramount stepped up to the deal and said they would take the risk, and it took a lot of guts to do that.

PREMIERE: *When acting as an executive producer, is it tempting to want to help direct?*

SPIELBERG: I've executive-produced only twice now, both times for Robert Zemeckis: once for *I Wanna Hold Your Hand* and once for *Used Cars*. And both times I just had such trust and faith in Robert Zemeckis that I could just fade into the distance while Bob made his movie. It was his film. And I just lent support when he asked for it, never voluntarily. It really depends on the circumstances and the director.

PREMIERE: *What about* Poltergeist*?*
SPIELBERG: I line-produced *Poltergeist.* That was my production; I was very involved with that from the beginning, from the storyboarding through the editing. *Poltergeist* is the story of a family, a normal, suburban family in California, that has a poltergeist experience revolving around their youngest child, five-year-old Carol Ann. And poltergeist experiences do revolve around children prior to puberty and often during adolescence. In the movie it develops into a chaotic nightmare for the family.

PREMIERE: *And* E.T. . . .
SPIELBERG: *E.T.* is a personal film because it's about people and personalities and relationships that I have some experience in. My childhood is still fresh in my memory. I'm sure when I'm seventy and eighty, my childhood will be even fresher in my memory then. But it comes from some of my experiences growing up, and it also evolves out of my wanting to make a movie about the relationship between a ten-year-old boy and a nine-hundred-year-old extraterrestrial outer-space person.

PREMIERE: *Directly from your childhood?*
SPIELBERG: Directly from my childhood fantasies. Part of it evolves from my childhood and my friends as I knew them growing up, and the other part of it evolves from a yen to bring outer space down to earth for a very personal, seductive meeting of minds. *Poltergeist* was just something I conceived while I was doing *Raiders.* I always wanted to make a ghost movie, ever since I was a kid. I loved what happened in *Close Encounters* when the child was kidnapped by the mother ship and taken away by his friends of equal proportion. So I kind of blended a little bit of the kidnapping of the child in *Close Encounters* with the research I had done about poltergeists, and made a movie about a child who's kidnapped by ghosts in her own suburban home in middle America.

PREMIERE: *Do you storyboard all your movies?*
SPIELBERG: All of my movies prior to *E.T.* were storyboarded. I designed the picture visually on paper and then shot the paper, embellishing things

as I went along, because a piece of paper with a one-dimensional sketch is only a starting-point. You have to breathe life into that sketch through characterization, atmosphere, movement, sound and all sorts of things. I'd always designed my movies on paper, up to and including *Poltergeist*. After I designed *Poltergeist* I decided I was tired of spending two months with a piece of paper and a pencil and a couple of sketch artists interpreting my stick figures. I decided to wing *E.T.* Winging *E.T.* made it a very spontaneous, vital movie. Not that the other ones aren't, but I surprised myself. I realized I didn't need the drawings for a small movie like *E.T.* I would never wing *Raiders II*, but I could improvise a more personal picture like *E.T.*, which was essentially more about people and relationships. It was much better to start with personalities and let the personalities suggest where the camera goes as opposed to setting the camera in cement and instructing an actor where to sit, stand and move because that's what the little doodles suggested. If I ever made a picture like *One Flew Over the Cuckoo's Nest*, I certainly wouldn't draw four thousand sketches; I would allow the rehearsal and the characterization to stimulate my visual response to it.

PREMIERE: *Do you enjoy working with children?*
SPIELBERG: I love working with kids.

PREMIERE: *Do you follow what happens to them after your films? For example, what is Cary Guffey (of* Close Encounters) *doing now?*
SPIELBERG: I get updates and pictures. I haven't talked to him in a couple of years, but I know he's still working and he's growing up strong and friendly.

PREMIERE: *Did you discover Heather O'Rourke "Lana Turner-style?"*
SPIELBERG: Yes, I did. Except it wasn't Schwab's, it was the MGM commissary. For *Poltergeist*, I wanted a "beatific" four-year-old child . . . every mother's dream. While having lunch, I looked across the room and there was little Heather sitting there. I kept staring at her. After lunch, I walked over to the table and I said, "Who's the proud mother or agent of this child?" And two hands went up—the mother's and the agent's. So I pulled Heather aside, and I think we made her deal the next day. She's wonderful. *Poltergeist* centers around two children in a family of six, so working with

Heather and some of the other kids on *Poltergeist,* and then, after only five weeks off, stepping right into work with three other kids on the soundstage directing *E.T.,* actually eleven kids, altogether, well, it was a wonderful summer. I'm a frustrated father; I don't have any kids of my own. It was the summer I realized that I wanted to have kids of my own. I told Kathy Kennedy (the producer) before I started shooting *E.T.* and *Poltergeist* that the summer would tell me once and for all if I was suited to being a father. It was going to go one of two ways: I was going to come out of it either pregnant or like W. C. Fields.

PREMIERE: *You realize, of course, that now you will have a lot of mothers and agents parading their kids by you in commissaries.*
SPIELBERG: Right. I'll have to avoid commissaries. I have a great kid in *E.T.* His name is Henry Thomas and I found him when I saw him play Sissy Spacek's older son in *Raggedy Man.*

PREMIERE: *An underrated movie.*
SPIELBERG: Yes, I thought so too. Henry Thomas read for me, but after the reading he did, I asked him to do an improvisation with Mike Fenton, the casting director. The improvisation was so heartfelt and honest that I gave him the part right there. You can hear my voice on the videotape before we could turn the camera off, saying, "You've got the job, kid." I was blown away by this nine-year-old. Then I came to realize that he's an adult actor, not a nine-year-old. He's a very controlled, methodical performer who measures what he does and feels what he does and yet broadcasts it in a totally subtle way. His performance is so controlled, unlike most kid performers, who seem to be giving you 150 percent on every shot. Henry's performance is just a bread crumb at a time, but he takes you in a wonderful direction to a very, very rousing catharsis. He's just a "once in a lifetime" kid.

PREMIERE: *Did you talk to people who had poltergeist experiences before making the movie, similarly to talking to a lot of people who had U.F.O. sightings before* Close Encounters?
SPIELBERG: No, I didn't, really. People think I did. I didn't talk to many people regarding U.F.O.'s, I talked to friends of mine who had experiences with U.F.O.'s. George Lucas had an experience with a U.F.O. Gary Kurtz,

the producer of *Star Wars,* had an experience with a U.F.O. A U.F.O. experience doesn't necessarily mean that they were convinced that it was a space craft from off this planet. It means they saw something unidentified and quite phenomenal in its display.

PREMIERE: *How do you distinguish science fiction from science speculation?*
SPIELBERG: That's a very good question. I've always found that science speculation was about the preternatural. It is more or less what the name implies. It's elements of nature that we know exist; we're just not sure how they exist or how to measure their existence. But they're things that we know are around us in everyday waking life. Science fiction, of course, is just boundless. It's to the limits of one's imagination. And so far it hasn't been discovered where those limits reside.

PREMIERE: *Although you've sometimes been criticized for the frequent use of high technology in your films, the hero usually outwits the opponent with resourcefulness, not a laser gun.*
SPIELBERG: You know, to me humanity always comes first. If there wasn't humanity, nobody would like my movies. I think that every movie that succeeds, succeeds on a humanistic level. You have to like the people of your story; it's very important, and if you don't like the people, no matter how technologically superior a film is, it's just not going to succeed.

PREMIERE: *Are you going to be working with Industrial Light and Magic a lot on future films?*
SPIELBERG: If I make special-effects movies again I will. I certainly will use them on *Raiders II.* Using special effects is only another way around something that can't be created naturally. A special effect is an alternative to making a direct deal with God and asking him to part the Red Sea or create a fantastic light-show in the sky or allow us to see spirits of the past floating through space. It's just another way around that. Failing that, you need special effects. I find the most successful special effects are when it appears that you did make some sort of "special arrangement." The worst special effects to me are the kind that cause the audience to say, "Look at that great effect." The best special effects cause the audience to truly suspend their disbelief and watch wonders unfold right before them. Just like

Spencer Tracy spanking Katharine Hepburn in *Adam's Rib*. While they're watching that sequence, nobody says, "Did he really hit her? Did he really hurt her or did he pull his punches?" Nobody thinks like that when they are totally involved in the storytelling. It's the same with special effects.

PREMIERE: *Do you still always like to print your first take?*
SPIELBERG: I always print my first take, unless the camera crashes into the set wall, or the film breaks or the ship sinks with the crew on board.

PREMIERE: *Is that the one you usually go with?*
SPIELBERG: Not always. But it's always nice to get it right off, because the awkwardness is in the first take. I often go for the awkward moments rather than the rehearsed glossiness because I kind of like the mistakes actors seem to make at first.

PREMIERE: Sugarland Express *was very natural in that respect.*
SPIELBERG: That was very natural. I did a lot of printing of the early takes. I also like to print later takes after the actors have done a scene many times. I suddenly throw in something that throws them off. Then I watch them scrambling for their confidence and scurrying for the focus of the scene. During that searching, some very exciting things can happen in front of the camera. I include accidents as much as possible, especially working with kids, as on *E.T.* Most of the movie is accidents. Henry Thomas' performance certainly isn't, but I play tricks on a number of the actors just in order to keep them spontaneous and fresh.

PREMIERE: *No mean tricks like some directors. . . .*
SPIELBERG: No, no mean tricks, never mean tricks, never on kids. Only on adults. In *Raiders*, I dropped snakes on Karen Allen's head because I didn't think she was screaming for real. I was nicer to Cary Guffey in *Close Encounters* when I opened up a big gift box and pulled out a toy car in order to get him to react to the UFO's approaching his home. He reacted to the present being opened and the toy being offered him. But it just depends on the mood I'm in. If I'm in a playful mood, watch out. If I'm in a serious mood, don't worry about it.

PREMIERE: *In 1974 you said that eighty percent of what you contribute to films is in the selection of the actors. Do you still feel that way?*

SPIELBERG: Yeah, but I think the percentage is different. I really believe that casting is at least half of a movie. When I was younger I tended to exaggerate. As I began to hit my mid-thirties, I began to be more cautious in what I said. Anyway, I really believe casting is half the battle. Imagine *Kramer vs. Kramer* with anybody else but Dustin Hoffman and Justin Henry playing those parts. You can't. Certainly there are other people who could play the parts, but I think Dustin's time had come, and that movie's time had arrived, and it was destiny that put that chemistry together. Can you imagine *Dr. Zhivago* without Julie Christie and Omar Sharif? Or *Lawrence of Arabia* played by anybody other than Peter O'Toole? I don't believe *Lawrence of Arabia* would have been a successful picture with a lot of second choices. A lot of people feel that nobody else could play Indiana Jones, save Harrison Ford. I find casting to be really important. Not only casting the actor, but also casting the crew.

PREMIERE: *There seem to be some people you like to work with again and again.*

SPIELBERG: The only person that I've had a perfect association with is John Williams. I've never made a feature film without John's score. John not withstanding, sometimes I find it healthy to change. After doing three pictures with Joe Alves, I found that we could no longer work together. I was beginning to look around for new talent . . . new, young, untried people. You can't call Norman Reynolds, who just won the Oscar for Art Direction for *Raiders,* untried. But *Raiders* was really Norman's first picture on his own. And when you think about it, although he assisted John Barry on *The Empire Strikes Back* and *Star Wars* and *Lucky Lady,* essentially *Raiders* is Norman's first movie. And on *E.T.* I used a brand-new art director named Jim Bissel. That was his first feature. And I used a guy named Jim Spencer on *Poltergeist.* That was his first feature film too. In fact, *Sugarland Express* was Joe Alves' first feature film. I love giving people their first break. Because I got my break once. I know how valuable that first time is. People give you their best on their first, second, third, fourth time out of the box. And they put all that energy and ambition into their own work and, of course, into your movie. And that's why I find it so valuable to use very enthusiastic newcomers.

PREMIERE: *And actors?*
SPIELBERG: I think that Richard Dreyfuss and I work very well together. I would love to make another picture with Richard because we work wonderfully and we have a good time. When Richard and I work together, it's more vacation than job.

PREMIERE: *I guess that's one way of keeping spirits up during an exhausting shoot?*
SPIELBERG: Yes. By working with friends. And by creating families and friendships on the set. Although I'm usually the first person who loses his temper or gets a little pushy, because I run blind sometimes when I direct. I only see the work, and sometimes I forget that there are a lot of human people who are trying to contribute to your vision. And I sometimes become a little blind to that. But most of the time it's a very wonderful family. I'd much rather work with somebody like Richard Dreyfuss. I mean, he can be a prima donna for another director, but he can't get away with that with me. We know each other too well. And we share a similar sense of humor about those things.

PREMIERE: *Tell me about your unique method of casting while baking cookies.*
SPIELBERG: I only did that once. I'll tell you what happened. *Raiders* was to be my fifth movie. After having done a lot of TV shows and four feature films, involving many casting sessions all over the country, I realized that actors are really not given a good chance to show you who they really are. When they come into your office you only give them fifteen minutes to open up a portfolio and show you some eight-by-tens. As they talk, you're usually reading their resume and little eye contact is made. Then, just in the last few minutes of the meeting, an actor is required to make an impression that is everlasting, that will win him the part in your movie. I think that's pretty crummy, yet that's been the standard casting method for decades. I found the best way to cast was to make people comfortable. I couldn't think of any better way to make them comfortable than to have a bunch of flour on a table and eggs to be beaten, and dough to be kneaded, and frosting to be laid on. Right away you forget the portfolio. I found in five minutes, as opposed to fifteen minutes, whether I was on the right track. And the actors would all have a chance to let their hair down and be a little looser.

PREMIERE: *Did you do it a lot? Were there a lot of cookies baked?*

SPIELBERG: I went through Julia Child's cookbook twice. We baked every day, five days a week, for over fourteen weeks of casting. And often we baked two selections a day, one in the morning and one in the afternoon.

PREMIERE: *Who ate everything?*

SPIELBERG: The office. Lucas had a staff of a hundred people. They would smell the cooking from the kitchen in the office complex and suddenly reach in their lunch boxes and have an eleven a.m. lunch because they couldn't wait any longer. But that was the fun part, and I'll do it again. Unfortunately, we lost the office we were casting *Raiders* in, so I now have to find a place with a kitchen. I don't want to work off a hot plate or a Bunsen burner making tuna-melts in my Universal office. I need the cutting block in the center, the cupboards, the microwave...forget the microwave, never cook anything in a microwave. Make that a gas stove.

PREMIERE: *Do you believe in poltergeists?*

SPIELBERG: Yes, I do, I absolutely do. I believe in poltergeists and UFOs. In every movie I've made I've essentially believed in what the films were about. Even *Jaws.* I do believe there are sharks close to twenty-six feet long in the ocean. The largest ever caught is twenty-one feet. If I ever make a film about a fifty-foot woman, I'll believe that too.

PREMIERE: *Since 1941, it appears that everything you've done has come in under-schedule and under-budget. Is that true?*

SPIELBERG: Actually, that is sort of a new effort on my part. *Jaws* was justifiably over-budget and over-schedule. *1941* was more capriciously and lavishly over-budget and over-schedule, which was all my fault. *Close Encounters* was semi-justifiably over-schedule, but I believed in that movie and I would have done anything to make it as good as it possibly could be, no matter who was paying. But since then, beginning with *Raiders* and including *Poltergeist* and *E.T.,* all have been under-schedule and under-budget. I found with these movies that the compromises I made to deliver the films responsibly were actually better than the original ideas I started with. This isn't a rule, and maybe I'll change my mind later, but when I had to make a compromise to save some money, I found that the second idea was fresher and better for the movie.

PREMIERE: *Do you think we're better or worse off for no longer having a studio system?*

SPIELBERG: Well, the studio system filled a need as a center of incubation for an artform that was just coming into its own. It was very important as a hatchery for writers, directors, producers, stars and composers, and people in all sorts of arts and crafts. Then, it appears, the crafts people and the creative people began to outgrow their playpens, and they wanted to be more independent; they wanted to make their own decisions, as opposed to allowing a Jack Warner or Harry Cohn to make decisions for them. I think that, for a while, that was very, very healthy. I don't think that films like *Streetcar Named Desire* or *On the Waterfront* could've been made through the studio system that existed from the twenties through the late forties; and yet, by the same token, I kind of miss it today, only because there are some talented, creative people who aren't organized. They have loads of talent, imagination and a lot of creative ambition, but they are not a part of a system that would give them the sandbox to play in. Certain people work better when there are other people around who can discipline, even act as sounding-boards, as well as providing the technology that will help make movies better and more efficiently. A little of that is what George Lucas is doing up in Northern California. A little of that is what Francis Coppola is doing at American Zoetrope, here in Hollywood. I think that it's a great idea, yet, at the same time, everyone wants to be a part of a club but no one wants to join as a lifetime member. You know, when I was first getting started, I signed a seven-year contract with Universal Studios because I would do anything to get my break. But after tasting freedom and experiencing what it was like to make a movie and wear a lot of different hats, I was no longer happy pitching for just one ball club. I wanted to have my own company. Still, I work very well within the studio system . . . that system gave me my start.

PREMIERE: *While under contract at Universal you directed a lot of TV. Did that help you become organized as a director?*

SPIELBERG: Yes. Television taught me how to be a professional within a very chaotic business. Making movies is an unnatural act. Really, if God had meant for man to make movies, Thomas Edison would have been born a thousand years ago. It's usually contrary to nature, contrary to human behavior, and often Murphy's Law and the Peter Principle prevail. If I'd had my 'druthers back in 1968, I would have started in feature films, but nobody would give me a job. Yet there were jobs in the offing as a television director. So I began working on *Night Gallery* and *Columbo* and established a small reputation. Then I branched out into feature films after a few successful TV movies. But I found that TV taught me how to do homework. It taught me how to sketch out ideas and taught me how to make a shot-list in the morning. I'm really happy to have started in a disciplined arena such as television. I really admire directors like Arthur Penn, John Frankenheimer and Sydney Lumet, who began in live television. That's something that my generation has never experienced. I hope that live television comes back, because that was what the word "event" was coined for.

PREMIERE: *Have you ever screened a film and recut it after that?*
SPIELBERG: Recut's not the right word because it implies that a movie's a disaster and you have to start from scratch, reworking every frame. I have previewed a film and revised it, juxtaposed certain things and deleted or even extended certain moments. I use previews the way theatrical directors use rehearsals. They listen to the reaction; they change things. If there's a huge laugh and pertinent dialogue is about to occur they'll hold for the laughter. I use previews that way. The difference is, there's a lot more time in theater than there is in film. When you get down to the preview stage, there's probably about three weeks left to do everything before the film is released. The previews of both *Close Encounters* and *Jaws* really helped me. Two very successful previews, by the way—the kind of previews where all the studio people say, "Gee, don't touch this; it works great." And after this extraordinary preview in Dallas of *Jaws,* I still didn't feel I had a big enough reaction in the second act of the movie, so I designed the head coming out of the hole in the boat, which I shot in a friend's swimming pool. And that became the big scream of the movie. I felt the movie needed an explosive surprise at that point. I thought things were beginning to get a little too expository. The preview helped to expose a weakness so I could fill the gap. On *Close Encounters,* I had a very important decision to make: whether or not to use the Walt Disney song, "When You Wish Upon a Star" at the end of the movie, with Jiminy Cricket's actual voice performing it. And the only way I could tell was to have two different previews, on two different nights: one night with the song, one night without it. I then analyzed the preview cards very carefully, inter-

viewed the people who left the theater, and made a determination that
the audience wanted to be transported into another world along with
Richard Dreyfuss as he walked aboard the mothership. They didn't want
to be told the film was a fantasy, and this song seemed to belie some of
the authenticity and to bespeak fantasy and fairy tale. And I didn't want
Close Encounters to end just as a dream.

PREMIERE: *Recently, there have been a number of lawsuits by people claiming
their ideas were stolen by famous filmmakers. Does this make you hesitant to
read material sent to you?*

SPIELBERG: It's the unknown people you've never heard of, whose material you've never read, who usually crawl out of the woodwork like cock
roaches to sue you. But if you're worried about lawsuits, you shouldn't read
material. You know, you only hear from them after a film is making millions
of dollars every week. You rarely hear of people coming out of the woodwork
after a *Heaven's Gate* or *1941* claiming you stole their ideas. It only happens
when a film is very successful. I've never been gun-shy about it. I've just
been very careful to use my own material and my own ideas, especially in
recent years. It's more satisfying to make up the story from thin air than it
is to adapt someone's novel or buy a short story that's been, perhaps, floating around for forty years. I'd much rather make my own movies, from my
own ideas. A lot of people have original ideas. I really believe that an idea
is kind of like a spore from a dandelion; you know, it gets into the air and
it can pollinate the universe. But there is only a handful of people who
know how to take an idea and develop it into something, and only a few
others, a lower percentage of creative individuals, who can take that developed story and make it into a movie. Ideas are always going into the air for
anybody to just reach up and grab at. That's why so often you see, say,
three gang movies coming out at the same time. There's a virus in the air;
everybody catches it, but perhaps only a half-dozen people can develop it,
only a few people can get movies made from it and maybe only one of
them is any good. And this happens constantly.

PREMIERE: *A lot of meanings have been read into your films. Do people try to
pin you down regarding your intentions?*

SPIELBERG: Well, I'm always surprised at certain symbolic references or
cross-parallels to other experiences, or other films, that people bring up,

saying, "Gee this is like . . . " or "Hey, this is existential." Sometimes I'm pleasantly surprised. It's always nice to see a movie not only through your own intuitions but through someone else's perception. I love anybody who thinks beyond the butter in their popcorn. I really do.

PREMIERE: *Speaking of popcorn, do you like to go to the theatre and watch other people's reactions to your movies?*
SPIELBERG: No. Never.

PREMIERE: *Why is that?*
SPIELBERG: Because once I finish a movie it's done. It's not mine anymore. The actual release of the picture is all but anticlimatic. I'd seen *Raiders* innumerable times and was very tired of it by the time it hit the screen. When people were just discovering *Raiders* and throwing up their hats, I was exhausted from the experience of having made the movie. I never saw *Raiders* with the general public until it opened at the Cinerama Dome after its forty-fourth week in movie theaters. This was the first time with the public, and almost a year had passed since I'd last seen it. I was able to watch the picture semi-objectively and to enjoy the film as entertainment. But there was still a feeling of, "Why did I do it that way? Why didn't I do it this way? Gee, why did I use those syphilitic camels?"

PREMIERE: *Are you usually so critical of your work?*
SPIELBERG: I'm very critical of my work. "I should've spent more time on that sequence; oh my God, that was take two, I hated take two, why didn't I use take four?" I mean, it was that sort of thing. I can watch my own movies up to a point and then I become too critical about choices, and missed opportunities, and better shots that a year later seem more vivid in my mind than what I'd remembered a year before. So it's traumatic for me to sit in my own film and watch it. I marvel at John Williams because he can conduct his own music over and over again. I can't do that. I'll dedicate two or three years of my life to one film. But then I want to move on and try something new.

PREMIERE: *After* Jaws *was such a phenomenal success, was its immediate effect positive or negative?*
SPIELBERG: It's strange, because at first it had a very negative effect on me. I thought it was a fluke. No movie had ever grossed a hundred million

dollars in the U.S. and Canada. On its way to making what it eventually made, four hundred million around the world, it was regarded by everybody as a kind of carnival freak. They said it must have been the heat of that summer that gave the shark legs, that took him inland so far, gobbling up the country like little Pac-Men. So I began believing it was some kind of freak and agreeing when people said it could never happen again. They were saying it was the timing and the climate that created the success of *Jaws* more than what I had done to make the movie a success. What vindicated me was when *Star Wars* came out and became the second film to gross over a hundred million. And what doubly vindicated all of us, including George, was when *Raiders* grossed over a hundred million. But I do think I was a little set back by that thinking early on in the experience. Later, I realized we made a movie that was just super-intense and somehow struck a chord around the world.

PREMIERE: *Do you like to rehearse your actors much?*
SPIELBERG: It depends. Only if the scene calls for rehearsal. I've never really been involved in a project that was less visual and more performance-oriented. I've had good performances in all my films, but the films have been somewhat larger than the people in them. And often, in certain scenes, the people have had to play second clarinet to this cathedral organ of a mothership from *Close Encounters*. At the same time, I found that rehearsal really helps periodically within a very large movie. I actually rehearsed Dreyfuss and some of the other actors on *Close Encounters*. I actually rehearsed Robert Shaw, Richard Dreyfuss and Roy Scheider for *Jaws*. These are films you wouldn't imagine having rehearsals for. But they came over to my house to rehearse lines like "That's a twenty-foot shark," and Dreyfuss saying, "Yo ho ho." I mean, you can imagine us sitting in a room together, rehearsing "Yo ho ho" for three hours. But in fact, all the dialogue for *Jaws* came from improvisation because I was not one hundred percent happy with the script that I had developed and was responsible for. I was very happy with the structure, but not with some of the characterization and dialogue. So I sat with these three talented actors at my house every day, and we improvised and rehearsed until we found a way to play the scene. Often, I would just take the lines right from the tape recorder, transcribe them to script form, pass out the pages the next morning and we'd shoot the scene later that day. I would never have rehearsed

E.T., because there's nothing that can kill spontaneity faster than rehearsing youngsters. They're natural and you don't want to lose that electric spark.

PREMIERE: *Were you considered weird or at least different as a child?*
SPIELBERG: I think I was never considered really weird, the way the philosophy majors were weird. But I was considered different by the neighbors who saw me making movies on the weekends with twelve- and thirteen-year-old kids dressed up as adults with fake mustaches and beards, army uniforms and sometimes monster suits. And I think that probably several of my friends were warned about playing with me—that nothing good could come of knowing somebody who makes movies in eight millimeters at twelve years old. Although some of the neighbors took exception with my hobby, other people thought it was great. I had a good time growing up. I can't complain about my childhood.

PREMIERE: *Is it true that your parents kept a blanket over the TV set?*
SPIELBERG: Yeah. Yeah. I was ten years old and was forbidden to watch TV. They knew that at night, when the babysitter would be there, I would sneak and turn the TV set on and watch late movies. And so they would put a blanket over the screen and arrange plants and things on top with precise measurement. Sometimes my father would attach hairs in exact positions so he could tell if I had lifted up the dust ruffle over the RCA nineteen-inch screen and snuck a peak at *The Honeymooners* or *Dragnet.*

PREMIERE: *Well, did you accept the challenge? Did you....*
SPIELBERG: Yes, I always found the hair, memorized exactly where it was and rearranged it before they came home.

PREMIERE: *Was your dad terribly disappointed that you didn't become a computer engineer?*
SPIELBERG: Well, I don't know; it's hard to say. I think my dad wanted me to follow in his footsteps and get involved in electronics and computers, but as it turned out I'm getting involved in electronics and computers anyway by being a "Pac-Man" and an "Asteroid" and a "Missile Command" freak. Hopefully, I will eventually design software for video firms.

PREMIERE: *What other media do you want to work in?*

SPIELBERG: I want to do stage work...maybe a Broadway musical. I'd love to do live television. And, as I said, I'd like to design software which I intend to do. And eventually, I want to find new, more economical ways of recreating cinema. I want to do everything that has to do with visual arts and media, but you only have so much time in which to do everything. It's very hard to squeeze all that energy and ambition into the time it takes to make one movie, because making one movie, in itself, is close to impossible, as anybody who has made a movie knows. I'm not exaggerating when I say it's like going to war. You're under siege; your positions are attacked. I've never come onto a set where I had a day completely free of problems. That's never happened.

PREMIERE: *So do you see yourself having to direct less so you can do the other things?*

SPIELBERG: Probably, at some point, I will have to direct less so I can do the other things, especially if I want to explore theater and video programs, but I'm sure that will be part of my own evolution in growing up and I'll come back to film.

PREMIERE: *Would you like to do a musical?*

SPIELBERG: Funny you should mention that. I'm planning one right now. Quincy Jones and I are developing it. I've got to be secretive about it, though. I never really discuss my ideas until they've been fully realized, usually in scope and stereophonic sound. I'm a big fan of Quincy's. I thought this would be a perfect opportunity to combine what he does best with what I do well and make a "dangerous" movie.

PREMIERE: *When you were starting out did you sneak onto others' sets?*

SPIELBERG: Yes.

PREMIERE: *And were you bodily ejected?*

SPIELBERG: A couple of times, just like I've had to throw spectators off my sets. The security is usually really tight on my sets. I don't usually invite observers to come and watch. I was thrown off *Torn Curtain* when I was a teenager. Then, after *Jaws* came out, I was thrown off another

Hitchcock movie, *Family Plot*. So I've been tossed off two Hitchcock films. I never met Hitchcock, I'm sorry to say. It was very eerie the second time I was thrown off his set. I walked onto the stage and Hitchcock was sitting with his back to me watching the action. All of a sudden it was as if he sensed an intruder in his reverse vision. He couldn't have seen me but he leaned over to an assistant director and whispered something. A few moments passed and the A.D. came over to me and said, "Sir, this is a closed set." I was escorted off the set and it was actually quite thrilling. That was the closest I came to Hitchcock. I learned that he had eyes in the back of his head.

PREMIERE: *You once described yourself as a very enclosed person who makes open, impersonal movies.*

SPIELBERG: Well, I might have said that at a time when I was feeling kind of closed-off. I am kind of closed-off when I'm in the middle of a production. I'm open to the recycling of the real world, which has to go through the moviemaker to get into the movie, to ring true. But by the same token, I kind of shut down my personal life and put everything into my movie world. It's like having an affair with my film while I'm making it. I think as time's gone on I've sort of learned how to make movies and live life all at the same time. I think I'm very demanding when I make a movie. I kind of become a two-star General, then a nice guy, after the experience is over. I've had crews at wrap parties say, "Why can't you be this way every day on the set?" Sometimes, when I work, all I can think about is the results and how to get those results. It is very hard for me to really enjoy myself while making the film. I'm too single-minded. But whatever high pressure I exude is unconscious on my part. I don't design friction just to bring the best out of people. I'm naturally demanding. If I think I can do somebody's job better than they can, sometimes I try to do the job. And it just automatically makes people work harder at what they do. When I work with somebody, I try to bring the best out of them, because I'm always trying to bring the best out of myself with every movie I make. So I get very demanding, and that demand either provokes some kind of friction or it invites a kind of creative sympatico. Making movies is hard work. The creativity is sometimes only realized in the editing, or later when the audience laughs where you want them to laugh or cries where you thought they might. That's the reward. And that's when you say, "Gee, we all did a pretty good job." Until then, it's just a lot of hard work.

I get my jollies when I'm cutting and when I'm storyboarding. In between the storyboarding and film editing, it's a nightmare. When I'm editing and under no pressure, I can come in at ten and eleven o'clock and work until two, three a.m. My editor, Michael Kahn, who has been with me for five movies, loves working at exotic hours. He won the Oscar for *Raiders* as much for his personal commitment as for his skills. I think maybe I enjoyed cutting *Raiders* with Michael more than I've ever enjoyed editing any movie before. We had a great time, especially in tightening the film until it began to exceed the speed limit for a movie of this nature, and once the film exceeded the design in terms of forward velocity, that's when I stopped and said, "Okay, I'm finished." Then I showed it to George, George made some adjustments, and we showed it to Paramount and then released the movie.

PREMIERE: *How did you manage to escape drinking, smoking and doing drugs?*
SPIELBERG: Movies are my sin; my major sin is filmmaking. I find the people who drink excessively, or take a lot of drugs, aren't really happy with their lives and with what they're doing. But I've always been very happy making films and that is all the stimulation that I've needed. Well, I also need a good social and home life. My home life is as important to me as my filmmaking life. With this in mind, I usually can stay pretty normal.

PREMIERE: *Paul Schrader recently said that the business was dying. You don't share that. . . .*
SPIELBERG: No, I don't think the business is dying at all. I think that the business is flourishing. With cable and satellites, and feature films and TV. . . . It's unsettled right now, but it's all going to flourish and it's going to be good for everyone.

PREMIERE: *Do you see a future of being indoors more?*
SPIELBERG: Listen, the world is going indoors, and it's a fact we'll all have to face. Because the world is withdrawing to the safety and protec-

tion of the home, you're going to find a lot of advancement in television broadcasting, high resolution and sound. And screen size. It's just the next natural step. The world is going inside. But they'll go out if you make it worth their time. All the pressure is on us.

PREMIERE: *You seem to be prepared for it. How many video games do you have between your home and your office?*
SPIELBERG: At home I have four. In my office, I have six, and here (studio) I have four. I've got about fifteen. I only own four; the rest I rent. When I get tired of them, we send them back and get a new game.

PREMIERE: *Do you have other gadgets?*
SPIELBERG: I've got the regular stuff, only what every boy should have in his house. Several home computers with modems to update what's happening in the office. By the way, we're linking up my facility down here with George's facility up in San Rafael and marrying our computers. So when we're working on projects together such as *Raiders II,* we can exchange memorandums and ideas quickly via computer.

PREMIERE: *Don't you also have a special desk?*
SPIELBERG: Yes. I do. It's rather outdated now, but when I first got it five years ago, it was a real scream. It has built into it a papershredder, tape recorder, telephone, TV set to monitor who's at my front and back doors, pencil sharpeners, night light, a radio . . . a lot of things.

PREMIERE: *How far ahead do you have your work schedule projected?*
SPIELBERG: Actually, my life isn't planned out that much. I have a lot of things in development. I don't call those plans because a lot of the things we put into development are often turned back to the writers or never made, or made with other people at other studios. So the things I have in development don't really count until I'm on the floor with them. The only thing I know I'm positioning my time for, because I'm turning down a lot of things in order to clear the time-space, is *Raiders II.*

PREMIERE: *And when will shooting begin?*
SPIELBERG: That will start shooting in May of '83. I'll start preparing in January of '83. And it'll be out summer of '84.

PREMIERE: *And that will be completely storyboarded?*
SPIELBERG: Oh, yeah, just like the last *Raiders*. George is a great influence over me in terms of economics and budgets and schedules. He's a great producer and he's taught me a lot about creative compromise, about how you don't have to spend thirty million dollars to get fifteen million dollars on the screen. George shortcuts with little . . . I call them little "Pac-Man" detours. He's been very good, not only with me in *Raiders*, but with himself, á la *American Graffiti* and *Star Wars*. So he's his own best producer and he's a very good producer for anybody else who works with him.

PREMIERE: *How many episodes of* Raiders *are planned?*
SPIELBERG: Four.

PREMIERE: *And you're going to do them all?*
SPIELBERG: No. I'll probably do the next one, maybe the third one. But it just depends. If I have as much fun with the second one as I had with the first one, I might do the third one; or maybe George will. We'll just have to wait and see what happens.

PREMIERE: *Which film of yours has given you the most personal satisfaction?*
SPIELBERG: I can unequivocally say that my most enjoyable experience and the best result came out of the *E.T.* experience. It is the closest I've been to really being satisfied with a picture and not wanting to go back in and change it.

PREMIERE: *Do you have any trouble finding new challenges?*
SPIELBERG: Every movie I make is a new challenge. I'll have big hit movies and I'll have films that aren't big hits and that's just what happens when you're a filmmaker and you're putting your things out there for the public to either applaud or yawn at. Through all that, I just hope I don't lose my ambition and my love for starting something new and seeing it right through to the end. I just hope I don't lose that. That seems to be the main cause of atrophy among filmmakers who have been around for a while. They tend to forget how exciting that spark is that first gave them all the energy to make their first five or six or seven movies, and then they seem to get a little tired. John Ford never did because he just kept his instrument tuned up. He worked all the time, sometimes making as many

as three movies a year. A lot of other directors were part of the studio contract system and made movies the way construction workers build condominiums. It was a job, albeit a very stimulating and creative one, but still a job, and they just lived hard and lived long. Today, because movies mean so much more to the individual filmmaker than they ever had before, because so much is riding on even a ten- or twelve-million-dollar movie, because it still costs seven to ten million to sell it, make the prints and pay for the advertising; because so much rides on it, it seems that each movie becomes a life-or-death struggle. And I kind of like the old-fashioned attitudes of some of the "workhorse" directors of the thirties and forties. When every movie was a job, a personal commitment too, a love, perhaps more like an affair, you did the best you could possibly do within the limited amount of time you were given and within the confines of the budget.

PREMIERE: *Do you work well in crisis situations?*
SPIELBERG: Absolutely. I create problems for myself just so I can get creatively turned on. I don't create serious problems for myself, but I worry a lot. I tend to sweat the small stuff. I figure that if I anticipate the small things as being disasters, I'll be prepared for the larger, more obvious crises. I just find that I think better..., I'll give you an example. One scene in *Raiders* called for Harrison to fight the swordsman in a duel lasting three minutes. I had two days to shoot it in, but Harrison couldn't stand up because he had a bad case of the Tunisian Touristas. I suggested that he take his gun out and just shoot the swordsman. The solution was quite possibly an inspired compromise. So I think I work better when I'm pinned down, more than when I have all the money in the world and all the time and all eyes watching my next move. I work much better when I'm not being focused upon.

A Conversation with Steven Spielberg

MICHAEL SRAGOW/1982

AT THIRTY-FOUR, STEVEN Spielberg is, in any conventional sense, the most successful movie director in Hollywood, America, the Occident, the planet Earth, the solar system, and the galaxy. Three of his movies—*Jaws, Close Encounters of the Third Kind,* and *Raiders of the Lost Ark*—are action-fantasy classics that rank among the biggest moneymakers of all time. Before the summer is out, they may well be joined by *E.T. The Extra-Terrestrial,* a lyrical piece of sci-fi about the human, and alien, condition (conceived, coproduced, and directed by Spielberg), and a crowd-pleasing shocker, *Poltergeist* (coproduced and cowritten by Spielberg but directed by Tobe Hooper).

Spielberg is the scion of a suburban upbringing and a public-school education. His mother was a concert pianist and his father a computer scientist who moved his family of four children "from Ohio to New Jersey, Arizona, Saratoga, and Los Angeles." From age twelve on, Spielberg knew he did one thing best: make movies. When college time came, he enrolled in film school at Cal State Long Beach. In 1969, on the basis of a twenty-four-minute short called *Amblin',* Spielberg was able to sign with Universal, where he directed episodes of *Night Gallery, Marcus Welby,* and *Columbo,* the terrifying TV-movie *Duel;* his first feature, *The Sugarland Express;* and his breakthrough, "primal scream" thriller, *Jaws.*

E.T. The Extra-Terrestrial is another breakthrough for Spielberg. His previous movies have all been spectacles of some species, even the out-of-control slapstick epic *1941*. Their escapism grew out of Spielberg's childhood fantasy life: "When I didn't want to face the real world," he says, "I just stuck a camera up to my face. And it worked." Making *E.T.*, however, compelled Spielberg to face the reality of his childhood pain and left him feeling "cleansed." Now, he says, "I'm trying to make movies by shooting more from the hip and using my eyes to see the real world."

The day after a triumphant out-of-competition screening of *E.T.* at Cannes in May, I spoke to Spielberg in his New York City hotel suite. He exuded casualness, from his NASA cap to his stockinged feet, as well as confidence that his most intimate movie might also prove to be his best loved. Talking about *E.T.*, *Poltergeist*, his favorite contemporary directors, and the troubled state of the motion-picture business, Spielberg seemed itching to take on the world.

Everything seems to have come together for you with E.T. *Certainly few filmmakers have had such a good shot at being both profoundly personal and phenomenally popular.*
You know the saying, the book wrote itself. This movie didn't make itself, but things began to happen from its inception in 1980 that told me this was a movie I was ready to make. I'm not into psychoanalysis, but *E.T.* is a film that was inside me for many years and could only come out after a lot of suburban psychodrama.

What do you mean by suburban psychodrama?
Growing up in a house with three screaming younger sisters and a mother who played concert piano with seven other women—I was raised in a world of women.

In a lot of your movies, the women or the girls are the more elastic characters, emotionally.
That's right, they are. I like women, I like working with women. *E.T.* had a plethora of them. A woman coproducer, a woman writer, a woman film editor, a woman assistant director, woman costumer, woman script person,

women in construction, women in set design, a woman set dresser. I am less guarded about my feelings around women. I call it shoulder-pad syndrome; you can't cry on a shoulder that's wearing a shoulder pad. This is something from my school days of being a wimp in a world of jocks.

How much of a wimp were you?
The height of my wimpery came when we had to run a mile for a grade in elementary school. The whole class of fifty finished, except for two people left on the track—me and a mentally retarded boy. Of course *he* ran awkwardly, but I was just never able to run. I was maybe forty yards ahead of him, and I was only 100 yards away from the finish line. The whole class turned and started rooting for the young retarded boy—cheering him on, saying, "C'mon, c'mon, beat Spielberg! Run, run!" It was like he came to life for the first time, and he began to pour it on but still not fast enough to beat me. And I remember thinking, "Okay, now how am I gonna fall and make it look like I really fell?" And I remember actually stepping on my toe and going face hard into the red clay of the track and actually scraping my nose. Everybody cheered when I fell, and then they began to really scream for this guy: "C'mon, John, c'mon, run, run!" I got up just as John came up behind me, and I began running as if to beat him but not really to win, running to let *him* win. We were nose to nose, and suddenly I laid back a step, then a half-step. Suddenly he was ahead, then he was a chest ahead, then a length, and then he crossed the finish line ahead of me. Everybody grabbed this guy, and they threw him up on their shoulders and carried him into the locker room, into the showers, and I stood there on the track field and cried my eyes out for five minutes. I'd never felt better and I'd never felt worse in my entire life.

You once said you managed to win over some of the jocks by starring them in a film called Battle Squad. *By making films like* Jaws, *were you still trying to ingratiate yourself with hard guys?*
Yeah, hard liners. Hard, cynical liners. But not just three or four jocks in my elementary or junior high school. I'm talking about millions of people.

Do you mean that making movies is a way of showing off?
With the exception of *Close Encounters,* in all my movies before *E.T.,* I was giving *out,* giving *off* things before I would bring something *in.* There

were feelings I developed in my personal life...that I had no place to put. Then, while working on *Raiders,* I had the germ of an idea. I was very lonely, and I remember thinking I had nobody to talk to. My girlfriend was in California, so was George Lucas. Harrison Ford had a bad case of the *turistas.* I remember wishing one night that I had a friend. It was like, when you were a kid and had grown out of dolls or teddy bears or Winnie the Pooh, you just wanted a little voice in your mind to talk to. I began concocting this imaginary creature, partially from the guys who stepped out of the mother ship for ninety seconds in *Close Encounters* and then went back in, never to be seen again.

Then I thought, what if I were ten years old again—where I've sort of been for thirty-four years, anyway—and what if he needed me as much as I needed him? Wouldn't that be a great love story? So I put together this story of boy meets creature, boy loses creature, creature saves boy, boy saves creature—with the hope that they will somehow always be together, that their friendship isn't limited by nautical miles. And I asked Melissa Mathison, who is Harrison Ford's girlfriend and a wonderful writer, to turn it into a screenplay.

Did you hire her because you admired her work on The Black Stallion*?*
I did admire *The Black Stallion,* but it was more because Melissa was one of the few people on the *Raiders* location I could talk to. I was pouring my heart out to Melissa all the time.

In E.T., *the view of growing up is both uplifting and painful. If Elliot hadn't befriended E.T., he'd still be one lonely kid.*
To me, Elliot was always the Nowhere Man from the Beatles song. I was drawing from my own feelings when I was a little kid and I didn't have that many friends and had to resort to making movies to become quasi-popular and to find a reason for living after school hours. Most of my friends were playing football or basketball or baseball and going out with girls. I didn't do those things until very late.

Is E.T. *your imaginary revenge—turning the Nowhere Man into a hero?*
Oh yeah, absolutely. When I began making *E.T.,* I thought that maybe the thing to do was to go back and make life the way it should have been. How many kids, in their Walter Mitty imaginations, would love to save the frogs or kiss the prettiest girl in class? That's every boy's childhood fantasy.

Have you been able to fulfill your own childhood fantasies?

Let me tell you an interesting story. The German director Wim Wenders called me yesterday and said, "Do an interview for me; I'm asking one question: what is the future of the movie business?" I agreed and showed up at three in the afternoon at the Carlton Hotel in Cannes. I walk into the room, and there's a 16-mm movie camera, a microphone, a Nagra [tape recorder] and lights and a crew of six people. They turn on the equipment and they leave me all alone in the room! Finally, I answer the question—straightforward, analytic, sort of like the *Wall Street Journal*. I'm proud of myself until I talk to Harrison Ford. He says *he* would have taken off all his clothes and sat there in the nude, not said a word for ten minutes, then, when the film had run out, walked out fully dressed and thanked them all for a pleasant experience. After all, they weren't going to see the film for forty-eight hours—it takes that long to process it! Now, that just shows me that I'm not as far along in my development as Harrison is. I guess I still haven't been able to shake off the anesthetic of suburbia.

The anesthetic of suburbia—that implies that it protects you from pain and from any kind of raw feeling.

And real life. Because the anesthetic of suburbia also involves having three parents—a mother, a father, and a TV set. Two of them are equilibriums, but one of them is more powerful, because it's always new and fresh and entertaining. It doesn't reach out and tell you what to do.

To me, the key suburban feeling is claustrophobia. Sitting in the den, waiting for the Good Humor truck to come.

I love that. Remember Pinky Lee? I used to sit in the den, listen for the Good Humor truck and watch Pinky Lee on TV. There was no privacy in suburbia because my mom's friends would come in the morning, drink coffee and gossip. And it *was* claustrophobic. It's a reality to kids; in suburbia you have to create a kids' world apart from an adult world—and the two will never eclipse. In an urban world, the adult world and the child world are inseparable. Everybody gets the same dose of reality every day. On the way to school, on the way to the drugstore, on the way home, on the way shopping, it's all the same. In suburbia, kids have secrets. And that's why I wanted *E.T.* to take place in suburbia. What better place to keep a creature from outer space a secret from the grown-ups?

How heavily did you base the movie on contemporary suburban experience, as opposed to your own memories?
In today's world, a twelve-year-old is what we were at sixteen and a half. So a transformation happened once I cast the film with real kids. Not stage Hollywood actors, you know—kids who've never been in a casting director's office or an art director's room. Real people, just real people—that's who we cast.

Dialogue changed considerably. I never would have called my brother, if I'd had one, "penis breath" in front of my mother. It's not the most popular word in the Pac Man generation's vernacular, but it's a word that's used every once in a while, and it conjures up quite gross and hilarious images. I wanted the kids to say something that would shake up the mother, 'cause I wanted her to laugh first, then reprimand, instead of just saying, "How dare you say that in my house!" *That's* the Fifties mother, the one who got attacked by the Martians who ate the dog. *Today's* parent, being my age, would burst out laughing and then suddenly realize, "Omigosh, I'm the father, I can't laugh at that. Sit down son, and never say that word again, or I'll pretend I'm *my* mom and dad back in the Fifties, and you'll have to learn from them."

I think kids tend to look at adults as just melodramatic excuses for people. A lot of kids look up to look down. And I found, even when I was giving Henry Thomas [Elliot] direction, that if I was out of touch with his reality, he would give me a look that seemed to say, "Oh brother, he's old." I could always tell when I was reaching Henry. He would smile and laugh, or he'd say, "Yeah, yeah, right." I was constantly being rewarded or corrected by people three times less my age. I was moving *faster* than the kids. So I slowed myself down and began to metabolize according to them instead of Steven Spielberg.

Did that scare you?
The thing that I'm just scared to death of is that someday I'm gonna wake up and bore somebody with a film. That's kept me making movies that have tried to outspectacle each other. I got into the situation where my movies were real big, and I had a special-effects department and I was the boss of that and that was a lot of fun. Then I'd get a kick out of the production meetings—not with three or four people, but with fifty, sometimes nearer to 100 when we got close to production—because I was able to lead

troops into Movie Wars. The power became a narcotic, but it wasn't power for power's sake. I really am attracted to stories that you can't see on television and stories that you can't get every day. So that attraction leads me to the Impossible Dream, and that Impossible Dream usually costs $20 million.

François Truffaut helped inspire me to make *E.T.* simply by saying to me, on the *Close Encounters* set, "I like you with *keeds,* you are wonderful with *keeds,* you must do a movie just with *keeds*...." And I said, "Well, I've always wanted to do a film about kids, but I've got to finish this, then I'm doing *1941,* about the Japanese attacking Los Angeles." And Truffaut told me I was making a big mistake. He kept saying, "You are the child."

To me, your biggest visual accomplishment is the contrast between suburbia in the harsh, daytime light, when everything looks the same, to the mysterious way it looks at night. By the end, you get a mothering feeling from the night.
Yeah, it *is* Mother Night. Remember in *Fantasia,* Mother Night flying over with her cape, covering a daylight sky? When I was a kid, that's what night really looked like. The Disney Mother Night was a beautiful woman with flowing, blue-black hair, and arms extended outward, twenty miles in either direction. And behind her was a very inviting cloak. She came from the horizon in an arc and swept over you until everything was a blue-black dome. And then there was an explosion, and the stars were suddenly made in this kind of animated sky. I wanted the opening of *E.T.* to be that kind of Mother Night. You know, you come down over the trees, you see the stars, and suddenly you think you're in space — wow, you're not, you're in a forest somewhere. You're not quite sure where; you might be in a forest on some distant planet. It was Melissa's idea to use the forest; at first, I thought of having the ship land in a vacant lot. But she said, "A forest is magical ... there are elves in forests."

Poltergeist seems to be the antithesis of E.T. *in just about every way.*
E.T. is my personal resurrection, and *Poltergeist* is my personal nightmare. A lot of things in both movies really come from my growing up. *Poltergeist* is about my fears — of a clown doll, of a closet, of what was under my bed, of the tree in New Jersey that I felt moved whenever there was a wind storm and scared me with its long, twiggy fingers. But *Poltergeist* is just a suburban ghost story. It's meant to be a thrill a second, with humor. The

most important thing that I wanted to do with this movie was portray a simple, suburban American family that has a sense of humor about life and about science. They enjoy science a little too much. The mother becomes too curious about the poltergeist phenomena for her child's own good, and then is put into the responsible position of rescuing the child. My favorite part of the movie is from the beginning until they get the kid back. My least favorite is the last fifteen minutes. It was fun; I really didn't take it that seriously. After most movies, you can return to the safety of your house. For this movie, I would have liked to steal the ad line from *Jaws II:* "Just when you thought it was safe to go home . . . *Poltergeist*."

You've coproduced both E.T. *and* Poltergeist. E.T. *seems to have gone very well,* Poltergeist *seems to have had trouble. How did you react to facing turmoil as a producer?*
Well, the turmoil is essentially created by wanting to do it your own way and having to go through procedure. That is why I will never again *not* direct a film I write. It was frustrating for Tobe Hooper [the director], and it was frustrating for the actors, who were pretty torn between my presence and his on the set every day. But rather than Tobe's saying, "I can't stand it. Go to Hawaii, get off the set," he'd laugh and I'd laugh. If he'd said, "I've got some ideas that you're not really letting into this movie, I would love you to see dailies, consult, but don't be on the set," I probably would have left.

Has a producer held you in line and helped you in the way, say, Darryl Zanuck is supposed to have helped John Ford?
George Lucas, on *Raiders.* He didn't come in and cut my movie or dictate policy or style or substance. But he was always available to talk, and he was never lacking in ideas. You'll laugh at this: the only other similar experience I've had with somebody I trust and believe in is Sid Sheinberg [president of MCA]. Through the years he's been an invaluable support and sounding board. But he's corporately so high up that he actually has to struggle down the ladder to roll up his sleeves.

You've said that you want to start a children's crusade, leading new talent into the Movie Wars. Does it make sense to do it on your own? Or do you have a chance of making a huge and lasting change only if all the guys with power do it—you, George Lucas, maybe Francis Coppola—joined forces?

I don't know what it would be like to put George Patton, Omar Bradley, Mark Clark, Napoleon, Margaret Thatcher, and Stonewall Jackson in a room together and say, "Okay, now we have to put our heads together and hire a great army." I don't know whether it would blow up in our faces or whether we would be able to consolidate and transform the motion-picture business. Right now, we've all got our own universes to make movies in. Francis lives in a world of his own, George lives in a galaxy far, far away but close to human audiences, and I'm an independent movie-maker working within the Hollywood establishment. But all of us share one thing: each of us would like to do to the film industry what Irving Thalberg did to it fifty years ago.

Is it possible to do that in Hollywood today?
Let's put it this way: if I decided to take two years off from my life, I'd do it only to run an independent studio for a couple of years. And somebody's gonna have to gamble along with me; somebody's gonna have to give me maybe $150 million. And they'll either never see that money again, or they will multiply it by a factor of a hundred, maybe a thousand. It's just a matter of whether Francis or George or I decide to step into the shoes that have been worn by agents for the last eight, nine, ten years and try to apply what we know about how important ideas are, and how important execution is, and how important the casting is, and hire the kinds of directors that would allow us to have as much input as the David O. Selznicks, the Louis B. Mayers, the Jack Warners and the Howard Hughses of the past—not by being tyrants, but by being experienced parents.

I don't know of more than four executives in this town who know how to cut a movie and how to execute one. The people who are in charge today wouldn't know how to save a *Heaven's Gate* if indeed it needed saving. Now, I'm of the school that doesn't think that *Heaven's Gate* needed to be saved. I think that the overall attack that was launched on the director, Michael Cimino, is more interesting and worthy of analysis than the *Heaven's Gate* cataclysm. Because *Heaven's Gate*, which is a very, very flawed movie, is one of the most carefully *crafted* movies of all time. Nobody wrote that *Raise the Titanic* cost around $30 million; everybody destroyed Cimino because his movie cost $30 million. Way down deep, I think the outcry was a primal scream from movie lovers, saying "Please bring the budgets down, please give us better ideas and more entertainment, and give us more intellectual stimulation as well as the pleasure of butter on the popcorn. Don't crush yourselves under the weight." I wish Cimino had been left alone, because, of all the new guys coming up, Michael's got a chance to be David Lean [*Lawrence of Arabia*]. Michael has a showman inside that doesn't know where he's at yet. Michael is maybe as technically skilled as Billy Friedkin, Francis Coppola, Brian De Palma, and Martin Scorsese. And once he gets himself a story that's accessible to the masses, he's gonna be hard to stop.

Do you see any other directors breaking away?
The thing is, anybody who is being given the chance to make a movie has already "made it." That's why making films today is like walking a tightrope over a crocodile pit. The crocodiles are not the critics, they're the economy. If a movie doesn't make money, it's harder to launch a second picture.

But to answer your question, Robert Zemeckis and Bob Gale [*Used Cars*], Hal Barwood and Matt Robbins [*Dragonslayer*]—mark my words, they'll break through. Bob Towne [*Personal Best*], Ridley Scott [*Alien*], Hugh Hudson [*Chariots of Fire*], John Carpenter [*Halloween*] will get there. De Palma certainly will, if he's not already. John Milius [*Conan the Barbarian*] will have his breakthrough some day. Certainly George Miller [*The Road Warrior*]. I like this guy Michael Mann [*Thief*], and Allan Parker [*Shoot the Moon*]. But they are more of the Scorsese-Coppola school than . . . our group.

You say that with a twinkle in your eye. You don't mind there being . . .
I don't mind having two groups. I think the business is one big melting pot anyway. I'm just saying that there are different sensibilities. I think George Lucas and I and some of the others—the Chicago to California group as opposed to the Chicago to New York group—are more frivolous with their imagination. The West Coast has different sensibilities than the East Coast.

I think the other group—Francis and Marty and some of the European filmmakers—bring a lot of their urban development into their movies and take their films very seriously. They internalize who they are and express that on film. I think if you put everybody together and rated them, Marty would have to be the best *filmmaker* of our generation. George Lucas is the best *moviemaker*. You see, George and I have fun with our films. We don't take them as seriously. And I think that our movies are about things that we think will appeal to other people, not just to ourselves. We think of ourselves first, but in the next breath we're talking about the audience and what works and what doesn't.

How do you respond to the idea that what Scorsese does is more adult than what you guys are doing?
Well, it *is* more adult, because it appeals to our anxiety-riddled, darker side. It appeals to the unknown persona. My movies and George's appeal to things that are lighter in nature. I think the difference is terrific. Can you imagine if everybody made *Raiders of the Lost Ark* last year? I think studios were spoiled the first day *Gone With the Wind* made more money than any movie ever. I think from that moment on, decision makers wanted movies that would be hugely successful. So every time I see a small picture take off, whether it's *Animal House* or *Diner,* I cheer. I think it's bullshit when people say the success of *Raiders* precludes the success of *Diner.* I think a success like *Raiders* feeds the pocketbook that's gonna finance *Diner.* You can't have a *Diner* without *Raiders.* But you can't have good movies without *Diner.* So, we need each other. Should we all join hands and sing, "I'd like to buy the world a Coke"? [*Laughs.*]

You talked about your group deferring to the audience occasionally. But in the case of E.T., *it seems you didn't have to do that.*
Well, when I started *E.T.,* I was fat and happy and satisfied with having the films I had on my list. And I just didn't feel I had anything to lose. I actually had *nothing* to lose. I had nothing to prove to anybody except myself—and any people who might have wondered if I ever had a heart beating beneath the one they assume that Industrial Light and Magic [the Lucasfilm special-effects company] built for me.

Does it give off a red glow?
Yes, that one.

Do you think it will help, hurt, or make no difference to have Poltergeist *and* E.T. *come out at the same time?*
I think it might help. I think one gives life to the other. They don't compete. Had I made *Forbidden Planet* and *E.T.*—those films compete. But

Poltergeist is a thrill-a-minute roller-coaster ride through ghosts and haunted houses and various kinds of non-violent bloodletting, "polter-letting," let's say. And *E.T.* is just a whisper from my childhood. These films aren't gonna clash at all.

What comes next?
Well, I know I'm gonna backpedal for about a year because I want to do *Raiders II* next. I'm gonna have a lark this summer by doing a twenty-two minute episode of *The Twilight Zone* in color and wide-screen. All I've got is about ten shooting days and a million bucks to make my show, including postproduction. I've put together a group of directors: John Landis [*Animal House*], Joe Dante [*The Howling*], George Miller [*The Road Warrior*], and myself. Two of us are doing remakes of old episodes, and two of us are doing originals. It'll come out as a quartet this Christmas titled *The Twilight Zone*.

Will you and George Lucas collaborate on Raiders II*?*
Just like the last time. George has the story, I'll have a lot of the scenes. Willard Huyeck and Gloria Katz, the grown-up kids who did *American Graffiti*, will be doing the script. Harrison Ford will continue, but there'll be a new cast.

Raiders II *is for Lucasfilm and Paramount,* The Twilight Zone *is for Warners.* Poltergeist *was for MGM, E.T. for Universal. Why do you go to different studios all the time?*
A moving target is harder to hit [*laughs*]. That's probably it.

So it's a way of reasserting your independence. . . .
Actually, after *E.T.*, most of the movies I'm involved with, I'm gonna own the copyright and the negative. The studios will provide distribution services for a negotiated fee and a piece of the profits. I want to eventually own my own movies. I want to control when they go to cable and when they don't. I want to control when they go to free TV. I don't want to have an inspiration like *E.T.* fall on my head out of the sky and then have all the business and financial decisions about it taken over by a bank.

I won't be able to do this every time. If I come upon a story where the budget's gonna be $20 million or $25 million, then I'll finance it with a

major studio because I wouldn't want to raise that money by selling off
territories overseas. Nobody can raise that much independently. I just
want to keep moving fast, so nobody can say, "I know what makes h
work. It's easy. Anybody can do it."

Don't let them get too comfortable with the resident genius.
Nobody's a resident genius, but being a resident *anything* bothers me. Once
you're at a studio for more than three weeks, you're just another name on
a directory at the dead end of a corridor. That goes whether you're Fellini,
Francis Coppola or just getting started out of NYU.

Spielberg Films *The Color Purple*

GLENN COLLINS/1985

STEVEN SPIELBERG WAS PACING his midtown Manhattan hotel room, cracking walnuts. "Look at this, I'm so nervous, I'm cracking walnuts," he said with a hint of exasperation. "Directors waiting for the returns on new movies are reduced to babbling babies." He sat down, none too tranquilly, and began discussing the film he thinks of as his greatest gamble. "The biggest risk, for me, is doing a movie about *people* for the first time in my career—and failing," he said. "The risk that people will not respond." He paused, squeezing another walnut in his palms. "It's the risk of being judged—and accused of not having the sensibility to do character studies."

Mr. Spielberg's new film, *The Color Purple,* is based on the Pulitzer Prize-winning best seller by Alice Walker, whose epistolary novel witnessed the rural black experience in the first half of this century. A marked departure for Mr. Spielberg, and the first feature film he has directed in two years, the movie has been trumpeted as the movie event of the year. It opens this Wednesday at four theaters in Manhattan.

The Color Purple is devoid of such Steven Spielberg signatures as gleaming suburban kitchens, cuddly aliens and the vibrato of hovering motherships. In fact, there are no special effects. The film spans four decades in the life of its indomitable protagonist, Celie, who transcends the degrading realities of her life in Georgia through relationships with her sister Nettie, who is a missionary in Africa, and with Shug Avery, a blues singer who becomes Celie's lover.

It is a saga that marries elements like family violence, incest, racial discrimination and lesbianism with the power of redemptive love and the triumph of the human spirit. It is a film destined to draw comment regarding its depiction of whites, even as it raises questions about the way in which Hollywood portrays blacks. The film has provided important acting roles for black performers, such as the actress and comedienne Whoopi Goldberg, in her film debut, as Celie, as well as Danny Glover, Adolph Caesar, Margaret Avery, Rae Dawn Chong and Oprah Winfrey.

For Mr. Spielberg, who will be 38 this week, the making of *The Color Purple* spanned a time of cinematic and personal challenge. Married since Thanksgiving eve to the actress Amy Irving, with whom he has a 6-month-old son, Mr. Spielberg has seemed to be a ubiquitous presence this season. A new, critically praised "Steven Spielberg Presents" film, *Young Sherlock Holmes,* is in the movie theaters, although Mr. Spielberg's NBC television anthology series, *Amazing Stories,* has not yet found the audience he had hoped for. However, Mr. Spielberg can look back on six months marked by hits he produced like *Back to the Future* and *The Goonies,* and by the re-release of another film he directed: the biggest money-earner in movie history, *E.T. The Extra-Terrestrial.*

Was 1985 the year when Mr. Spielberg grew up? "I've always been a grown-up," he replied. "I've been playing in the sandbox for years—as a grown-up. But there was always something I was holding back. Something in me would say, 'Go for the easy challenge and not the hard task.' So what I went for was the fast-paced, energetic entertainments. And I won't stop doing them! But I thought that I could also satisfy my own curiosity—about my adult side.

"It's as if I've been swimming in water up to my waist all my life—and I'm great at it—but now I'm going into the deep section of the pool."

Mr. Spielberg added that "for a long time I'd been wanting to become involved with something that had more to do with character development." He explained: "I really wanted to challenge myself with something that was not stereotypically a Spielberg movie. Not to try to prove anything, or to show off—but just to try to use a different set of muscles.

I wanted to work in the same arena as directors like Sidney Lumet and Sydney Pollack—and Paddy Chayefsky, in terms of what he'd done as a playwright and writer."

Previously, Mr. Spielberg said, his closest encounter with a "character-oriented" movie was *E.T.* "The big difference in *The Color Purple* is that the story is not larger than the lives of these people," he added. "I didn't want to make another movie that dwarfs the characters. But here," he said of the new film, "the characters are the story."

The Color Purple is not wholly alien to the Spielberg oeuvre. "It links to my previous movies in that it portrays an urgency to fulfill a dream," he said. "Celie has an urgency to fulfill her own destiny, to discover the things that belong to her self."

In addition, he said, Celie shares an ordinariness with his previous film protagonists. "She is someone who, when she's on the streets of town, well, you wouldn't look twice," he said. "There's a bit of the ugly duckling here—she's called ugly by almost everyone when, in fact, she's beautiful."

But unlike his previous heroines, "Celie doesn't have I.L.M. at her disposal," Mr. Spielberg said, referring to the poltergeists at the Industrial Light and Magic studio who cast Mr. Spielberg's special-effects spells. "All she can call on—all she has—is God, and memory, and love for her sister, and the eternal wisdom dormant inside her."

Mr. Spielberg denied that his new movie had been simply a "property." "I didn't sit down with my associates and say, 'Find me a people project,'" he said. "Kathleen Kennedy, my partner and associate who runs my company, came to me and said, 'Here's something you might enjoy reading,' and slipped me the book."

"If she'd presented it to me as a potential project, I think I'd have felt challenged and defensive," Mr. Spielberg said. "But I started reading it and I couldn't stop. I came away from it very much in love with Celie. I was also obsessed with Mr.," he said, referring to the man Celie writes about as "Mr. —," the cruel widower to whom Celie is given by her stepfather.

The book "kept gnawing on me," he continued. The possibility of bringing it to the screen intrigued him, and when he discussed it with the composer Quincy Jones, who was one of the film's producers, Mr. Spielberg said, "I told Quincy, 'I don't know that I'm the filmmaker for this. Don't you want to find a black director, or a woman?' And Quincy asked, 'You didn't have to come from Mars to do *E.T.*, did you?' He said this movie should be directed by the person who loves it most—and I loved it more than anyone else."

Mr. Spielberg said he also wanted "to bring Celie's story to a wider audience than the one reading the book," adding: "It seemed to me that the audience reading the book was mostly female and white."

The Color Purple cost $15 million, Mr. Spielberg said, and to meet the budget he took no salary "except for the Directors Guild minimum, $40,000," the contractual minimum for directing a film. "And I spent *that* on overages. I'd say I want something done, and Kathy would respond, 'You know how much that costs?' and then I'd tell Kathy, 'Well, take it out of the D.G.A. minimum.'"

At first, after reading the book, Mr. Spielberg said he didn't know if it would be possible to adapt so literary a work for the screen. The novel's text is a sequence of letters written by Celie to God, and to and from Nettie.

"My own letters to the deity began, 'Dear God, how can I make this book into a movie?'" he said, smiling. "But finally I realized that the book left me with a residue of emotion, and I decided to deal with that— that made it possible to work with. And it struck me from the beginning that the book was Dickensian." He alluded to the novel's harrowing plot attended by a magical restoration of fortune at its denouement. Mr. Spielberg added a scene to the film showing the reading of *Oliver Twist.*

While he was considering directing the film, Mr. Spielberg said, Mr. Jones introduced him to Miss Walker at her home in San Francisco. "Basically, I was going to be interviewed," he said, "as I hadn't been since 11 years before when I was up for jobs, starting out as a director." They went out to dinner, and she gave him her approval. Ultimately, Miss Walker became a consultant on the production's design, made casting suggestions—including that of Miss Goldberg—and visited the set during filming.

"Alice was a spiritual presence throughout the movie," he said. "She was there about half the time. A couple of times we'd go over to her and say, 'We're adding something here and we'd like to ask, could you help us?' and she'd write a line or two."

This sunny portrait contrasts with the original worries Miss Walker aired in interviews on the set concerning her reservations about entrusting *The Color Purple* to a white director working within the white male Hollywood power structure. The screenwriter who adapted the book, the Dutch-born Menno Meyjes, is also white.

"My color was never an issue after she selected me as the right guy for the picture," said Mr. Spielberg. "The issue was not the color of my skin, but whether I'd make a good movie out of the book."

What is Miss Walker's reaction to the film? "She's seen it and she thinks highly of it," Mr. Spielberg said. Miss Walker declined to be interviewed about the movie or to issue a statement about it, save for a spokesman's explanation that "she wants to see it again."

Some of those who attended preview screenings have wondered if audiences will feel that the film reinforces racial stereotypes. "I never saw the movie in any way as reinforcing those stereotypes," Mr. Spielberg said. "This is a human story, and the movie is about human beings. It's about men and women. This is a movie about the triumph of the spirit—and spirit and soul never had any racial boundaries."

"Sometimes black men in the movie abuse black women," said Whoopi Goldberg in a subsequent interview. "Now, people see lots of movies where white men abuse white women, and they never think, 'This movie stereotypes whites.' Steven has made a fantastic movie about the human experience. There is not a 'mammy' or a 'nigger' in this film. I resent the fact that people think we actors would be involved in something that shows stereotyped behavior. Do people think that neither I am capable of judging what's exploitative, nor Danny Glover nor Oprah Winfrey?"

Others who have seen it have observed that the film is hardly a bouquet for the whites it depicts, who are portrayed as being oppressive, weak, or vindictive. Mr. Spielberg commented: "Because this was not a movie about race or racial issues, we did not feel that we needed to give equal importance to white characters. The few white people in the film are part of the storytelling process. They are people representing circumstances."

Mr. Spielberg said he had attempted to make the film true to the spirit of the book, although he has added scenes and truncated the original plot. One significant change is that the relationship between Celie and Shug Avery is less explicitly physical than in the book. Was he going for the PG-13 rating? "It was an artistic decision," he said. "I didn't categorize it as a lesbian relationship so much as a love relationship of great need," he said. "No one had ever loved Celie other than God and her sister. And here Celie is being introduced to the human race by a person full of love. I didn't think a full-out love scene would say it any better."

Both Mr. Spielberg and Miss Goldberg believe that the character of "Mr."
is more sympathetic in the film than in the book. "I wanted him to learn
something," Mr. Spielberg said. "That, by the end of the film, his soul had
changed."

The making of *The Color Purple* is intricately connected to his family, in
Mr. Spielberg's mind. It was during the filmmaking that he and Miss Irving
decided to marry, "and I'll always remember how Max was born—Amy
went into active labor on take three of the birthing scene," he said,
of the moment when Celie gives birth. Mr. Spielberg's own amazing story
happened June 12, after Miss Irving had already gone into labor. "The assistant director broke in to tell me that Amy was on the phone. Amy said,
'O.K., come home to deliver *my* baby now.'"

When the conversation turned once more to Mr. Spielberg's anticipation of reaction to *The Color Purple,* his smile faded and he began cracking
walnuts again. Was this movie his bid to be taken seriously as a director
by the film community? "I think I am taken quite seriously as a director,"
Mr. Spielberg responded. "I feel I've already been accepted, with over 40
nominations in technical and creative categories," he said of the Academy
Awards. But in 1983, Sir Richard Attenborough's *Gandhi* beat out *E.T. The
Extra-Terrestrial* for most of the major Oscars, including best picture, actor,
director and screenplay.

Did this still rankle? "People read too much into that," he said of the
1983 awards. "They think it was more of a blow than it was. Of course, it
means a lot, winning anything, being recognized for your work—anyone
who denies that isn't speaking from the heart. An Oscar would be wonderful, but for me, not the last goal."

Which is what? "Well I hope, in the movie life, there is no last goal.
That you make movies until your teeth fall out and you've retired to the
Motion Picture Home in the country." Mr. Spielberg cracked the last walnut, eyed the contents benignly, and smiled again. "The good thing about
a walnut," he said, "is that when you get tired of worrying, you eat it."

Spielberg at 40: The Man and the Child

MYRA FORSBERG/1988

IN THE FIRST PART of Steven Spielberg's sprawling new epic, *Empire of the Sun,* a boy dressed in a party costume discovers a derelict fighter plane in a field near Shanghai. The adventurer, resembling Aladdin, instantly climbs into the rusted cockpit and gleefully imagines he is stalking enemy aircraft.

The whimsical sequence starring a precocious child recalls magic moments in past Spielberg fantasies. But when the boy—a few seconds later—ventures farther afield, he does not experience close encounters of the wondrous kind. Instead, he bumps into a phalanx of grim Japanese soldiers patiently waiting for the next battle to begin.

This jarring episode that segues from the twilight zone of the imagination to the earthbound realities of wartime China evokes one of the movie's basic themes—a boy's head-on collision with manhood.

But the taut scene also aptly symbolizes the recent odyssey of Mr. Spielberg himself, the director and producer whom many have called a cinematic Peter Pan. From *Close Encounters of the Third Kind* and *E.T.* to *Back to the Future, Gremlins,* and *Goonies,* Mr. Spielberg has spun stories featuring children and teenagers that appealed to both the young and the young at heart. But while many of these movies reaped high praise and huge grosses, critics started wondering when the Wunderkind was going to finally grow up. His 1985 movie addressing more mature themes, *The Color*

From *New York Times,* 10 January 1988. Copyright © 1988 by *The New York Times.* Reprinted by permission.

Purple—about a black woman's struggles in the South—drew decidedly mixed reviews and seemed to raise even more questions about whether the director could jettison his child's-eye view of the world.

For *Empire of the Sun,* Mr. Spielberg returned to filming a child protagonist, but with dramatically different results. Instead of introducing the boy to beatific aliens who phone home, the director has sentenced him to a Hades filled with prison guards and scavengers, malaria, and misery. And while the story offered Mr. Spielberg another opportunity to collaborate with a young actor—and embodies many of the director's own childhood obsessions and traumas—it has helped him make a transition to what he calls "grown-up stories."

Acknowledging that turning 40 recently "ain't been so easy," he says it has forced him to reassess his work both as a director and producer: "I suddenly realized that, 'God, maybe I should please a part of me I haven't pleased before—that *Empire* has just started to please, which is a side that doesn't necessarily think of the audience with every thought and breath, but thinks about what I need to be satisfied.'"

Mr. Spielberg is not the only one pleased by *Empire.* Based on J.G. Ballard's semi-autobiographical book, the movie has won critical acclaim for both the director and Christian Bale, the 13-year-old star of the saga.

"I was attracted to the main character being a child," says Mr. Spielberg, sitting in a spacious office at Warner Bros., which is distributing the $35 million film. "But I was also attracted to the idea that this was a death of innocence, not an attenuation of childhood, which by my own admission and everybody's impression of me is what my life has been. This was the opposite of Peter Pan. This was a boy who had grown up too quickly, who was becoming a flower long before the bud had ever come out of the topsoil. And, in fact, a flower that was a gifted weed."

This "gifted weed" starts out as a rich British schoolboy living in Shanghai who dreams about God playing tennis. In between God lobbing a drop shot in 1941 and Man dropping the atomic bomb in 1945, young Jim Graham is separated from his parents and sent to a Japanese prison camp where he learns words like "survivor" and "pragmatist." Along the way he meets a Faginesque American who teaches him to steal shoes from the dead and soap from the living, and glimpses an eerie white light that may be a woman's soul or an atomic explosion. If this sounds more like a David Lean epic than a Steven Spielberg film, it is hardly surprising. For, according to Mr. Spielberg, the British auteur had indeed considered direct-ing it.

"He asked me to acquire the rights for him," recalls Mr. Spielberg, who would have served as producer on the film.

But by the time the rights became available, Mr. Lean was enmeshed in another project and encouraged Mr. Spielberg, who had read the Ballard book earlier, to direct it.

"From the moment I read the novel, I secretly wanted to do it myself," admits Mr. Spielberg. "I had never read anything with an adult setting—even *Oliver Twist*—where a child saw things through a man's eyes as opposed to a man discovering things through the child in him. This was just the reverse of what I felt—leading up to *Empire*—was my credo. And then I discovered very quickly that this movie and turning 40 happening at almost the same time was no coincidence—that I had decided to do a movie with grown-up themes and values, although spoken through a voice that hadn't changed through puberty as yet."

Another attraction was the plethora of images the work invoked. "Ever since *Duel*," says Mr. Spielberg, referring to his seminal television film about a sinister truck, "I've been looking for a visual narrative—a motion-picture story—that could be told nearly exclusively through visual metaphors and nonpretentious symbolism. And nothing had come along until *Empire*. And the book was so much from the point of view of this very confused child who becomes a thoroughly indoctrinated young man—it's such a character journey for him—that I said, 'This is wonderful. It's like a large coffee-table picture experience. The images say more than nine pages of dialogue ever could on stage.' "

But there were other attractions—attractions that symbolize Mr. Spiel-berg's own childhood. For example, there's Jim's fascination with planes. "As a child I used to build model planes," the director recalls, "and I was attached to flying the way Jim is."

And the very era the story covers—World War II—has been revisited in other Spielberg films, from the crazed California populace in *1941* to the missing bomber pilots in *Close Encounters* to the Nazi schemers in *Raiders of the Lost Ark:* "I'm closer to the '40's personally than I am to the '80's. I love that period. My father filled my head with war stories—he was a radioman on a B-25 fighting the Japanese in Burma. I have identified with that period of innocence and tremendous jeopardy all my life. I collect

Dennis Weaver, *Duel*, 1971

Robert Shaw, Richard Dreyfuss, and Roy Scheider, *Jaws*, 1975

Richard Dreyfuss, *Close Encounters of the Third Kind*, 1977

Harrison Ford, *Raiders of the Lost Ark*, 1981

Henry Thomas and E.T., *E.T. The Extra-Terrestrial*, 1982

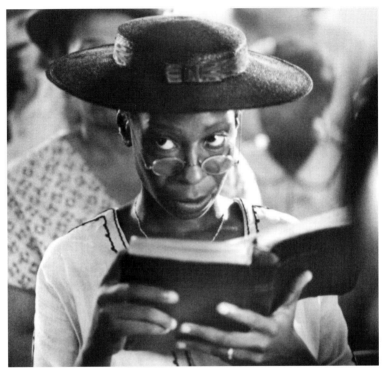

Whoopi Goldberg, *The Color Purple*, 1985

Jeff Goldblum, Richard Attenborough, Laura Dern, and Sam Neill, *Jurassic Park*, 1993 (Photo: Murray Close)

Liam Neeson and Ben Kingsley, *Schindler's List*, 1993 (Photo: David James)

Djimon Hounsou, *Amistad*, 1997 (Photo: Andrew Cooper)

Matthew McConaughey, *Amistad*, 1997 (Photo: Andrew Cooper)

Tom Hanks, *Saving Private Ryan*, 1998 (Photo: David James)

Jeremy Davies, *Saving Private Ryan*, 1998 (Photo: David James)

documentaries, and I think I have every one made on that period. It was the end of an era, the end of innocence, and I have been clinging to it for most of my adult life. But hitting 40, I really had to come to terms with what I've been tenaciously clinging to, which was a celebration of a kind of naiveté that has been reconfirmed countless times in the amount of people who have gone to see *E.T., Back to the Future* and *Goonies*. But I just reached a saturation point, and I thought *Empire* was a great way of performing an exorcism on that period."

And in depicting the dawn of the atomic age, Mr. Spielberg says, "I wanted to draw a parallel story between the death of this boy's innocence and the death of the innocence of the entire world. When that white light goes off in Nagasaki and the boy witnesses the light—whether he really sees it or his mind sees it doesn't matter. Two innocents have come to an end and a saddened world has begun.

"I don't think I've made a dark movie," he insists. "But it's as dark as I've allowed myself to get, and that was perversely very compelling to me."

Perhaps one of the most familiar Spielbergian motifs in *Empire* is that of a child's separation from his parents. It is a crucial theme in the Ballard novel, but it also reverberates in some of Mr. Spielberg's major works: the natural parents seeking their baby in *Sugarland Express*; a boy wrenched from his mother in *Close Encounters*; an alien separated from his mothership in *E.T.*; a little girl abducted by ghosts in *Poltergeist*. In *Empire*, in one of the film's most apocalyptic scenes, a boy is torn away from his parents by a stampeding crowd of Chinese refugees fleeing the Japanese.

Mr. Spielberg sees personal strands in the separations painted on those canvases: "My parents got a divorce when I was 14, 15. The whole thing about separation is something that runs very deep in anyone exposed to divorce, especially when you're cognizant of what it means to not have a routine—no matter how stressful or antagonistic that routine may have been. The breaking up of the mother and father is extremely traumatic from 4 up. All of us are still suffering the repercussions of a divorce that had to happen.

"But the whole idea of being taken away from your parents and forced to adapt to a new routine—I'm *not* good with change, personally speaking. Possibly that's why it has taken me so long to get out of the habit of just trying to appeal to audiences between the ages of 6 and 15. Because it's nice having the kids coming up to you and saying I love this and I love that. And it's taken me all this time to learn that that no longer satisfies me as much as I thought it did."

This desire for a change was yet another factor in Mr. Spielberg accepting the challenge of externalizing a novel that is, as Mr. Ballard himself describes it, "almost entirely an interior narrative." It was a painful process: "I was very disturbed making this movie," the director says. "This was not a happy experience, not because it was such a difficult film to make—I'm accustomed to working through problems in logistics. It was my attitude. It was that I was doing things against not the grain of my intuition, but against the collection of my own experiences as a director. I was making a movie that when I would discover how to slightly subvert the drama through humor, I would have to count to 10 or hold my breath—and not do it.

"I'm always trying to infuse humor into any situation. The more dramatic the situation, the more fun I have trying to find the lighter side to the darkness. And in this case, I had to really bite my lip to drown out where my kick reflex from all my other films was taking me. It was a real internal struggle to get this thing on the screen and not mess it up."

He has more pleasant recollections when discussing Christian Bale. Mr. Spielberg's direction of child actors has resulted in several luminescent performances in past films, with critics comparing his expertise in this genre to Truffaut's. But this may be the most virtuosic collaboration yet, for Mr. Bale dominates almost every frame.

"There was something about Christian that was purely intuitive, and that's how I work too," Mr. Spielberg explains. "We really got along on that level. We didn't do a lot of intellectualizing. I found the best way to work with Christian was just imitation. I would get in there and play the scene myself and we would mix it up and become friends.

"This is essentially how I work with all young people. With adults, when they say lunch for one hour, the adults go back to their trailers and I go back to mine. But with Henry Thomas during *E.T.*, we would play video games for the entire hour. And with Christian, I bought him a radio-controlled racing car so every lunch hour we would go out with our cars and have races."

While Mr. Spielberg may indulge in childhood games during lunch hours, he has permanently abandoned the idea of filming *Peter Pan*. "I am up to here with 'I don't want to grow up,'" he says, motioning to his head. But he is "consciously regressing" and will start shooting the second sequel to *Raiders* in April. He cites an obligation to George Lucas, "but the real reason I'm doing *Indy III* is because I want to have fun."

"I'm still a showman," he explains. "I have that real pull between being a showman and being a filmmaker and there is a tough netherworld between both titles. It's filled with contradictions and bad choices."

Nevertheless, after the thrills and spills of *Indy III,* he intends to continue making films with more mature themes: "I'm still interested in making *Schindler's List,*" he says, referring to Thomas Keneally's book about a German businessman who saved more than a thousand Jews during the Holocaust. "And I'm developing an original screenplay with my sister Annie that has not a kid in it."

More important, Mr. Spielberg says, he has turned over the administration of his production company, Amblin Entertainment, to his longtime associate Kathleen Kennedy to allow himself more time to direct.

"I'm tired of producing," says the filmmaker, whose company suffered a bumpy summer—two of its releases—*Harry and the Hendersons* and *Innerspace*—were domestic box-office disappointments.

"I can't eat any more candy or it will ruin my health. I have been in the candy factory for the last three years as a producer making sugar substitutes, and I've gagged on it myself—even though I'm proud of most of the stuff I've given a green light to."

"But I want to stop having kids on the screen and have them in real life," says the director, who has a 2½-year-old son with his wife, Amy Irving. "And that's been a catharsis for me in that I really want to leave that all behind and move into other areas."

He calls himself a victim of his own Xerox machine: "I followed my own trends a bit because it was seductive to have something succeed so well and to suddenly follow it up with something else that succeeded almost as well. Yet by the same token, it doesn't challenge me."

But while he does crave challenges, there are inherent economic risks—illustrated by the fact that *Empire* is doing respectably, but not spectacularly, at the box office thus far. "I'd like to take more chances," he says, "but I would hope those risks don't cost the distributor a lot of money."

"I'm trying to grow up in increments," he reflects. "I don't want to come up to the surface so quickly that I'm going to have a terrible case of

the bends. I'm trying very gently to step up to a different kind of movie—
not saying that I will then make *that* movie for the rest of my life, but I
want to test the envelope. I want to see how far I can push it in each direction. And I felt that *Empire,* which was emotionally the most difficult film
I've made, still had a boy in it to help with that transition to a kind of genre
I would like to play around with—that all my friends are saying, 'Come
on, this is fun. Play with the grown-ups for a while. There will always be
children's stories, but this is real good for you.'"

Always: An Interview with Steven Spielberg

SUSAN ROYAL/1989

STEVEN SPIELBERG'S SPECTACULAR CAREER includes directing four of the ten highest-grossing films of all time: *Jaws, Raiders of the Lost Ark, Indiana Jones and the Temple of Doom*, and *E.T.* Taking into account films he has produced, seven of the twenty top-grossing movies in history are his. In 1982 he directed *E.T.* which ultimately grossed $720 million worldwide theatrically and shipped over 14 million home videocassette units, making it the most successful movie ever. In the interview which follows, Spielberg talks about the films he has made since *E.T.* — in particular, his latest release, *Always* (starring Holly Hunter, Richard Dreyfuss, and John Goodman).

Before we talk about Always, *I'd like to touch on some of the films you've made since I interviewed you at the time of* E.T.'s *release.*
Okay.

Let's start with The Color Purple. *How did you know Oprah Winfrey could act?*
There was no way to really know, but I did know she was extremely willing to try anything. What she brought to our first meeting was a great deal of enthusiasm for the book and the screenplay...and for herself as a beginner. She wasn't afraid of anything; she didn't bat an eye, I had seen tapes

---

From *American Premiere*, December/January 1989–90. © 1989 by Susan Royal. Reprinted by permission of the author.

of her early talk show—before she went into syndication. I saw this fearlessness in those tapes. The figure I had in my imagination to play Sophie was exactly who Oprah was when I met her. I certainly wouldn't cast her today because she is svelte and picturesque, which is not the physical image of Sophie. She was very courageous in the meeting. She said, "I know this person and I really want this part. I've had experiences like her experiences." Which is not to say that every actor who tells me they really want the part necessarily gets it, because everybody says that. It's just that Oprah convinced me that she *was* this character in our very first meeting. And then she tested and it was a wonderful test. I cast her and she was wonderful. She has remained a good friend over the years, too, which is nice.

You once told Gene Siskel that you used two film models for The Color Purple: Grapes of Wrath *for the emotional tone and look and* Best Years of Our Lives *for successfully juggling several people's stories. Do you frequently use old films or feelings from old films as reference points while directing?*
I might talk to my DP about the lighting of Gregg Toland, for instance, in *Citizen Kane* or *The Magnificent Ambersons.* I might say, "Gee, I love those low angles where they would shoot past the people to the ceilings." I make a lot of these kinds of references to the technical people in my movies. In trying to make a point about color photography, I often make references to black and white. If I want to contrast colors in a scene, I'll refer to the great black and white movies, where contrast was an art form.

Was your son born just as you were shooting the birth scene in Color Purple?
Yes, when Celie was giving birth to Olivia. Just as we were pulling the rubber baby out from the bed—the little rubber baby that you had to shake to make it look like it was alive—the phone call came and one of the assistant directors ran in and said, "Your baby's on the way. Your *real* baby is on the way." It was wonderful moment in my life.

Before Color Purple, *some people criticized you for not making "grown-up" movies and after* Color Purple, *there was still some criticism . . .*
I feel that there is plenty of time for me to get to everything. I can't let other people determine my life or, at the very least, my next subject. I've got a lot of time and I just feel that I'll make that grown-up movie when

I'm grown-up enough to make it. And if I make a grown-up movie it'll be because I *am* grown-up. I don't want to pretend to be someone I'm not right now. A movie is only a sort of indication of who the filmmaker is at any given time. And so, if I make a movie some day and people say, "My goodness, what an adult, mature, restrained work," I might look back at those accolades and say, "Well gee, I'm insulted. Where's the kid in me?" But I kind of feel that I'll just take my time and sort of let myself continue to decide what movies to make next based on what interests me, not on what I think I *should* be doing.

When I last interviewed you, you said you wanted to direct less and produce more. Since then you've done a lot of executive producing. Do you now want to direct more?
Oh yeah, I'm swinging back the other direction. I'm definitely directing more.

What was the producing experience like?
Producing was a bit frustrating, because a producer is only there to pretty much agent a project and to cast it, perhaps. More importantly, to cast the director. But once the director's been selected, he becomes the decision maker. And if you can get a very, very good director, well, most good directors are single-minded and have their own ideas. I haven't found a lot of directors who are as collaborative as I am. And there's not a lot of room for me or other producers in the picture. I found that even though some of those movies turned out really well, it was a bit frustrating for me and I really felt I wanted to get back to calling the shots.

I admire good producers. But good creative producers often turn to directing themselves, out of sheer frustration at not being able to get their ideas across to their directors. It's the only way for them to really kind of chaperone an idea right onto the screen.

You've often said you like George Lucas as your producer.
My favorite producer, really, is Kathy Kennedy. Kathy and I have a very healthy collaboration. With George producing for me or when Kathy's producing for me, there's no ego involved among any of us. We just set out to make the best movie possible. Kathy has good taste and she's rational. And she understands what it takes to make a movie. She's a very good sounding board.

And what does Frank Marshall do?
Frank's also a producer for the company. Frank works primarily pre-production and post-production. And Kathy works mainly—at least in my movies—during the actual principal photography. But they work as a team. They're kind of interchangeable at times. Sometimes Frank works the production and Kathy works the pre-production. It really all depends. The three of us are sort of a commando team and we've actually found a way, with just the three of us, to make five movies a year. I don't know how we do this, but we get it done. But the effort, the real work on a day-to-day basis, is done by Kathy and Frank as the heads of Amblin Entertainment, with Kathy as the president. So she takes most of the workload. And she did this to free me up to direct more.

How did you become involved with the restoration of Lawrence of Arabia?
I think *Lawrence of Arabia* is the film that inspired me to become a motion picture director. More than any other single movie in my memory, that was the one movie that sort of decided my fate. And so, I've always honored and cherished that film and when there was a chance to restore it to David Lean's original version, Scorcese and I, along with Columbia, sponsored the restoration.

And you have had an ongoing friendship with David Lean since then?
He's like a great teacher who you hope will be your friend. I kind of look at David as the best professor whose class I ever attended.

What was that story about him wanting six months to shoot an Amazing Stories?
He was joking. I brought him on the *Amazing Stories* set when I was directing and said, "Would you like to do one of these?" and he said, "Well, dear boy, how many days do you give a director?" And I said, "Between six and eight." And he said, "Oh my, well, if you perhaps add a zero after the six or the eight, I'll consider."

Let's go on to Empire of the Sun. *You've been quoted as saying, "For one time I thought maybe I would not think of the audience with every thought and breath, but think about what I need to be satisfied as a director." Did you say that?*
Yes I did.

Can you elaborate on that a little bit?
I knew going in that *Empire of the Sun* wasn't a very commercial project, it wasn't going to have a broad audience appeal. But it was a story about a courageous survivor who was only 13 years old. And I so identified with him in the novel. I knew I had to make this movie despite my producer hat, which kept nagging at me that this was not a movie to spend a lot of money on because you're not going to make any of it back. And yet some things need to be done regardless of the commercial return.

So, you're allowed that once in a while?
Well, look, I've earned the right to fail commercially, I said to myself. And I said this is a movie I really want to make for myself and I will be forever in debt to Warner Bros. for risking all that money to sort of recreate the Second World War in China between the years 1941 and 1945. It was a horrendous risk. But they pretty much let me make my—what would you call it—my large canvas personal film. And for me, anyway, at least up to this point, it ranks among the most satisfying experiences I've had directing.

You seem to be attracted to the 1940s.
I like the period because it was naive and it was somewhat innocent and it represented the growing pains of the 20th century. And it's a very fertile time for movie stories.

That was also the era in which Raiders of the Lost Ark *and its sequels were set. You were kind of tired of* Raiders *by the time it was released...*
It's not so much that I was tired of *Raiders,* it was just that I had done it once. I made George Lucas a promise that if the first one was successful I would do two more. It wasn't a contract, it was just sort of a friendly handshake, but George is one of my closest friends, and I take that as a promise. When the first one was successful, I signed on to do a second one. And when that was successful, I fulfilled my promise to George and did number three. Although, with number three, almost four screenplays were developed before I was satisfied. I wasn't going to just go ahead and fulfill my obligation. I was going to make every effort to end the saga with a very unique and very thrilling finale.

The only thing that would have gotten me to break my word to George was if everybody's attitude was "Let's get it over with. We're going to make money on it, anyway. Let's just play it safe and give the audience exactly what we think they want." I wanted to take a risk and I wanted to do a father-son story from the very beginning. After three and a half screenplays had been written and the third was about to be abandoned, I said, "Look, I'll direct it, but it's going to have to be a father-son story." And George said, "Well, I want it to be about the Holy Grail." And I said, "Yeah, but I want it to be about a father and son. I want to get Indy's father involved in the thing. I want a quest for the father." And George said, "Yeah, I want a quest for the Grail." And we both looked at each other and we said, "Hey, how about we do 'em both?" So we combined my idea with George's and the icing on the cake was casting Sean Connery. He's wonderful to work with; he's a wonderful guy.

Young Indy was a Boy Scout, as were you. Didn't you recently receive a special award from the Boy Scouts?
It was the Distinguished Eagle Scout Award from the National Counsel of the Boy Scouts of America at the National Jamboree in Arlington, West Virginia. It was the highlight of 1989 for me . . . the best memory from the entire year.

I believe you've told stories on yourself about being a rather inept Boy Scout.
Well, I guess I was pretty inept. I couldn't cook, I couldn't tie knots well and I sliced open my finger while demonstrating ax sharpening to about 500 scouts during summer camp. But I learned a lot from scouting. I learned a lot of basic human values and American values that I otherwise wouldn't have so early in life.

You recently created a cinematography merit badge. How does a Boy Scout go about getting that badge?
It's really no harder than getting an animal husbandry badge. Instead of milking a cow, you make a movie with a Super 8 or on videotape. Hopefully, it will do for some scouts what it did for me, which is open up a whole lot of possibilities for discovering what talent you might possess. Earning badges provides very early incentives in young kids. It really teaches you how to go for a goal. And because the merit badge program covers such a wide variety of topics, it exposes kids to fields they would otherwise not be

exposed to. Everything in scouting has to do with adventure. If you get 25 merit badges, that means you've had 25 adventures that you would otherwise never have experienced in your life.

Let's move on to Back to the Future *and its sequels. Did you save a lot of money by shooting Parts II and III back to back?*
We thought it was going to save money but, in fact, it didn't. But it did accomplish a couple of things. Michael Fox won't age five years between II and III. And who knows, one of these days Michael just might wake up and start looking his age. He's very fortunate to have such a young looking face, but in five years, who knows? So one good thing was that Michael and the rest of the cast get to stay the same age without heavy makeup. The other thing is that we probably would have lost Bob Zemeckis. I don't think he would have directed III if we hadn't done II and III at the same time. Bob is moving on. He's like where I was five years ago. He wants to test himself and push the envelope and see what other things he's good at. He knows he's pretty good at *Back to the Future*. Now he wants to test the unknown. He wants to stretch and mature as a filmmaker and I think that we probably wouldn't have gotten Bob to direct III.

And then Part III comes out next June?
Yes.

How does this affect the release of the home videocassettes?
I'm not sure how we're going to do that yet. Maybe we'll release the video of II after III is out. I'm not sure, we've had very little discussion about it.

Do people understand Back to the Future Part II *if they didn't see the first film?*
Not really. But most of the people who see Part II have already seen the first one. Also, we showed *Back to the Future* on NBC four days before the sequel came out. It was like a primer for those who never heard of *Back to the Future*. For those who had seen the first one it was a refresher course to remind you who Biff is and who the McFlys are and who Lorraine Baines is. It was a very highly rated two hours on NBC. We got millions of people to watch it and then the people who went to the theater to see Part II understood how it interwove with the original *Back to the Future*.

Did you shoot all new footage or use some from the first film?

There were a couple shots from the original movie of Crispin Glover who played George McFly. And a couple of those were angles that weren't used in the original film, but were dusted off and used in the sequel. But most everything was recreated fresh.

And the next one has a Western motif.

Yes. At the end of Part II we have a little preview of the coming attractions. The saga resumes. The idea was to offer the audience a very satisfying conclusion to the dilemma in the second movie, but then create a new dilemma that will only be solved in the final installment. And nobody wants to wait five years for that to be resolved.

You were unable to direct Rainman *because you were doing Part III of* Raiders. *Were you supposed to direct* Big, *too?*

Big was something I flirted with for a couple of months with Harrison Ford to play the part that Tom Hanks played. But my sister wrote the script and I felt that she'd been standing in my shadow long enough. Most of my life she's sort of been in the shade and this was a great screenplay she and Gary Ross wrote—with no help from me. I simply came on as a possible director. But I began to consider the fact that if I directed it, people wouldn't give Annie any credit. And so I quickly told Jim Brooks that I wasn't going to get involved because, essentially, I would have stolen Annie's thunder and I just didn't want to do that. This was Annie's chance to be successful—this was her coming out party. I had already had mine and I didn't need another one. And so, as quickly as I stepped into it, I stepped out of it.

With *Rainman,* I spent almost half a year developing it with Dustin and Tom Cruise and Ron Bass. I kept trying to get the screenplay to be better and better while having a stop date of the 12th of January at which time I would have to start shooting *Indy III* or we couldn't make our Memorial Day 1989 release date. When I saw that I was going to go past January 12th and that I would have to step down from *Indy III,* the promise I made to George was more important than making *Rainman.* So, with great regret because I really wanted to work with Dustin and Tom, I stepped down from the movie.

I understand that you turned all your notes over to Barry Levinson.
Yeah. I sort of debriefed in front of Barry and gave him all of my notes and everything. And Barry went his own way and made his own movie, but he appreciated the hours we spent together talking about my notes. But that's how I would have made a film and Barry's not me and he had his own way of making the picture.

And Martin Brest and Sydney Pollack both had other ways, too.
Everybody had their own way of making that film and it turned out Barry's way was the best.

I know you still want to work with Dustin Hoffman.
We're developing about five things right now.

And Meryl Streep.
Yes. I think Meryl can do anything. She's become a national treasure. So have Dustin Hoffman, Robert De Niro and some other people like that who I'd love to work with.

Let's talk about Always *now. Would you call it a remake?*
I wouldn't call it a remake. I've never looked at it like that. I think the film owes a great inspiration to the 1943 Victor Fleming film *A Guy Named Joe*. But it's not really a remake. It was the basis for a new story.

How would directing a film from a completely original idea compare to directing an adaptation of a play or of a book?
When you're directing from a novel, it's just words that conjure up images, but when you're directing a movie which is based on a film that's already been made, the images are on film. I chose not to look at *A Guy Named Joe* a lot when I decided I wanted to do a version of that story. With an original idea, there are no preconceptions out there. When the source material is from a book or previously made film, everybody has their own interpretation already. It's always a little more risky doing something based on a novel, a movie or a play because the original source material is represented and suddenly you are being compared to someone else's work.

How long have you wanted to make this film?
The first screenplay was written in 1980, so it's been about nine years.

Raising Arizona *is one of my favorite films. Did you think of Holly Hunter and John Goodman together after seeing that film or...*
You know what's weird? I loved John Goodman and Holly in *Raising Arizona*, but I completely forgot they were in it together. I cast John Goodman after having already cast Holly. It only dawned on me later that they had both shared a set. And that was very interesting.

They are both very natural, very real actors.
Yeah, so is Dreyfuss. I didn't want to make this movie with glamour queens or the icons of stardom of the 1990s. I wanted real people that we could relate to. People about whom we could say, "Gee, I'm like her" or "People think I look like Richard Dreyfuss, people think I laugh like him," that kind of thing. Or "I have a best friend like John Goodman." Everybody has a best friend like John Goodman in life or should.

You were quoted recently as saying that Holly Hunter is an architect of character and that you learned more from her than any other actress.
Yeah, true. She's a builder. She starts at the foundation, and she makes a plan for her character. This includes a history of the character's life and the character's sincerest desires, likes and dislikes, how she sounds and the kind of scent she might exude, just with different moods. Holly plots and builds her character like someone would build a house from the ground up. And as a director and a collaborator—which I feel I am as a director— I kind of had to run a little faster to jump aboard Holly's house which was already moving and under construction by the time I got there. She had a lot of ideas about Dorinda, the character she plays. And they were all wonderful ideas. And she's a great builder.

This was your third film with Richard Dreyfuss [after Jaws *and* Close Encounters of the Third Kind*] and you two are very good friends. Is it difficult to direct a good friend?*
No. The more I've grown to know Rick the easier it is to not mince words. I have to say much less to Richard than I would, for instance, with Holly. And I think if Holly and I work together—I'm certain we will—a second

time, there'll be even less verbal communication. And I found with Richard there was less verbal communication because we've worked together twice, we've known each other very well for years, and I could just make a little gesture—almost like a conductor with a baton—just raise my hands or lower them and Richard would know exactly what I was talking about. I would go over to Richard and he would say, "How was that?" and I'd just look at him and lower and shake my head. And he'd say, "That bad, huh?" And I'd kind of nod my head and he'd say, "One more time." Jokingly, I mean, jokingly. I didn't know Holly that well, though I knew her very well by the end of the shoot and we would joke around a lot together. I don't like taking a lot of this stuff seriously. You know, I don't believe in whispering the words of God into the ear of an actor just before they go on and expect them to perform miracles. I just think that directing and acting is simply about communication. And communication can take many forms. Sometimes it's simply the desire to ask the actors to do one more take and not say anything at all and see what happens. Other times, it's a lot of discussion, a lot of rehearsal, a lot of experimentation. It gets like directing a play. Hitchcock used to spend many takes never talking to his actors. He never indicated to his actors whether he liked or disliked what they had just done. But he made them do it over and over and over again. The actors began trying to please Hitch by sheer panicked invention. And it was some of those inventive moments in an attempt to please Hitchcock that turned into great moments in film.

You've compared the chemistry of Richard Dreyfuss and Holly Hunter to that of Tracy and Hepburn.
Well, that's just sort of a nice way to say that they seem to belong together in movies and not just this one; I see them doing other movies together. They're a team. I didn't realize how good of a team they were until they began acting together. They're sort of made for each other. They can do comedy, they can do drama, they can do love stories like they just did with *Always*. But I was fortunate to have found these two people who were very right for each other. They have an edge, both of them, when they act together. That's what makes the relationship interesting. It's not a roll-over-and-play-dead relationship; it's a real sassy, saucy kind of rapport they have with each other. They do a lot of needling. Both on and off camera.

And you've managed to bring Audrey Hepburn back to movies.
I fully expected her to turn it down for various reasons—mostly because she is so involved with UNICEF and travels the world. I know her time is precious, but she loved the script, she made the time and that was the biggest compliment she could have given any of us.

How did it occur to you that Hap didn't have to be played by a man?
Well, I kept thinking that Hap's not really God, and yet, why is it that God is always perceived to be male? I've never really agreed with that male understanding. I assume that men wrote the Bible and so God was always a man. Also, Audrey was closer to the maternal side of nature. And I thought that whether she's interpreted as being an emissary of God or Mother Nature or God itself, it just seemed right to me and I never thought twice about it when I decided to cast her in the movie. She has a compassion about her; and Pete, the character that Richard plays, needs a lot of compassion, because he's a single-minded, ornery type of guy. He needs all the help he can get to put his priorities in order. I would say Hap is his conscience. She's like the conscience of people everywhere . . . all sort of rooting for the Richard Dreyfuss character to be able to say the things he needs to say before he goes away.

Was this Brad Johnson's first major motion picture?
I think it was his first anything. He may have done a few car commercials.

I understand that when you first met with him he spilled his coffee. Was he trying to be the character for you or was he really a klutz?
When I first met him he was really a klutz. I don't know whether it was out of sheer nerves or perhaps he just likes to spill things, but he sure ingratiated himself to me. I gave him the part after he had tested two or three times, but I think the klutziness helped. I told him to put some of it into the character, when it wasn't there before. But for all the funny klutzy things he did, I should point out that he is a rodeo rider and a pilot. He's got shelves of rodeo trophies and he's obviously done things that take quick thinking and precision skills. So I think he saves his klutziness for when he sees a pretty girl and gets a little flustered and spills coffee all over himself.

And the character he plays . . .
He's sort of Holly's steppingstone back into the real world. I wouldn't say
he's the final answer in Holly's life, but he certainly helps her to free her
heart and get on with her life.

What attracted you to shooting in Montana?
Forest fires. You see, Montana was right next door to the Yellowstone burn
and, while we wanted to shoot actual forest fires, we didn't want to start
any new ones. We reburned areas of the Yellowstone fire that had already
consumed thousands of acres.

How did you do that?
The special effects people went in and rigged the trees that had already
burned. Once they're burning again you can't tell that they're not green.
Because of the flames, they're just all orange and yellow. So, even though
we were reburning already blackened trees, once the forest was ablaze you
couldn't tell. And we photographed some of the actual Yellowstone fire.
In a lot of the scenes where Richard and John Goodman are flying over
the fire, that's actually Yellowstone burning below. We sent our crews
out over two and a half years ago in preparation for this movie. The Forest
Service let us go in with our airplanes and shoot some of the actual
Yellowstone fire as it was happening.

And you also shot in Washington State?
Yes, Ephrata and Moses Lake were the areas where we shot the practice
field at which the firefighters learned how to drop the chemical retardant
on fires from their World War II bombers.

And your DP was Mikael Salomon who shot The Abyss.
Yes. Jim Cameron called me and said, "There's a new cameraman who just
came to this country a year ago and he speaks better English than I do and
he's got a better sense of humor than anybody that I know, and he's got a
uniquely American sense of humor for a Dane." And he said, "He's done a
great job on my movie." And so Mikael actually brought the film over to
my house. We sat down and looked at 25 minutes of *The Abyss* and, based
on that, I hired Mikael for *Always*. He's a wonderful man, too. I'll be using
him on a lot of films.

It's too bad you couldn't use Irving Berlin's song "Always" for the film. What was it he said to you. . . . He had plans for it?
Yes. He was 94 years old and he "planned to use it in the future." Well, it was interesting; he was making plans for the future, and I'm sorry I never met him and I'm also sorry I never could get his song in my movie. But it's not because I didn't try.

What kind of old guy do you want to be?
I'd like to be old, but not angry or bitter. And I'd like to be old and directing movies, not old and on the lecture circuit.

Why did it take nine years to get Always *made?*
My problem was my own threshold of courage. I could have made *Always* in 1981, I could have made it in '83, '85, '87. I just never quite had the courage to step up to the mark. It was a story that I've always loved. I couldn't think of anything better in that same genre that was original, so I relied on the old bones of the 1943 story. But I was not able to successfully update it. I did not want to go back and make it a World War II story. I wanted to make a contemporary story. I was afraid that if I set it in a period, people would say, "Well, that's just how people thought back in the old days. People don't feel that way in modern times." So I wanted this to be applicable to this generation. And it took a long time to adapt it to 1989.

Always is about love after death, but it's not a downer. It essentially says that true love survives death and can come back to haunt you in both good and bad ways. It's a story about a man who had a chance to say everything important to the one person he loved and didn't say it until it was too late. And now that he's gone, his mission—so to speak, even though he doesn't know what his mission is—is to come back and say all the things he was never able to say as a living human being. And the rules of the game are that none of the characters can see or hear Richard, but he can still somehow reach their hearts. And he can still somehow get through to them. The movie's really about inspiration. If you're writing a story and you think, "God, this is a great story," and your writing is just honed and concise and it's economical, you feel inspired. Or I'm directing a scene and I say to myself, "Gee, I'm on a roll, I feel inspired." Well, who's inspiring me? I mean, did Victor Fleming come back from the dead and stand behind me for part of *Always*? Or, when I was making *E.T.,* was Victor Fleming there, too, whispering in my ear? I couldn't see him, I couldn't hear him, I couldn't feel him or smell him, but there were days when I felt truly inspired. We all have those days when we feel inspired. What I'm saying is not to take any credit away from ourselves, because we do a lot for ourselves. But is it possible? Could there be people from our past or even strangers to us, who have come back at times not to haunt us, but help us? And that's the genesis for *Always*.

Let's talk about your future films. Are you going to make Schindler's List?
Schindler's List is definitely something my company is going to produce with Universal. But at the moment, I'm not directing it. It's been a burdensome subject. It's a subject that's dangerous, because it's a Holocaust story. And, unlike something you might do for TV like *War and Remembrance* or *Holocaust* itself, a feature film about the Holocaust is going to be studied through a microscope and it's going to be scrutinized from the Talmud to Ted Koppel. And it has to be accurate and it has to be fair and it cannot *in the least* come across as entertainment. And it's very hard when you're making a movie, not to violate one or all of those self-imposed rules. So that's why it's been stalled for so many years. It's a very delicate balance and I'm not sure we've pulled it off yet; so we're still in development.

You're definitely not doing Peter Pan *and you're not doing an* E.T. *sequel, right?*
Yes. Definitely not.

And what film will you next direct?
I don't know. I should develop a script called "I Don't Know," because I say this every time I'm asked.

You once joked about feelings of insecurity, saying you were afraid that one day Universal would want to take your offices back . . .
I'm not worrying about Universal taking my office back. I'm worried about somebody *buying* Universal and taking my office. (laughs)

Yes, it's a strange time. I can't get used to seeing the "Lorimar Pictures" sign on the old MGM Studios.
It's even stranger to go to Lorimar and see "Columbia Pictures" up there. But that studio will always be the MGM Studios for me. It is a museum of

the greatest movies ever made in the history of our industry, in my opinion. It's a haunted studio. I've felt very comforted by a sort of prevailing creative presence every time I step onto that lot, and it's just sad to see it with anything other than "MGM" on the water tower. But time changes the face of all architecture and it always has.

Do you think this is a particularly unstable time for the industry?
Well, it's a paradox. It appears to be unstable, in that companies that have no idea how to make a movie are buying movie companies. But movies are still getting made and they're more successful than they've ever been in their whole history. It's a time of great bounty while it's also a time of great instability, corporately. So you never know who's going to adorn your water tower tomorrow. As long as filmmakers remain dogged in their quest for the perfect movie and we just try to forget who's signing the checks — as long as the money's there to pay for the film and processing and everybody's salaries — it shouldn't matter who takes over the studios, as long as the corporations who don't have film savvy don't try to get involved creatively. And I don't think Sony will. I think Sony has completely divested their creative urges, if any, to Jon Peters and Peter Guber who, in my opinion, will do a fabulous job turning Columbia around and making it as successful as it was in the 1930s and '40s. I really think they're going to pull this off and do a smashing job. After all has been said and done, and all the jokes have gone around town, and they're out of Warner's and they're set up at Columbia, I think they're going to do great.

What do you think about Japanese investments in the movie business?
We can be jealous of the Japanese, but we've got to give them credit for turning out great cars and great entertainment tools like VCRs and television sets. Japan is the only country in the world that is seriously getting into high resolution television. We're going to eventually have to compete against them in that field, too, because that is going to overwhelm this country and in ten years people are going to be demanding HDTV. So, rather than complain about the Japanese, I think we need to compete more soundly with them.

There was a time when you felt that E.T. should not be a home video experience. Now, of course, it's the most successful one of all time. Was that hard for you to release it on home video?

Not really. I did once say that I could never envision *E.T.* going onto home cassette. But, over the last six years or seven years, I was sort of pummeled by parents and children asking me, "When is *E.T.* coming out on cassette?" One out of five people who recognized me on the street would ask me that. It got to the point that I just couldn't deny a very strong and popular demand. So it happened.

And the home video market has expanded so much since E.T. *was made.*
Oh yeah, it has expanded and, most importantly, there are many more players now. By releasing *E.T.* when we did, it could be appreciated because the players were out there. To have released *E.T.* a year after 1982, at the end of '83, would have been a complete waste of effort. The cassette would have been priced at over $100, and there were less than five million players around . . . which, in my opinion, was not enough to justify a cassette of *E.T.* I'm not talking financially, I'm just saying there were not enough players to justify the demand. Now there are. The market will grow and grow. The sell-through market is the biggest market and that'll grow and grow. And cable's growing like crazy. Eventually there's going to be so many choices.

What about the laser disc?
The quality is better—about 40 percent better. I have laser at home and I love it. When somebody says they have a film on laser, I'll choose laser over cassette. And the sound is better. I would hope people could get the state of the art to play our movies on, because we've worked and slaved to make our movies look and sound great. It's a shame to have them played back on bad hardware.

I read somewhere that you don't think much of music videos.
I love music videos. I just don't want to make one. I don't think I'd be any good at it. I'm a big advocate of music video. I just don't want to see video mentality creep into feature films.

Because they don't tell stories.
Yes, because they don't tell stories. They give you fragments of images and they sort of assault your senses and they change the way you perceive imagery. And I think that's fine when there's music accompanying it. But I

would not like to see 115 minutes of video technique in an attempt to tell a story. Unless it was Stanley Kubrick behind the camera. No matter what new techniques come, though, they often go; because nothing substitutes for a good story. And no matter where you put the camera or how many times you split the screen or whether you shoot it in slow motion or you undercrank it so it'll move around like Ben Turpin, all that means nothing if you've got a strong story. If you've got a strong story, automatically the sensibility behind the camera is to shoot normal speed, conventional presentation and just get the story onto the screen—clean, with style, and with compassion.

How did your appearance on the Tracey Ullman Show *come about?*
I got a call one day that they had written a script with me in it and would I play myself, or would I at least read the script and consider it? I was curious, so I read the script and I loved the little nine-minute segment of Tracey talking to my speaker box and trying to get into my house. I was really flattered by it, thought it was sweet, and on impulse said I would do it. Of course, five minutes later I regretted saying yes because I don't do real well in front of the camera.

Well, how did you do?
I did okay. Ted Bessel was a good director and he relaxed me. And Jim Brooks was there, and Jim was supportive, and Jerry Belson was there and he was supportive. And Tracey was the most supportive and she saw that I was a bit nervous behind the eyes and she said the right things to me and I suddenly realized, "Hey, is that what a good director does . . . simply to relax the actor and allow the actor to do his or her best work?" And that's pretty much what everybody did for me.

Did you first see Tracey in Plenty?
Oh, I loved her in *Plenty*. But I saw her before that in the Paul McCartney video. Before Jim Brooks actually wrapped a show around her, I was shouting her name all over town, trying to find something to put her in.

You've admitted to being a procrastinator. How do you achieve so much if you procrastinate?
Well, let's put it this way. If I didn't procrastinate, just imagine how much more I could achieve. (laughs)

Hook

ANA MARIA BAHIANA/1992

IT WAS ALMOST LIKE a mythical Hollywood tale, or
perhaps a running joke: Steven Spielberg wants to do a contemporary Peter Pan. Of course, like no other American filmmaker of
his generation, Spielberg seems enthralled by the possibilities of
eternal youth, by the cosmic resonances not only of childhood in
general but of his childhood in particular. It would only be fit-
ting that he would be the one to transport these visions—so
cleverly expressed by the Disney animators in its late-1950's *Peter
Pan*—to live action. But the years passed and Spielberg's most
obvious project never seemed to come to fruition. And as he
explains in this interview, that has more to do with personal
psychological reasons than with the usual Hollywood pitfalls of
complicated negotiations, tangled deals and high-rotation production executives.

Finally, in late 1990, it was announced that *Hook*, a modern-day retelling of
James Barrie's Peter Pan myth, was firmly under way, with Spielberg at the
helm, Dustin Hoffman in the title character, and Robin Williams—a natural Pan, if ever there were one—as a 1990s Boy Who Wouldn't Grow Up
(but eventually did and here lay the twist in the tale).

Written by Jim Hart (with additional material provided by several other
writers, even though only *Once Around*'s Malia Scotch Marmo gets on-screen

From *Cinema Papers*, March/April 1992. Reprinted by permission.

credit) and based on an original idea of his eight-year-old son ("What would happen if Peter Pan left Neverland and grew up?"), *Hook* proved to be a more arduous task than anyone envisioned. "We didn't really realize the size of the project until we were smack in the middle of it," says Hart, who is also the film's producer.

Building Neverland according to stage designer John (*Cats, Miss Saigon*) Napier's luxuriously complex blueprints was a gigantic task in itself. But then there were the matters of making grown-ups fly in a convincing way, controlling a dozen utterly uncontrollable pre-teens (who play the new, multi-ethnic Lost Boys) and, last but by no means least, handle the tangled overexposure of Julia Roberts (who plays Tinkerbell), her momentous unmarriage and sudden illness, right in the middle of the shoot.

Was it worth it? On the opening week in Los Angeles, Spielberg shows up for this interview wearing his signature pilot jacket and baseball cap, with the relaxed and glowing attitude of a content man. He brought *Hook* in at a whopping cost of $75 million (and counting) but the film, in spite of lukewarm reviews, is a hit in the rich holiday market: almost $100 million in tickets over a mere 6-week period. It is enough to make anyone fly.

What are your earliest memories of Peter Pan?
My mom read *Peter Pan* to me when I was, I guess, three-years-old. When I was eleven-years-old, I, along with other kids, directed a shortened version of James Barrie's *Peter Pan* in my elementary school, with all the parents watching in the audience. I actually staged it and did it as a kid, just like in the opening scene from *Hook*. I put that scene in almost only for that reason.

Peter Pan *stayed with you throughout your career. There are many references to it in* E.T. The Extra-Terrestrial, *for instance. In a way, it is surprising that you didn't do this movie earlier.*
I was going to do it as early as 1985. I had been pursuing the rights and in 1985 I finally acquired them from the London Children's Hospital. I was going to make a Peter Pan movie based on the novel, a live-action version like the 1924 *Peter Pan* silent movie. But then something happened: my son (Max) was born and I lost my appetite for the project.

Why?
Because suddenly I couldn't be Peter Pan any more. I had to be his father. That's literally the reason I didn't do the movie back then. And I had everything ready and Elliot Scott hired to do the sets in London.

In a way, my son took my childhood away from me. But he also gave it back to me. When he was born, I suddenly became the spitting image of my father and mother. All the parental clichés, all the things I said I would never say to my kids if ever I had them, I began saying to my own kids.

But, as I was raising my kids, the appetite for *Peter Pan* came back, and stayed with me.

What kind of childhood did you have that you seem to celebrate it so much?
I don't know that any of our childhoods were completely happy—from our own memories. My childhood was bad and it was good. It was chaotic; it was noisy; it was real loud. I have a big family, with three younger sisters. People yelled and screamed at each other.

Now that I'm a dad and have four kids—the fifth is on its way, actually—they scream and yell at each other all the time. I guess now I can appreciate even more whom my parents were.

What is, for you, the most enduring quality of the Peter Pan myth? Eternal youth, perhaps?
It's actually flying. To me, anytime anything flies, whether it's Superman, Batman, or E.T., it's got to be a tip of the hat to Peter Pan. *Peter Pan* was the first time I ever saw anybody fly. Before I saw *Superman,* before I saw *Batman,* and of course before I saw any superheroes, my first memory of anybody flying is in *Peter Pan.*

What does flight mean to you? There is a tremendous amount of flying in your films.
I am absolutely fascinated and terrified by flying. It is a big deal in my movies. All my movies have airplanes in them. You name the movie—they all fly.

To me, flying is synonymous with freedom and unlimited imagination but, interestingly enough, I'm afraid to fly.

I have two hundred hours in flight simulators. I love them, and once I even landed a two-engine Cessna based on my experience in the flight simulator. But it was more out of fear, abject fear, and the need to control that fear that I did it.

I'm only not afraid to fly in my dreams and in my movies, but, in real life, I'm terrified of flying. Just like the Peter Banning character in the beginning of *Hook*. That scene in the airplane? That was me; that's how I fly. I get white knuckles.

Have you ever analyzed your relationship with flying?
You mean psychoanalyzed? No, I haven't. I'm aware of the psychoanalytic implications of flight but, no, I have never been analyzed. I think we all need it, though. I think I need it, but I'm always afraid that if I get psycho-analyzed my movies will suffer because I'll become more intellectual about them. I'll all of a sudden figure out what it is I do and then I would proba-bly screw it up.

What made you pick up this specific project, Hook, *after all these years not tack-ling* Peter Pan?
I decided to do it when I read the Jim Hart script. It was a great idea, even though my first reaction was "This isn't exactly what I want to do, but this is a great idea for a movie." But then I took the idea and I rewrote the script with Jim and another writer [Malia Scotch Marmo] and, based on the rewrite, I went ahead and made the movie.

What was it about it that attracted you so much?
I guess I related to the main character, Peter Banning, the way Jim wrote him—a "type A" personality.

I think a lot of people today are losing their imagination because they are work-driven. They are so self-involved with work and success and arriv-ing at the next plateau that children and family almost become incidental. I have seen this happen to friends of mine. I have even experienced it myself when I have been on a very tough shoot and I've not seen my kids except on weekends. They ask for my time and I can't give it to them because I'm working. And I've been both guilty and wanting to do some-thing about it.

So, when Jim Hart wrote that script, and wrote a "type A" personality in Peter Banning, I related to it. I said, "Gee, that's quite a character arc for this character. Could this person ever have been Peter Pan? Wow, what an interesting challenge!"

Could it also be that you were interested in returning to youth-oriented pictures after a couple of adult projects?
It's not conscious. I don't sit down and say, "Now I have to look for a movie that is just for families," because I had made three films for adults. And we only got adult audiences, actually, for the last three films, except that I didn't think of them that way.

When *Hook* came by I was actually planning to direct *Schindler's Ark,* [*Schindler's List* in America] which is very much an adult film, and which I'm finally going to direct early in '92.

Hook *was also an extremely expensive movie to make. Was that a concern of yours at any point during the shoot?*
I'm real apprehensive about finances on every movie no matter what it costs. *E.T.* cost $10 million, and I was saying, "Gee, why can't we make it for $8 million?" But basically once a movie starts, the last thing you want to be aware of is the responsibility to the financiers because that would completely interrupt the idea that we're making a movie, that we're telling a story together. It would get in the way every day, so I don't think that was in my mind at all in the making of this movie.

When the movie is done the studio reminds me how much I've spent making the movie, and then, of course, I start to worry. I worry at the end but not during the making of the movie.

What was so expensive about it?
Well, creating a world is always expensive. And this is what I was trying to do: create a world. When George Lucas created a world for *Star Wars,* nobody had ever seen anything like that before. It was the same thing here. We all have expectations for Neverland so we needed to put our heads together to create a Neverland that you would believe in, that would look like Neverland and not just Laguna Beach [a beach suburb of Los Angeles].

You mentioned Schindler's Ark *as your next project. Would that be before* Jurassic Park?

Yes. I bought the book eight years ago, but I haven't been able to get a writer to do a script.

It's a drama about the Holocaust, about the real-life story of Oscar Schindler, who was a German Catholic profiteer who saved twelve hundred Jews in Poland. It's a fascinating story.

It's also interesting that I would pick, of all the Holocaust stories I could tell, the one that has one glimmer of hope.

Schindler's Ark has a very interesting statistic: there are six thousand descendants from the twelve hundred Jews that Schindler delivered to safety, and that out-numbers the surviving Jews in Poland. That's an idea worth making a movie about, I thought. We're shooting in Poland and Czechoslovakia, in black-and-white.

Why black-and-white?
Because I don't see the Holocaust in colour. I've been indoctrinated with documentaries and they're all black-and-white. Every time I see anything in colour about World War II, it looks too glamourized, too antiseptic. I think black-and-white is almost the synonymous form for World War II and the Holocaust.

A last and maybe obvious question: Are you Peter Pan?
No, no. I think my mom is the quintessential Peter Pan. She even looks like him. Seriously. My mother has a restaurant and she literally flies around it. She's 72 years old and she moves faster than I ever could.

Steven's Choice

JOHN H. RICHARDSON/1994

FOUR HUNDRED EXTRAS STAND freezing in the slanting snow.
They wear clumpy old boots, scarves on their heads, old hats, long beards,
and every one of them wears a white armband with a blue Star of David.
They stamp their feet as clots of snow slip off the steep Eastern European
rooftops, waiting for a Nazi officer in a gorgeous old Mercedes convertible
to drive through the square.

"Tell all the actors to take their hats off as the car goes by," says Steven
Spielberg, who is dressed for the weather in rubberized Sorel hiking boots
and a hat with earflaps.

This is Kraków, Poland, in the heart of the old Jewish ghetto. The air is
full of steam and smoke. Spielberg has been here for five weeks, shooting
Schindler's List, Thomas Keneally's account of the true story of a German
businessman who saved at least 1,100 Jews from the death camps—all while
drinking and whoring with the local Nazi elite. Very little has changed in
the past 50 years. Most of the buildings are just as the Nazis left them
when they emptied the ghetto to fill the death camps. Auschwitz was—
is—conveniently located 45 minutes away. According to the production's
Polish guide, so many people were killed there that even today the banks
of the nearby ponds are black with human ashes.

"Okay, here we go, stand by!"

Spielberg rides in the backseat of the Mercedes, looking through the
camera. A crew member translates his instructions to the extras through a

---

From *Premiere,* January 1994. Reprinted by permission of the author.

megaphone. Barking orders in his harsh, guttural Polish, he sounds like he's really ordering them to their deaths.

"Camera ready, and we're . . . *rolling!*"

"*Action!*" Spielberg shouts. The car pulls out, and the extras scatter.

Between shots, a gray-haired woman leaves a small group of gawking tourists and approaches Spielberg. She tells him that seeing the Nazis in the plaza gave her a shock.

"It's horrifying, horrifying, to see it again," she says.

Her name is Lorna, and she's a survivor on a pilgrimage to the death camps. Spielberg speaks to her very directly, as he does to everyone. "Were you ghettoized in Kraków?" he asks.

"Until the liquidation," she answers.

"Did you have a job?"

"We worked by fur, cleaning fur," she says.

Spielberg says this happens a lot. "They see the stars on the clothes and the armbands, and the costumes, and they go white." This gives him unmistakable satisfaction. "That's what it's all about," he says. "Creating an opportunity to remember. What is that famous line? 'Lest we forget.'"

Then without any pause at all, he turns to his first AD, Sergio Mimica: "Sergio, Sergio. What's holding us up? The sun's coming out, and I need to get this reverse in matching weather."

Schindler's List is a massive production: 126 speaking parts. 30,000 extras. 148 sets on 35 locations. 210 crew members, and another 30 for construction. Before it is over, they will shoot for two more months. Spielberg has come to the set almost directly from the shoot of *Jurassic Park*. For him the story of Oskar Schindler is the definition of a labor of love, a tribute to his Jewish heritage and to the heritage of black-and-white film, as well as a struggle to free himself from the commercial brilliance that has made him the most successful filmmaker of all time. He is shooting it without stars in black and white on a relatively small budget of $22 million, and he seems absolutely in love with every moment of the day, energized as he has rarely been in recent years.

The cast and crew are equally devoted. There is an almost consecrated gravity to this set. Because Spielberg was not able to find enough Jews left in Poland to fill out the cast, many of the actors are Israeli, either survivors themselves or the children of survivors. Producer Branko Lustig and Jewish tradition consultant Wlodzimierz Sztejn both lived through Auschwitz. The Gentiles are equally committed, like focus puller Steve Tate. Married to a Jew, he was producing his own movies when he heard Spielberg was ready to make *Schindler.* "I told him I'd do anything, even work for free, because I hope it will encourage other righteous Gentiles. Maybe one of them will save my children someday."

Before the shoot began, the troupe gathered at Auschwitz for a memorial service led by Sztejn. "He barely got through it," Spielberg recalls. "His voice was in an almost constant vibrato, a vibrato of choky tears. It was a sound I've never heard before, a sound of such anguish. I thought he reacted that way whenever he came here, and then I found out that he hadn't been back for 45 years."

Actor Liam Neeson did his first scene at Auschwitz. Playing Schindler, he rushed to the camp to save a group of his factory workers who were routed there accidentally. "It was a bleak fucking place," he says later. "I finished a play on Broadway [*Anna Christie*] on Sunday, and I was in there in front of the cameras on Wednesday morning. It was bitterly cold. I stood there, with the whole movie circus, and nothing entered my soul. Then Branko said, 'What do you think?' And I said, 'Branko, it's my first day.' He unrolled his sleeve and showed me his tattoo."

"To the right, many of the barracks have been torn down, but the chimneys are still there," says Spielberg. "It's a forest of chimneys. It was a city. It was an industry, an industry of death. It is a haunted killing field, and you feel it. Everybody was extremely edgy the couple of days we shot there."

Then he turns his attention back to the set. "Sergio," he says, "what I'd love to see is: Give the men cigarettes, and when the car goes past, have them put them behind their backs."

As he shoots, Spielberg talks. And talks. Maybe it's having spent five weeks in Kraków; maybe it's the prevailing mood of testimony. He says talking helps him burn off nervous energy. Much of his conversation is in the way of historical exegesis—he's become quite a scholar of the Holocaust. At other times it is more personal. Growing up Jewish in Arizona was tough, he says. "They threw pennies in the study hall, you know—in a real quite room, they threw pennies at me."

He was raised Orthodox for part of his childhood. "I kept wanting to have Christmas lights on the front of our house so it didn't look like the

Black Hole of Calcutta in an all-Gentile neighborhood—our neighborhood used to win awards for Christmas decorations. I would beg my father, 'Dad, please, let us have some lights,' and he'd say, 'No, we're Jewish,' and I'd say, 'What about taking that white porch light out and screwing in a red porch light?' and he'd say, 'No!' and I'd say, 'What about a yellow porch light?' and he said, 'No!'"

Spielberg and Universal Pictures bought *Schindler's List* eleven years ago, shortly after it was published. "In my burning desire to entertain," he says, "I kept pushing it back." At one point he fobbed it off on Martin Scorsese, and when he changed his mind, he ended up trading him *Cape Fear* to get it back. Part of the problem was dramatizing Schindler's gradual conversion from a Nazi party member to a hero who kept Jews alive by inventing jobs for them at his factory—he saved small children, for example, by telling the Nazis that only their tiny hands could polish the insides of bombshells. Several screenwriters worked on the script before Steven Zaillian tamed the sprawling narrative by paring it down to what cast members half-jokingly call "a buddy movie," focusing on the friendship between Schindler and Itzhak Stern, a Jewish intellectual played by Ben Kingsley. Stern fights with a charming Nazi killer named Amon Goeth for the soul of Schindler. "It's the perfect dramatic shape," observes Kingsley, "with Stern the good angel and Goeth the bad angel and Schindler in the middle."

As the script matured, so did Spielberg. Becoming a father helped prepare him. "I'm much more political now than I was before," he says. "Ten years ago when people interviewed me about *E.T.*, I was proud to say that I was a kind of political atheist, that I was six years late getting the Beatles, and that Vietnam went right over my head."

Spielberg also realized he'd gone somewhat astray in recent years, having been "seduced by my own success. I had always played to the adult audience who were able to remember their childhood and enjoy the movies along with their own children," he says, "but when I began playing to the kids directly, I found that I stumbled on my own shoelaces. Then I realized, when you're making movies, you can't do things consciously."

Schindler is different from anything Spielberg has done before, as far from the "movie" movie universe of *Jaws* as it could possibly be. Even *Empire of the Sun* was seen through the eyes of a boy and therefore was much more of a "visual feast," as Spielberg puts it. To make *Schindler* right, he knew he would have to try a radically different palette. "The authenticity of the story was too important to fall back on the commercial techniques that had gotten me a certain reputation in the area of craft and polish," he says.

This took a certain struggle. It ended up, as emotional struggles often do, with a new technique: "I threw a whole bunch of tools out of the toolbox. One of them was a crane. One of them was color film. I just limited the utensils, so the story would be the strength of the piece. There's nothing flashy in this movie at all...." He pauses. "I hope it's not too dull."

To keep the frame lively, Spielberg is shooting fast—sometimes 35 or 40 shots a day—and lavishly, doing more coverage in the first five weeks than in his last five movies put together, he says. And he plans on using it in rapidly cut montage. "I'm taking advantage of the speed with which we're shooting to be able to find more ways of shooting it," he says. He's also going for a documentary, cinema verité feel, employing a lot of wobbly hand-held shots. He expects the final product will be 30 percent hand-held, which will help "take a coat of wax off the finish."

Spielberg avoided using stars, although he says several were willing to play Schindler virtually for free. (The names most frequently connected with the project on the industry grapevine were Mel Gibson, Harrison Ford, and Kevin Costner.) "I was looking for the actual guy, as close to the actual man as I could find." Spielberg says. "Liam did a spectacular test for me, and I like the fact that although he's not an unknown actor, he's not a star either, and he won't bring much baggage to the character."

Curiously, Schindler is unlike most of Spielberg's previous heroes, who are much darker than generally perceived. From Roy Neary furiously building his mashed-potato mountain in *Close Encounters of the Third Kind* to Elliott frantically showing E.T. his toys, they have burned with troubled energy—Schindler, in contrast, is so much the "host of his world," as Spielberg puts it, that he even makes Indiana Jones look anxious. "Liam Neeson as Oskar Schindler is the most romantic character I've ever worked with. He romances the entire city of Kraków, he romances the Nazis, he romances the politicians, the police chiefs, the women. He was a grand seducer."

The movie will be dedicated to former Time Warner chairman Steven J. Ross, who became a father figure for Spielberg before he died in 1992. "Steve Ross gave me more insights into Schindler than anybody I've ever known," he says. "If Schindler were alive today, he would be running Time Warner.

Before I shot the movie, I sent Liam all my home movies of Steve. I said, 'Study his walk, study his manner, get to know him real well, because that's who this guy is.'"

In his darkest film, Spielberg has put his brightest character. No wonder he takes such pleasure in Schindler, speaking of him often and with great affection: "What's amazing is that Oskar managed to consort with this terrorist for the entire three years—drinking together, whoring together, making money together—without ever once letting him see the true side to his nature."

Ralph Fiennes, who plays Goeth, nods his head. "There's something in one of the documentaries about Schindler that may explain that. He could sort of let the pig out in himself. He used an interesting expression: 'I could always contact the *Schwein* in somebody else.'"

Spielberg grunts, a kind of laugh. "The pigs ate 6 million truffles," he says.

Hundreds of extras grab suitcases off the prop truck and line up in front of a gate shaped like one of Moses' tablets. The Jews are entering the ghetto. Horses pull carts with wooden-spoked wheels piled high with furniture. Nazis with machine guns line the street. The snow continues driving down in sheets, like a sweeping white broom, and steam rises from the horses, feathers out from every mouth.

It is so cold that every muscle tenses up and exhaustion comes quickly. But Spielberg never sits down. He wades into the crowd, positioning extras. "You'll stop them right here," he tells an actor. In the back he finds a very old man with a long wispy beard and puts him in the front. Two of the actors want to know what to do with their suitcases when they reach the head of the line. "Don't rehearse it," he says. "You can't plan for real."

The next shot catches the crowd of Jews lining up for their assignments. Spielberg tells the children to hold umbrellas over the Nazis at the tables to keep the snow off their uniforms, then decides to incorporate them into the shot. The kid in the foreground is too cute, so Spielberg replaces him with a plainer child. "I love umbrellas in a movie," he says. "Remember *Foreign Correspondent*? Everything was original about that, especially the high angle on all the umbrellas. When the shooter escapes, you can only tell what direction he's running because the umbrellas are being jostled one after the other. Remember that?"

Spielberg considers using a dolly. He tucks his chin in and stares at the ground. His baseball cap comes down at an oblique angle to his nose, like a resting bird. "The dolly shot would be a real Hollywood shot," he says, "a real movie shot on a normal 'movie' movie. On a movie like this, a pan is always the choice."

Constantly, Spielberg restrains himself. To dilute the satanic charm of Goeth, for example, he's had Fiennes play many of his scenes "behind dull, drink-shrouded eyes, because I don't want him to become the Hannibal Lecter of the Holocaust genre," he says.

This scene turns out to be difficult to choreograph, what with hundreds of extras approaching the desks, the horses cutting off to one side, Nazis stamping work orders—and all this must be timed to the dialogue. After the second or third take Spielberg starts getting . . . testy would be the wrong word. Insistent.

"What happened there?" he says. "They just flood through. The whole point of this scene is, they have to pause to get their assignments. That's not real. They have to be real."

He decides to go for a longer lens to get more of the crowd in the picture—but not too long. "A little closer and I can justify hearing the dialogue," he says. "And when they start walking, it justifies a dolly."

Having changed his mind, he orders up a dolly track.

Producer Branko Lustig is a cheerful man, solid and gray-haired. He calmly announces that he lost his whole family in the camps. "Everybody except my mother. We met up after the war."

And he continues smiling as he talks about working in Poland. "I must tell you, when I'm here, I'm not comfortable. They need our money so they are very correct. But I don't trust them. They were very anti-Semitic during the war. They are anti-Semitic for 600 years. Why they should change?"

Then why make a movie about a German, even if he happened to be a good German?

"You heard about this protest in Germany where 1 million people were with candles in Munich, Hamburg, Frankfurt?" he asks, speaking of recent demonstrations against neo-Nazi skinheads. "They say it should never happen again. I think Schindler, he was one of the Germans who held his candle, 50 years ago. But he was alone."

At around 5 P.M., Spielberg sits down on a box. Except for lunch, it is the first time he's sat down the entire day. There are no director's chairs—or actor's chairs or producer's chairs, for that matter—on this set.

With a few minutes to kill, Spielberg gives an impromptu lecture: "Black and white doesn't distract the way color distracts. Often even when you light a scene to look depressing, it comes across looking beautiful. Because if you use soft light coming in through a window—what an overcast day looks like—even if you print it toward the blue side, there's still a kind of Merchant-Ivory beauty about it. The beauty is in its frankness. It's completely unforgiving. Black and white is about texture; it's not about tone. If you wake up with a pimple in the morning, black and white will accentuate the blemish more than color will. So when you're in a ghetto like this, black and white details every single wall, all the bricks, all the chipped plaster on the facades of these ghetto dwellings. I knew the minute I read the book that I would be making this film someday in black and white."

How does the studio feel about that? Spielberg says the resistance went no further than a mild objection from Universal chairman Tom Pollock. "He said, 'Look, we're probably not going to make any money on this in its theatrical release. At least shoot in color so we can sell the cassettes and sell it to television.' I understood his plea, but it would have been bad casting."

Everybody is so cold and tired at this point that the actors keep blowing their lines. They end up doing about nineteen takes. Finally, some exhausted crew member says, "Are we finished? Can we go home yet?" And Spielberg's eyes dart around. "Who said that? No, we're not! Who said that?"

The instant one shot is finished, Spielberg and his core crew hustle across the plaza to grab another. This time the setting is a pharmacy so tiny that only Spielberg, the actors, and the cameraman fit inside. Spielberg studies the set. "Move that jar," he says. "The blue one. It's too skinny."

"Guys, we're losing the light," Spielberg says. "I can't see through my sunglasses...."

"Rolling and...action."

Then they move to another small room in another dark building. This time it's Kingsley forging work documents. "They used to forge diplomas from technical colleges," Spielberg explains, "so you could take a conductor of a symphony, who would be of no use to the Germans whatsoever, and make him a valuable metalworker."

While waiting, Spielberg speaks of his grandfather, a Jew from Odessa. As a boy, he says, his grandfather was prohibited from attending school. "They did allow Jews to listen through open windows to the classes, so he pretty much went to school—fall, winter, and spring—by sitting outside in driving snow, outside of open windows."

He pauses, recalling his grandfather in America putting on a leather phylactery every morning and praying in Hebrew. "I was so ashamed of being a Jew, and now I'm filled with pride," he says. "I don't even know when that transition happened."

Kingsley arrives, and they rehearse. "Spill a little coffee on the diploma and then shake it in the air," Spielberg instructs. A crew member interjects that the real forgers used to age the diplomas with tea. But Spielberg says coffee looks better on camera. Kingsley is serious, almost grave, as attentive as a stalking cat.

"Bite the edges off the paper," Spielberg suggests.

Kingsley sips the coffee before he spills it on the document. Each time he adds a little gesture. They are making something, building it up piece by piece almost as if it were a physical thing and not just gestures in a dark room.

Despite his gravity, Kingsley is a joker. When a costumer pulls a thread off his jacket, he reacts with mock severity. "That's my characterization," he says.

She drops it on the floor. "That's *my* characterization," she says.

They're shooting in artificial light now but still racing against their daily wrap time. Spielberg makes a grabbing motion in the air, but nobody responds. "Cut," he says, turning to Mimica. "When I do this, what does it mean?"

"You're catching flies?"

"I've been doing this for five weeks," he says. "It's a *cue.*"

"There's a fly in the room," Mimica says.

Spielberg allows Mimica his joke. "And I haven't caught that stupid fly yet."

The next day Spielberg gets genuinely upset for the first time. He's about to shoot part of the big *Aktion*—the slaughter that cleaned out the last people still hiding in the attics and closets of the ghetto—but he hates the Nazi uniforms. It's important, because there was so much bloodshed— 4,000 people were killed in one day—and the Nazis came prepared in thick, splatter-proof, silver gray coats. He wants a Darth Vader effect. Except these coats are dull, pea-soup green.

"I'll be frank," says a costume woman. "I don't like them either."

"I'll be really frank," Spielberg says. "I really hate these costumes."

The woman tries to explain she didn't have money in the budget...

Spielberg cuts her off. "It's your responsibility to come to me ahead of time and give me the option to spend a little more money to get what I want," he says. "This is not what I want or even close to it. This is really bad, and I don't know what to do now, because the whole thing was planned around *Einsatzgruppe* guys looking completely menacing and scary, and these look no different than the NCOs we have walking around the forced labor camps. So I don't know what the fuck to do." He pauses, disgusted. "They look like raincoats from the Gap."

Someone tries coming to the woman's defense. "It's gonna be so dark..."

"It doesn't matter," Spielberg says. "It's the glisten. They're not shiny, they're not thick, and we've got all this research."

Steve Tate suggests the coats some officers were wearing earlier, long gray coats with some of the thickness Spielberg wants. The director agrees to using the officer coats. Now he is starting to feel bad. "I lost my temper. First time on the picture I lost my temper."

Mimica interrupts with a technical question, but Spielberg is still upset at losing control: "I won't holler for at least 24 hours," he swears.

Israeli actor Jonathan Sagalle plays Poldek Pfefferberg, the man who inspired Thomas Keneally to write his novel by telling him the Schindler story in a Beverly Hills luggage shop. Like many young Israelis, he's just about had his fill of the Holocaust—he says he learned about Nazi atrocities the way geese get fattened, with a metal tube straight to the stomach. It's important, he says, to stay healthy, not to be morbid. Unlike most of the others, he hasn't yet taken the Auschwitz tour. And yet...in one scene he had to walk a gauntlet of anti-Semites. "They're shouting, 'Kill the Jews!'" he says, "and you know they're extras, but they're locals, red-cheeked Aryans, and they're spitting and throwing snowballs and mud. This one kid threw a snowball at me, and even though it's only a movie, I really wanted to take that kid and strangle him."

"Each day is really hard," says Spielberg's wife, actress Kate Capshaw, who has come to visit the set. "So many shots are so violent, emotionally violent. There have been a couple of days where I think he really struggled to stay the director—in particular the shower scene, all the women being marched in for disinfection in what was, as we all know, the gas chamber. The horror of the women and the actors who were doing it . . . but there was something about being naked that got everybody."

Along with Capshaw, Spielberg brought his five children and three of their friends. "We're all here for a reason," Capshaw says. "People said, 'Why are you going for three and a half months?' It's really about this movie. It's not a *Raiders* movie. The net has to be stronger."

An unexpected snowfall has upset the schedule. When Spielberg is annoyed, he has a peculiarly matter-of-fact, almost unemotional way of expressing his displeasure. The actual words he uses can be cutting, but they don't seem brutal because he doesn't give them any emotional sting. He takes Lustig and speaks in a quiet but insistent voice. "This snow has screwed everybody up," he says. "You guys are great when we've got a full week planned in advance, but when we have to change things overnight, everybody falls apart. We have the wrong uniforms, wrong costumes, machine guns that were never tested until five minutes before we shot, and they were jamming. I never want this to happen again. I'm not going to rely on you guys anymore to tell me what order we're shooting the picture in—if we have rain, I want a call at 2 o'clock in the morning. Wake me up and make me a partner, because I'm the director of the movie. This is never going to happen again. End of lecture."

Spielberg rushes from set to set, snatching shots of the *Aktion*. Under the arched entrance of a ghetto building he has arranged a tableau of sleeping Jews lying on the floor. Three bearded men stand praying in rays of morning light. He adjusts the bodies, admiring the "really great Eastern European Jewish faces" and talking of atrocities: "The SS had a lot of marksmen, and just for fun, placing bets, they threw babies out the windows alive and shot them like skeet. I wouldn't show that in the movie. I couldn't, even with dolls."

With the light fading fast, Spielberg hurries to another old building to shoot a scene where Nazis try to ferret out hiding Jews by applying stethoscopes to the ceiling—when they hear breathing, they open fire. "I'd like to start with two guys carried on two shoulders," Spielberg says. "We just see the legs over their faces. We don't know what's happening. We pan up, and we see the guy listening through the ceiling with a stethoscope. If he could have some kind of a marker in his hand or something...a piece of chalk?" The composition comes together quickly, and it's characteristically beautiful: One guy is up on a ladder and two others stand below him, making a dark pyramid framed by shadows and backlit by streetlights shining through lace curtains. Never mind that it's a gorgeous composition of Nazis about to murder Jews. "Ooh, nice," Spielberg says. "That's scary. That's scary."

With the daily wrap time fast approaching, the Nazis fire their machine guns. A special-effects guy runs an electrified clamp down a row of nails sticking out of a two-by-four, setting off the squibs in the ceiling. Another man outside pumps blood to the ceiling through pipes. There's a huge roar, and shards of plaster flutter down. The room fills with smoke. The ceiling is riddled with bullet holes. The Nazis point their guns and wait.

But where's the blood?

They wait.

It turns out the blood has frozen, and Spielberg decides to finish the shot the next day. If they manage to warm it up, he says, it'll probably come down too thin. A morose special-effects guy murmurs to himself, over and over, "You fucked it up, you fucked it up, you fucked it up."

Every night the actors congregate in the hotel bar, sometimes fanning out to hit the Kraków night spots. Tonight it's 11 P.M., and Ben Kingsley accepts a kiss from a concentration camp survivor, who inadvertently bumps his wineglass. "A kiss is still a kiss," he says graciously, "even though it spills wine all over you." The "Nazis" are here too. It's magical, in a way, Jew and Nazi reconciled in the lobby of a big cement hotel, just like François Truffaut's wonderful behind-the-camera movie, *Day for Night*. The actors' table is piled with beers and mineral water and wine. Snatches of conversation drift across the lobby: "Isn't she fantastic?" "It had to do with eggs; I'm sure it had something to do with eggs!" Neeson sits with actress Natasha Richardson, who's come to Poland to see him. Rich, well-earned laughter floats in a cloud of cigarette smoke. "We go out in the evenings and listen to loud music and eat and drink and hug each other," Kingsley says, "because at the end of a day in hell you treasure life and you treasure your loved ones."

Thought at 2 A.M.: Today Spielberg shot some of the most beautiful Nazi footage imaginable, and when the blood finally drips it is certain to drip beautifully. Hand-held, improvised, or shot with a shaky cam, Spielberg can't help himself. He loves movies too much to worry about making the Holocaust beautiful. In a way he is too pure for such thoughts. "Every time we go to a movie, it's magic, no matter what the movie's about," he argues. "Whether you watch eight hours of *Shoah* or whether it's *Ghostbusters*, when the lights go down in the theater and the movie fades in, it's magic."

But too much magic can be a problem, as Spielberg has learned. Striving after effects can end up turning attention to the effects, not the subject. A film like *Shoah* creates its effect by the accumulation of unlovely detail— the word *magic* even seems a violation of its pursuit after truth. It seems Spielberg is still struggling with what may turn out to be the great question of his later career: to dolly or not to dolly.

The answer isn't a simple either-or. Because magic, finally, is what draws Spielberg to Schindler. And unites them, though one is a hero and the other just an artist. For instance, the two days Spielberg and his crew worked at Auschwitz-Birkenau: They were there to shoot just one scene, that long, black train carrying its load of souls to certain death, but the World Jewish Congress vetoed their plans to shoot in the death camp itself. Spielberg couldn't give in because he needed the scene—because Schindler showed up to save them. With nothing up his sleeve, Schindler somehow made the nightmare go away. And in his lesser way Spielberg did too: He reached a compromise with the congress that allowed him to build a small but perfect mirror image of the death camp just outside the Auschwitz-Birkenau gate. He put the train inside the real camp and brought it through the gate into his fake camp. So although movie magic will make it seem that the train was arriving, as it did so many times, with such grim consequences, this time the train came *out* of Auschwitz.

Seriously Spielberg

STEPHEN SCHIFF/1994

AT THE CONSUMER ELECTRONICS Show in Las Vegas a couple of months ago, Steven Spielberg looked like someone who hadn't grown into his big brother's clothes. His jeans were baggy, and so was his salmon-colored sweatshirt; he wore a baseball cap that said "Brown University" on it (because his seventeen-year-old stepdaughter, Jessica, had just been admitted there), and the gray streaks in his beard might have struck one as improbable. He was being squired about by Lew Wasserman, the dapper chairman of MCA, and Sidney Sheinberg, the company's president. And around them blinked several lesser lights, mostly officials of Panasonic, which, like MCA, is owned by the giant Japanese conglomerate Matsushita. The caverns of the Las Vegas Convention Center were filled with squawking video games, stereos, wide-screen televisions, and scary-looking motion simulators, and Spielberg strode among them all with his hands clasped behind his back, like General Patton. For him, this was conquered territory: everywhere one looked, there were variations on themes from his movies *Jurassic Park, Raiders of the Lost Ark, E.T., Close Encounters of the Third Kind*, even *Jaws*. As he strolled, techies goggled at him, snapped pictures, aimed camcorders, and thrust little control panels and joysticks into his hands: "Play this one, Steven!" "Steven, you'll love this. It'd make a great movie!" Wasserman and Sheinberg, two of the most powerful men in Hollywood, hung behind like courtiers, attending to his needs and directing his gaze to whatever shiny gewgaw might amuse him, and every

From *The New Yorker*, 21 March 1994. Reprinted by permission of the author.

STEPHEN SCHIFF/1994   171

so often Spielberg would throw out a question about something juicy like ROM capacity or interactions per minute, and new minions would appear at his side with answers. As he played with a video game that traced the berserk journey of a runaway truck on a sere and distant planet, I overheard a pimply young techie murmur, "Look, it's God." His companion craned his neck, caught sight of Spielberg. "Hey, you're right," he said. "God."

There are limits to the dominion of a techie god. But when you turn on the television or go to the movies, when you play a video game or enter an amusement park or a shopping mall, there it all is: the Spielberg vision, imitated, replicated, and recycled — the upturned faces awaiting miracles, the otherworldly white backlighting, the here-comes-the-shark music, the mischievous but golden-hearted suburban children, the toys that fidget and romp by themselves, the Indiana Jones jungles and deserts and hats. That Spielberg is the most commercially successful movie director in history, with four of the top ten all-time box-office hits, is widely recognized; less so is the enormous influence that his vision has had on all the other visions the entertainment industry purveys. For better or worse, Spielberg's graphic vocabulary has engulfed our own. When car manufacturers want to seduce us, when moviemakers want to scare us, when political candidates want to persuade us, the visual language they employ is often Spielbergese — one of the few languages that this intensely fragmented society holds in common. We all respond to the image of "a place called Hope" when it's lit like a Spielberg idyll; we understand what we're being told about a soda can when it arrives in a Spielberg spaceship; we get the joke when an approaching basketball star shakes the earth like a Spielberg dinosaur. The way Steven Spielberg sees the world has become the way the world is communicated back to us every day.

Still, prophets are without honor in their own country, and in Hollywood, a town famous for its vindictiveness and Schadenfreude, the supernal glow around Steven Spielberg had, by the beginning of last year, begun to fade. The word was that industry people hated him for his wealth, his sharp business practices, his happy-go-lucky-kid demeanor. The memory of the dreamlike *E.T. The Extra-Terrestrial,* which had become the most successful film in history, was a decade old, and Spielberg had slipped up several times since that movie's release: with *The Color Purple,* his unconvincing first foray into the world of grown-up cinema; with *Empire of the Sun* and

the wildly overblown *Always,* a pair of flops also aimed at adults; with
Indiana Jones and the Temple of Doom, which some thought too sadistic
to be any fun; with *Indiana Jones and the Last Crusade,* which some thought
too tepid to be any fun; and finally with *Hook,* his lumbering Peter Pan
saga, which cost more than any other movie he had ever made, and which
practically no one much liked—including Spielberg. Throughout the
eighties, Spielberg's films often seemed like imitation Spielberg films, only
preachier. Even in the summer of 1993, after the release of the dinosaur picture *Jurassic Park,* which swiftly replaced *E.T.* as the largest-grossing film in
history, Spielberg could still be shrugged off by his less charitable contemporaries much the way that they had always shrugged him off: as a kind
of adolescent savant doomed to accomplish nothing beyond Spielberg
movies—in other words, boys'-book fantasies, light shows, theme-park
rides. You could be smug about a filmmaker like that, even if he was richer
and more powerful and more famous than you, because the gap between
his technological gifts and his artistic maturity seemed almost comical; his
limitations were clear.

But that was before the release of his masterpiece about the Holocaust,
Schindler's List, a work of restraint, intelligence, and unusual sensitivity,
and the finest fiction feature ever made about the century's greatest evil.
Adapted from Thomas Keneally's superb book about Oskar Schindler, a
Nazi businessman who began by employing Jews in his Kraków factory
and wound up saving eleven hundred of them from the death camps,
Schindler's List is the sort of film that fashions of taste and politics won't
soon dislodge; it will take its place in cultural history and remain there.
And for Spielberg it has had the effect of a giant bar mitzvah, a rite of
passage. Prince Hal has become Henry V; the dauphin has emerged a
king.

"I had to grow into that," Spielberg told me recently. "It took me years
before I was really ready to make *Schindler's List.* I had a lot of projects on
my shelves that were of a political nature and had 'social deed' written all
over them—even had 'politically correct' stamped on top of them. And I
didn't make those films, because I was censoring that part of me by saying
to myself, 'That's not what the public will accept from you. What they
will accept from you is thrills, chills, spills, and awe and wonder and that
sort of thing.' I was afraid people would say, as some of them did say about
both *Empire of the Sun* and *The Color Purple,* you know, 'Oh, it's the wrong

shoe size. And it's the wrong style. What's he doing? Who does he wanna be like? Who's he trying to become—Woody? Or is he trying to become David Lean? Is he trying to become Marty Scorsese? Who does he think he is?' And I listened to that criticism. It gets to you. I certainly felt that everybody had sent me the message loud and clear that I was, you know, bad casting. I was a kid for life. And I almost slept in the bed they made— no, I made the bed for myself. But when I wanted to wake up and do something different many people tried to get me to go back to bed. 'Go to your room. And don't come out until it's something my kids will love, young man.' "

Yet, paradoxically, Spielberg's coming of age has been celebrated nowhere more ardently than in Hollywood—cynical, envious Hollywood, the community that has for so long denied the neighborhood rich kid its highest accolade, the Academy Award.

Anyone who has spent any time there lately will have noticed that it has become voguish for the movie industry's prominent players to display a disdainful indifference to the films they make. The formulation that runs, "It's only a movie; it's not a cure for cancer," has been popular, even when the movie in question was budgeted at a cost precisely suitable to a cure for cancer. So the mood was right for *Schindler's List,* which not only was a very great film, but seemed itself to be a kind of worthy cause. Still, there have been worthy-cause films before, and the impact of *Schindler's List* has outstripped nearly all of them, because, to so many people in the movie business, it seems an inexplicable phenomenon. Hollywood understands talent, but it is baffled by genius; it understands appearances, but it is baffled by substance. Spielberg's genius is all the more bewildering because he gives very little outward sign of having any. In a town obsessed with surfaces, Spielberg wears goofy clothes, collects goofy art (he has twenty-five Norman Rockwell paintings), makes wide-eyed, goofy conversation, and maintains a personal style that is unpretentious to a fault. It has been almost preposterous that this awkward prodigy—not a child of Holocaust survivors, not previously steeped in the literature, not even terribly Jewish—has turned his famously gaudy light on this darkest and most difficult of subjects and come back with a masterpiece. In the end, Hollywood couldn't dismiss it, couldn't resent it, could barely even digest it. Instead, people there fell back in flabbergasted awe, sputtering wildly, the way they often do at fund-raisers and award ceremonies.

"I think *Schindler's List* will wind up being so much more important than a movie," Jeffrey Katzenberg, who runs the Walt Disney film studios, told me. "It will affect how people on this planet think and act. At a moment in time, it is going to remind us about the dark side, and do it in a way in which, whenever that little green monster is lurking somewhere, this movie is going to press it down again. I don't want to burden the movie too much, but I think it will bring peace on earth, good will to men. Enough of the right people will see it that it will actually set the course of world affairs. Steven is a national treasure. I'm breakin' my neck lookin' up at this guy."

Whether or not *Schindler's List* really is Santa Claus, the tooth fairy, and Dag Hammarskjöld rolled into one, a number of Spielberg's friends think that making the film has transformed him, or, rather, that it marks the latest and largest advance in a seasoning process that began around 1985, when he had his first child, Max—whose mother is his first wife, the actress Amy Irving—and has developed throughout his second marriage, to the actress Kate Capshaw. Spielberg has become more outgoing lately, more clubbable, more capable of intimacy. "I don't think Steven's had this many friends in his life since I've known him," Capshaw says. "He's got real buddies—he's never had that." These days he hangs out, often with prominent show-biz figures who more or less answer the same description: child-men, many of whom have settled down with take-charge, family-oriented, often relatively unglamorous wives, to raise children of their own—Robin Williams, Dustin Hoffman, Tom Hanks, Robert Zemeckis, Jeffrey Katzenberg, Martin Short. Together, these grown-up kids form a benign aristocracy, very different from the one that once dominated Hollywood—not dangerous, not druggy, not sexy, not wild. Their boyhoods are etched in their faces. These aren't the guys who passed their youths rat-packing around the neighborhood and getting into mischief; these were the wimpy guys, the nerds who spent their days in the vicinity of Mom, alone in the sandbox or playing in their room, developing the inner world that would one day conquer the outer one.

"The thing about Steven is he's still the A.V. guy in junior high school," Tom Hanks says. "You know, the guy who brings the movie projectors around and knows how to thread them, and all that kind of stuff. And I was the same way. So when we go out and do 'guy' things, it's not like we're out, you know, parasailing. We're not spearfishing, or anything like that. We're out just talking about a bunch of stuff and waiting to pick up our kids. We were out walking around on Friday, and a young girl approached him, and she said, 'I just had to tell you,' and she talked to him about *Schindler's List*. And within forty-five seconds this girl had emotionally come undone, because she was saying, 'My Nana used to tell me stories,' and she had connected this movie to her grandma. And Steven, as best he could, reassured her. He put his hand on her shoulder and said, 'I made this movie so that people like yourself would realize . . . '—something that was very appropriate and not very astute. And then she collected herself and she went off. And then we walked across the street, and Steven came emotionally undone. It took him a while to collect himself. And I assume it was because, just as that girl was not prepared for the power of what she had seen Steven do, Steven hasn't been quite prepared for the emotional power of what he has done."

Now, though, he is not doing much of anything—at least, not by Spielberg standards. True, his MCA-based company, Amblin Entertainment, is producing several feature films, some animation, some TV. And Spielberg himself is dabbling in extracurricular activities—designing rides for the Universal theme park in Orlando, for instance, and investing, with Katzenberg, in a new restaurant chain called Dive, which will sell submarine sandwiches. But, for the first time in his career, Spielberg doesn't know what his next directorial project will be. There are those who, like the Warner Bros. president, Terry Semel, believe that Spielberg will now direct an adaptation of the Robert James Waller best-seller *The Bridges of Madison County*, which Amblin is producing. But Semel may be disappointed.

"I have no idea what to do next," Spielberg says. "And, more important, I don't care. And that's what allowed me to go to that Consumer Electronics Show in Las Vegas. I mean I would never have done that—I would have been so driven to do the next project. So I feel I can treat myself to some time off. Right now there's nothing that's inspired me, nothing that makes me want to work in '94 at all. I'm not really interested in making money. That's always come as the result of success, but it's not been my goal, and I've had a very tough time proving that to people. I've never been in it for the money; I was in it for the physical pleasure of filmmaking. It's a physical pleasure being on a set, making a movie, you know—taking images out of your imagination and making them three-dimensional and solid. It's magic."

Spielberg is a fast talker, and the way he stammers and burbles, swallowing some of the words, makes the impression of boyishness even more pronounced: he's like an excitable prepubescent, his hormones zinging, his thoughts scooting by so fast that his mouth can't trap enough language to express them. Beneath the round Armani glasses and the patriarchal beard, Spielberg has the face of the forty-six-year-old man he is; there are deep creases in his neck now, and a genuine gravity in his heavy-lidded eyes. But he is also squirmy and coltish: he bites his fingernails; he twiddles his thumbs. Energy leaks out of him everywhere.

"Maybe when I made *Indy Two* and *Indy Three* were the two times I could have been motivated by making money, by an easy slide into home plate," he says. "And if I do a sequel to *Jurassic Park,* that would be an easy choice. I have no embarrassment in saying that with *Jurassic* I was really just trying to make a good sequel to *Jaws.* On land. It's shameless—I can tell you that now. But these days I'd rather make the more difficult choices. I just was so challenged by *Schindler's List* and so fulfilled by it and so disturbed by it. It so shook up my life, in a good way, that I think I got a little taste of what a lot of other directors have existed on all through their careers—people like Altman, people like Kazan, even people like Preston Sturges, who made fiercely independent films. I suddenly saw what some of the tug was to the real filmmakers, who are always drawn to the subject matter because it's dangerous. I made *Schindler's List* thinking that if it did entertain, then I would have failed. It was important to me not to set out to please. Because I always had."

Of course, the almost unmentionable secret of *Schindler's List* is that it does entertain: that part of its greatness comes from the fact that it moves swiftly and energetically, that it has storytelling confidence and flair, that it provides pain but also catharsis—that it is not, in short, a lecture but a work of art. I ask Spielberg whether, in the past, his propensity for pleasing an audience had interfered with his pleasing himself. "Yes, definitely," he replies. "It was like believing your own publicity. Everybody kept trying to equate my name with how much money the movie made on opening weekend or in the long run, as opposed to how good the movie was. So if I could stay successful and my movies made money I could stay Steven Spielberg. I would be allowed to keep my name. And I've always had an urge to please the audience, to please people other than myself. I never thought about compromising my own self-respect. I was beyond self-respect. I was into putting on a great show and sitting back and enjoying the audience participation. I felt more like P. T. Barnum than John Ford, for a lot of my career. And I wasn't ashamed of that. I've always thought that filling every seat in every theatre in America was the ultimate vindication and validation. And the thought of pleasing myself only came to me recently."

As we talk, Spielberg is showing me around Amblin, a moviemaking haven like no other in Hollywood. Built in 1983, this place is perhaps the most visible emblem of Spielberg's power: twenty-five thousand square feet of offices, editing rooms, and conference rooms, with a palatial day-care center, a screening room (with popcorn-and-candy counter), a full-scale gym, a video-game room, a restaurant-size kitchen, and a separate building for directors called Movies While You Wait. The style is Santa Fe pueblo, and though the bricks are genuine baked adobe, the whole complex manages to look kitschy and unreal, like a movie set—or the world's fanciest Taco Bell. It sits in a remote and unnaturally quiet corner of the Universal lot (the corner nearest Warner Bros., for Warners and Universal are the two studios Spielberg generally works with), and its oasislike atmosphere is enhanced by lawns, palm trees, and a small Japanese garden: bubbling brook, fake-looking boulders, even a school of koi, the colorful Japanese fish, which Spielberg likes to capture on videotape—he sets their hungry gaping to Puccini, so that they appear to be singing *Madame Butterfly*. Nothing here is higher than two stories, because Spielberg has a phobia about elevators (though that hasn't stopped him from keeping an apartment in the upper reaches of New York's Trump Tower), and Spielberg's own office sits above a sunny courtyard; walking there, you feel as though you were padding from the pool back to your room at some Mexican resort hotel. Although Spielberg has been known to be steely in his business dealings and sometimes insensitive about dispensing gratitude, the denizens of Amblin appear to be happy campers.

"I began wanting to make people happy from the beginning of my life," Spielberg says. "As a kid, I had puppet shows—I wanted people to like my puppet shows when I was eight years old. My first film was a movie I made when I was twelve, for the Boy Scouts, and I think if I had made a different kind of film, if that film had been, maybe, a study of raindrops coming out of a gutter and forming a puddle in your back yard, I think if I had shown that film to the Boy Scouts and they had sat there and said, 'Wow, that's really beautiful, really interesting. Look at the patterns in the water. Look at the interesting camera angle'—I mean, if I had done that, I might have been a different kind of filmmaker. Or if I had made a story about two people in conflict and trying to work out their differences—which I certainly wouldn't have done at twelve years old—and the same Boy Scout troop scratching the little peach fuzz on their chins had said, 'Boy, that had a lot of depth,' I might have become Marty Scorsese. But instead the Boy Scouts cheered and applauded and laughed at what I did, and I really wanted to do that, to please again."

Of course, he may want to please again now, especially when, as is virtually certain, his latest film receives the Best Picture and Best Director Oscars (an eventuality he is too superstitious to talk about but has long coveted). And it occurs to me that his reluctance to take on a new directorial project may be tinged with fear. In making *Schindler's List,* Spielberg threw away all the usual contrivances of his trade—his reliance on drawing storyboards to map out complex shots, his cranes and zoom lenses—and went against his propensity for excess and overemphasis. The movie is inspired; it looks and feels as though it had been directed in a kind of fever, and fevers are difficult to conjure on demand. Spielberg may not know quite how he made *Schindler's List.* He may not know where the muscles that built it are, or how to find them again, and that could make him hesitate a very long time before plunging into something fresh. Besides, what *can* he direct now without tumbling from his new Olympus? Surely not *The Bridges of Madison County.*

On the screen, what has always made Spielberg Spielberg is his peculiar combination of technical mastery and playfulness. As a director, he had all the heavy artillery of a Major Motion Picture Maker like David Lean, or a master of spectacle like Cecil B. DeMille: he could manipulate vast landscapes and tremendous crowds; he could fill the screen with intricately choreographed activity; he could make a camera fly across immense expanses and deliver intimacy along with the grandeur. No one since Hitchcock has been better at visual storytelling, at making images—rather than dialogue or explanation—convey the narrative. And no one since Orson Welles has understood so deeply how to stage a shot, how to shift the viewer's eye from foreground to background, how to shuttle characters and incidents in and out of the frame at precisely the right moment, how to add information unobtrusively. Watching his elegant tracking shots—of an enormous archeological dig in *Raiders of the Lost Ark,* for instance, or of a posh house party in Shanghai in *Empire of the Sun*—one absorbs the sort of sweep and detail a nineteenth-century novelist might pack into a long, magisterial chapter. And yet the viewer never loses sight of the character who is guiding him through the scene—never becomes aware of the camera's dexterity, never spots the holes that are being opened up at just the right moment for just the right line of dialogue, never loses the urgent pressure of the plot against one's back. No technical challenge appears to be beyond Spielberg. In his cumbersome Second World War comedy, *1941,* he used miniatures to stage dogfights and submarine attacks with a deftness that few practitioners of that technology had ever imagined possible. He made platoons of cars seem to flirt and shimmy in his first feature, *The Sugarland Express*; he staged two of the sassiest, most high-spirited musical numbers ever seen on film in *1941* and *Indiana Jones and the Temple of Doom*; he created the most convincing and sympathetic outerspace creature in movie history in *E.T.* and built dinosaurs that looked as real as house cats in *Jurassic Park.*

But perhaps what has most charmed the fans of Steven Spielberg (and what most surprised them when he made *Schindler's List*) is how lightly he has worn his gifts. Has anyone else ever deployed so much know-how in the service of mere play? The better Spielberg movies are jokey and spry: long passages in them have a refreshingly tossed-off, improvisatory feel, and his approach to pleasing an audience teeters between wowing us and tickling us. When Spielberg arrived, in the middle of the seventies, his films were like a balm. Amid the sourness of a culture so recently bullied by Vietnam, Watergate, and recession, here was a filmmaker who soft-pedalled his obvious power, who could scare the living daylights out of you or thrill you to the marrow but always grounded his vision in the reassuring bedrock of suburbia—of brand names we recognized and jokes we knew. If George Lucas's *Star Wars* films imagined an extraordinary world and peopled it with ordinary characters, Spielberg began with the ordinary and then revealed its astonishments. That felt like a generous gesture; and it was generosity, above all, that marked Spielberg's movies. He seemed to know in his bones what his audiences expected, and he always delivered more—more danger, more thrills, more wonder, more light.

And he was generous in another way as well. For every macho blowhard crushing a beer can, like the Robert Shaw character in *Jaws,* Spielberg provided a likable doofus crushing a Styrofoam cup, like Richard Dreyfuss. His movies made it O.K. not to be remarkable by telling us that we already were. In that sense, *Schindler's List* itself is not so much a departure as a deepening of a central Spielberg theme, for the story of Schindler is not the story of a born hero, like Raoul Wallenberg, but the story of a common—even a base—man. Just as Richard Dreyfuss is "chosen" for transformation by the aliens in *Close Encounters,* just as Christian Bale is chosen by John Malkovich in *Empire of the Sun* and young Henry Thomas by E.T., so Oskar Schindler is chosen, in a sense—whereas a more outstanding and therefore more scrupulous or obtrusive man might not have been. Before the war, the movie tells us, Schindler had been something of a ne'er-do-well; after the war, he was a failure. And yet under the right circumstances he becomes a savior. It is only the presence of monstrous evil that makes Schindler a good man—and, finally, an exceptional one.

Spielberg, of course, rather resembles these ordinary characters of his. And as you race with him through his day it is not necessarily apparent that he is in command of an empire. Amblin has about forty-five employees, nine of whom report directly to Spielberg. There is a TV division (run by the veteran television executive Tony Thomopoulos); a merchandising division; an animation department, with offices in London and at Warner Bros. in Los Angeles; and a motion-picture division, with three development executives and their staffs. For the most part, Spielberg leaves the television and merchandising departments alone, but he's deeply involved in the animation, which, unlike most of the TV and movie production, has not just Amblin's name on it but his own. "It's just selfish," he says. "I get a real pleasure out of animation and less pleasure out of doing TV shows and looking at dinosaur toys."

The movie division, meanwhile, has been leaderless since the departure of Amblin's president, Kathleen Kennedy, early last year. (She left to start her own production company with her husband, Spielberg's sometime producer Frank Marshall.) But in May the screenwriter and producer Walter

Parkes will become Amblin's president, and his wife, the producer Laurie MacDonald, will become his executive vice-president.

"Walter has extremely good taste as a producer and as a writer," Spielberg says. "And I really wanted Amblin to be more writer-driven. I think the weak link of some of our produced movies has been in the screenplays, and I think it's partly because in recent years we've had a tendency not to stay with one writer for a long enough time. If a writer flamed out, we would just give up on him and go to another writer.

"Here's an example. *Schindler's List* went through many, many stages of development, but I always stuck with Steve Zaillian, and Steve stayed on the project even when he and I both thought the best thing for *Schindler's List* was for me to go south and Steve to go north. I liked Steve's screenplay, but I wanted the story to be less vertical—less a character story of just Oskar Schindler, and more of a horizontal approach, taking in the Holocaust as the raison d'être of the whole project. What I really wanted to see was the relationship between Oskar Schindler—the German point of view—and Itzhak Stern—the Jewish point of view. And I wanted to invoke more of the actual stories of the victims—the Dresners, the Nussbaums, the Rosners. At first, Steve resisted, but then we went to Poland together, and the plane ride back was cathartic. We went over the script page by page, and Steve was having a second vision. So, even when Steve was stubborn and resistant to change and I threatened to bring somebody else on, we went through all those sorts of marital strife, but we succeeded with each other. And I wouldn't have succeeded if I had switched and gone to somebody else."

Zaillian says, "I had made a rule for myself that any scene that didn't involve Schindler wasn't in there. Schindler didn't have to be in the scene—the scene just had to have some effect on him. But there are now some scenes that resulted from our work together that don't do that. The biggest change when Spielberg got involved was the liquidation-of-the-ghetto sequence, which in my original script was about two or three pages, and which finally ended up to be about thirty pages. Spielberg said, 'I want to follow everybody we've met up to this point through this sequence.' So that was something that changed in a big way. And then, as we got closer to filming, one of the survivors might talk to Spielberg about something or there might be something in the book that he particularly responded to, and that would go in. I think his changes were good. The thing is, when he reads something he sees it visually. I mean, there are three hundred and fifty-nine scenes in this movie, and every one of them has to have a visual idea. And from my very brief experience of having directed one film, *Searching for Bobby Fischer,* I know that after a certain point you run out of ideas. And he didn't. His great strength is really in being able to visually interpret a script."

It is a sunny Tuesday during the week before the earthquake, and Spielberg and I are on our way to a "punch-up" session for *Casper the Friendly Ghost,* which Amblin is adapting from the Harvey Comics series. The movie was written by Sherri Stoner and Deanna Oliver, veterans of the Warner Bros. animation group, but Spielberg is putting the screenplay through a process more common to sitcom production than to film—a roundtable. In this one, Stoner and Oliver join eight other writers to go over the script, adding new gags and polishing old ones. Spielberg first tried this technique on an Amblin production of *The Flintstones* (whose director, Brian Levant, has been drafted to run the roundtable); the resultant dispute over *Flintstones* writing credits has become a bit of a nightmare. But as we enter the conference room the atmosphere is jolly: the assembled company is singing, practically in unison, "We had joy, we had fun, we had seasons in the sun." Spielberg pretends shock. "I turn my back for five minutes, and now it's a musical?" he says.

The matter at hand is a scene in which a ghost enters the mouth of a sleeping middle-aged man; the man wakes up, looks in the mirror, and sees his face metamorphosing into other faces before his eyes. But the scene's particulars are growing fuzzy, and Spielberg, sitting in a chair a few feet away from the conference table, calls out, "Don't lose the good stuff, you guys! Remember, I committed to the script four drafts ago."

"So what was the good stuff then?" somebody yells.

Spielberg grins and shakes his head. Then he turns to me. "What I prefer to do is let them create all this," he says, "and then they give me pages to read, and I come in with my comments. They're mainly logic comments. I'm a little bit fastidious about that, because when you do fantasy it has to be based on common logic. When my kids see movies, they'll buy anything if it sort of makes sense. But if they're confused they get pulled out of the movie. You know, when I was seven years old it used to piss me off in serials when in Week 14 the car would go over the cliff and it would blow up and in Week 15 you see a shot you didn't see in Week 14—the hero jumping out of the car before it went over the cliff and blew up. I was pissed off that they cheated like that. They tell you the truth in Week 14 and lie to you the next week."

"Sort of like being engaged," an eavesdropping writer adds.

"Steven? Could I ask you something?" It's Sherri Stoner. "O.K., we've got him waking up after the ghost enters him and then he looks in the mirror."

"Yeah," Spielberg says. "And what he sees is that he's Mel Gibson, or whatever movie star will let his face be used for seven seconds. At a billion dollars a second." General laughter. "And then he says, 'Lookin' good.' And listen, you guys. Now you have the ghost entering through the guy's ear. It's gotta be through his mouth. You have to have the guy snoring, and have him enter through the mouth. Ear's no good. Mouth's much better."

"O.K.," Stoner says. "So then after he turns into Mel Gibson we want him to turn into, like, a monster face, right? And then he screams?"

"No, no," Spielberg says. "See, it's much funnier if he sees three different faces, including a monster face, and he *doesn't* scream. He's just looking at them and making little comments. And then he sees his own face. And that's when he screams. *That's* funny."

"So what's the best monster face?" Stoner says.

"I thought Mike Ditka was next," another writer says.

"Well, he could go from Mel Gibson to Mike Ditka," Spielberg says. "The problem with Mike Ditka is my wife thinks *he's* handsome, too."

Another writer: "Rodney Dangerfield."

"To go from Mel Gibson to Rodney Dangerfield is interesting," Spielberg says. "And then a monster, like someone like Wolfman. And then he sees his own face and he screams. That's the broad arc."

"How about Jerry Lewis?" Deanna Oliver says. "Jerry Lewis is a lot scarier than Rodney Dangerfield."

As if on cue, all ten writers unleash their Jerry Lewis imitations, crossing their eyes and screaming the word "Lady!" over and over again.

"Come on, come on," Brian Levant yells. "Let's focus."

As the dust settles, an older writer named Lenny Ripps turns to me. "*Schindler's* would have been a lot funnier if we'd done it this way," he says.

If you ask Spielberg where his ideas come from, he pleads ignorance. "Those images aren't coming from any place in my head," he says. "I guess it's just something that happens. I can't explain it, and I would be fooling everybody to say that I have a lot of self-control over what I do. Basically, I don't. I don't have a lot of experience in really talking and really dealing with my life in an analytical way. I just kind of live it. A true artist works from someplace inside himself that he is not capable of confronting when he's having breakfast. When I'm having breakfast, I read the cereal box. I read the top, the sides, the front, the back, and the bottom, just like I did when I was a kid."

He admits to watching too much television — "I junk out on bad TV movies," he says — and he has an insatiable passion for video games. Sometimes he plays them by modem with Robin Williams, who lives in San Francisco. Sometimes he just plays by himself. He plays after the kids go to bed, and on weekends, and sometimes on movie sets.

"He has little hand things," Dustin Hoffman says. "On *Hook,* while they were lighting, he shut everybody out, and he sat on the camera dolly and he played those — what are they, Game Boy? And then for a while he was getting all the flight information from L.A. International Airport, so he's sitting on the dolly and he's listening to the pilots. And he's doing that *while* he's playing Game Boy."

Here he is at lunch with Janusz Kaminski, the Polish-born cinematographer who directed the extraordinary black-and-white photography of *Schindler's List.* Kaminski is not the brooding artiste one might expect. He is a whimsical thirty-four-year-old moonfaced character with prodigious dimples, and he has spent much of the morning hanging outside Spielberg's office saying things like "This Holly Hunter — maybe I meet her. I like very much. She is wonderful girl." But now we are eating fish at a restaurant in the Universal CityWalk mall, and he and Spielberg have been reminiscing about filming *Schindler's List* in Poland. Spielberg suddenly changes the subject. "You know what you should try, Janusz?" he says. "I did this last night — it was amazing. You take a piece of Saran Wrap and put it over a flashlight, and wrinkle the Saran Wrap up. What I do is, I do shadow shows with my hands for my kids. I lie in bed with my kids — we have a white ceiling — and I put a flashlight pitched between my legs and I do these shows where my hands are huge on the ceiling. I do T. rexes attacking lawyers — I do everything. They really enjoy that. And then last night I had put the flashlight down, and it happened to be next to some Hanukkah wrapping that was clear like cellophane. And I saw the pattern against the wall with the flashlight. I thought it was fantastic, so I grabbed the cellophane, put it on the flashlight, and began making patterns on the walls. And it was amazing—it's like ocean waves on your wall. I don't know how you use it, but it was *amazing!*"

Can we understand how amazing? Perhaps not. Even Kaminski, who is nearly as boyish as Spielberg, looks a little puzzled beneath his grin. But then that has always been Spielberg's problem, ever since the beginning— the simultaneous urgency and impossibility of communicating what it is he sees. You can feel it in the oddly repetitive way he explains himself to an interviewer, stating and restating, doubling back on his sentences, laboriously spelling things out, so that everything is perfectly clear. His films, too, are, above all, emphatic. His signature storytelling devices insist that we get the point: the thunderous John Williams music; the famous reaction shots that cue the audience to feel fear or wonder; the brilliant light that Spielberg shines in our eyes, forcing our attention, hiding things or revealing them or enrobing them in awe. The entrance of a hero is announced by framing him in a doorway, silhouetted against the light, the camera looking reverently up at him, even rushing in to greet him. At its best, this sort of thing comes across as bounty; at its worst, as egregious overkill. Except for *Schindler's List,* Spielberg's movies are based on the power of more.

He is harsh with his film crews, even ruthless, and for similar reasons— he's impatient with them when they don't deliver what he thinks he has communicated. "Oftentimes he's thinking so far ahead that he doesn't want to waste the time explaining to anybody what he's trying to do," Kathleen Kennedy, who ran Amblin from 1983 until last year, says. "He needs people around who will just do it, and not question—be there and just execute, and not try to understand every little detail—because he's on the fly. When we were doing the big airplane sequence in *Raiders of the Lost Ark,* where they have the fistfight under the wing—that whole time from when Indiana Jones runs out to the wing until the airplane explodes is about a hundred and twenty cuts. They can only go together one way. And he knew already in his mind exactly what every single shot would be. And he just *sees* all of that. And what happens is he gets impatient, because once he sees it he doesn't want to lose what he sees."

He is also, it is said, an unusually tough businessman, a ferocious, canny, and obsessively secretive negotiator, and not a terribly generous one. Although Spielberg has long been the wealthiest director in America—and, indeed, one of the wealthiest men in the entertainment business (*Forbes* estimates his earnings over the last two years at seventy-two million dollars)—even his sister Anne Spielberg, who co-wrote and co-produced the movie *Big* and has several projects brewing at Amblin, says, "He's a very tough bargainer. He's a hard man to deal with on those things. There are times I'd be tempted to take things other places, where I know that I would get a better deal."

Spielberg is still a demon negotiator, but when he developed his close friendship with Steve Ross, the late chairman of Time Warner, his pockets began to open. "After I met Steve," Spielberg says, "I went from being a miser to a philanthropist, because I knew him, because that's what he showed me to do. I was just never spending my money. I gave nothing to causes that were important to me. And when I met Steve, I just observed the pleasure that he drew from his own private philanthropy. And it was total pleasure. And it was private, anonymous giving. So most everything I do is anonymous. I have my name on a couple of buildings, because in a way that's a fund-raiser. But eighty per cent of what I do is anonymous. And I get so much pleasure from that—it's one of the things that Steve Ross opened my heart to."

Ross, Spielberg has said, was like a father to him, and for Spielberg that designation carries considerable emotional freight. One can sense it in his films, which are full of yearning for home and family, and especially for fathers—departed fathers (as in *E.T., Empire of the Sun,* and *Indiana Jones and the Last Crusade*), failed fathers (*The Sugarland Express, Hook,* the grandfather in *Jurassic Park*), fathers who become distant, evil, or unrecognizable (*Close Encounters, Indiana Jones and the Temple of Doom, The Color Purple*), and fathers who return to save the day (*Jaws, Jurassic Park, Hook*). Even *Schindler's List* can be viewed as a story of patriarchy—of Schindler, an irresponsible child-man who must become father enough to protect his immense "family" from the enormity that will otherwise destroy it. In Spielberg's movies, fatherhood has a mystical shimmer.

His relationship with his own father, though, was rather bumpy. Arnold Spielberg was a computer pioneer and something of a workaholic; Steven's mother, Leah, was a former concert pianist. The marriage was never a very happy one, and the Spielbergs finally split up in 1966, when their son was eighteen. "My dad was of that World War Two ethic," Spielberg says. "He brought home the bacon, and my mom cooked it, and we ate it. I went to my dad with things, but he was always analytical. I was more passionate in my approach to any question, and so we always clashed. I was yearning for drama."

The boyhood of Steven Spielberg has been recounted so often that it has become a minor American legend, an urmyth for the age of the triumphant dweeb: how the pencil-necked Jew at a suburban Gentile school won over the local bully by starring him in his films, how dissecting frogs made him sick in biology class (and inspired a classic scene in *E.T.*), how gawky young Steve purposely lost a road race so a retarded boy could beat him, how the cruelties visited upon him by his smooth Wasp classmates drove him into the arms of his art. His sister Anne, who is two years his junior, recalls some of it a little differently. "He had more friends than he remembers having," she says. "I don't think he realized the crushes that some girls had on him. Some of my friends had major crushes on him. If you looked at a picture of him then, you'd say, 'Yes, there's a nerd. There's the crew-cut, the flattop, there are the ears. There's the skinny body.' But he really had an incredible personality. He could make people do things. He made everything he was going to do sound like you wished you were a part of it."

That gift served him well from the time he began making 8-mm movies in his Scottsdale garage at least until 1969, when Sidney Sheinberg, then the head of Universal's television department, saw Spielberg's rather saccharine short film *Amblin* and signed him to a seven-year contract as a TV director. The producer Richard Zanuck, who with his partner, David Brown, gave Spielberg his first stab at a feature film, remembers much the same quality. The movie they made together was *The Sugarland Express,* and Spielberg was only twenty-four when he started shooting it. Zanuck says, "I was thinking, Well, let's take it easy. Let's get the kid acclimated to this big-time stuff. But when I got out there the first day he was about ready to get this first shot, and it was the most elaborate fucking thing I've ever seen in my life. I mean tricky: all-in-one shots, the camera going and stopping, people going in and out. But he had such confidence in the way he was handling it. Here he was, a young little punk kid, with a lot of seasoned crew around, a major actress" — Goldie Hawn — "on hand, and instead of starting with something easy, he picked a very complicated thing that required all kinds of very intricate timing. And it worked incredibly well—and not only from a technical standpoint, but the performances were very good. I knew right then and there, without any doubt, that this guy probably knew more at that age about the mechanics of working out a shot than anybody alive at that time, no matter how many pictures they'd made. He took to it like—you know, like he was born with a knowledge of cinema. And he never ceased to amaze me from that day on."

Although *The Sugarland Express* was a box-office flop, Zanuck and Brown immediately hired Spielberg to direct another picture—*Jaws*. The project was star-crossed from the beginning. On the third day of shooting, the mechanical shark sank. By the time it could be made functional, the movie was a hundred days behind schedule and more than a hundred per cent over budget. "I was panicked," Spielberg says. "I was out of my mind with fear—not of being replaced, even though people were trying to fire me, but of letting everybody down. I was twenty-six, and even though I actually felt like a veteran by that time, nobody else felt that way about me. I looked younger than twenty-six. I looked seventeen, and I had acne, and that doesn't help instill confidence in seasoned crews."

In the end, of course, *Jaws* proved to be a terrific movie, a cheeky, unpredictable thriller that set the tone for a generation of cheeky, rather more predictable thrillers—and became, at the time, the highest-grossing film in history. Spielberg collected three million dollars, which in 1975 was enough to make him very rich—even Hollywood rich. But he was also movie-obsessed, to the exclusion of everything else; like his father before him, he didn't have a life. Although the memoirs of Julia Phillips, the co-producer of *Close Encounters,* mention his dating such Hollywood tigresses as Victoria Principal and Sarah Miles, Spielberg says, "I didn't stop to notice if women were interested in me, or if there was a party that I might have been invited to. I didn't ever take the time to revel in the glory of a successful or money-making film. I didn't stop to enjoy. By the time *Jaws* was in theatres, I was already deeply into production on *Close Encounters,* and by the time *Close Encounters* was released I was deeply into production on *1941,* and before *1941* was over I was severely into preproduction on *Raiders of the Lost Ark.* So I never had a chance to sit down and pat myself on the back or spend my money or date or go on vacations in Europe. I just haven't done that, and I just haven't done that because I put my moviemaking ahead of some of the results. I thought that if I stopped I would never get started again, that I would lose the momentum."

The momentum? The ability to make hits? To keep the ideas coming?

"No, the momentum of being interested in working. I was afraid that if I stopped I would be punished for enjoying my success by losing my interest in working. Like I feel right now. If I felt ten years ago what I'm feeling today, I would panic. I would really panic. I wouldn't know how to handle these feelings."

But Spielberg appears to have socialized more than he remembers, and in 1976 he met Amy Irving, the daughter of the actress Priscilla Pointer and the actor-director Jules Irving, who was one of the founding directors of the Lincoln Center Repertory Theatre. Spielberg was immediately smitten. He and Irving carried on a tempestuous and troubled relationship, breaking up around the time she made the 1980 film *Honeysuckle Rose* with Willie Nelson, and finally reuniting dramatically in 1983, when Spielberg flew to India to scout locations for *Indiana Jones and the Temple of Doom.* Irving, who had been filming *The Far Pavilions* there, surprised him at the airport. They were married in 1985, and Max was born the same year, but the marriage was stormy almost from the start.

"I like Amy a lot," Spielberg's old friend Matthew Robbins says. But, he adds, "when Steven decided to marry her I was very worried. It was no fun to go over there, because there was an electric tension in the air. It was competitive as to whose dining table this is, whose career we're gonna talk about, or whether he even approved of what she was interested in— her friends and her actor life. He really was uncomfortable. The child in Spielberg believed so thoroughly in the possibility of perfect marriage, the institution of marriage, the Normal Rockwell turkey on the table, everyone's head bowed in prayer—all this stuff. And Amy was sort of a glittering prize, smart as hell, gifted, and beautiful, but definitely edgy and provocative and competitive. She would not provide him any ease. There was nothing to go home to that was cozy." Spielberg and Irving remain good friends (Irving now lives with the Brazilian film director Bruno Barreto), but they divorced in 1989. Irving's settlement was reported to have been a recordbreaker—though she has denied rumors that it was in the neighborhood of a hundred million dollars.

During the ups and downs, there had been other women, and one of them was Kate Capshaw. Spielberg had met her in 1983, when she auditioned for the role she eventually won in *Indiana Jones and the Temple of Doom,* and though friends say that for him their early relationship was essentially a fling, Capshaw was resolute from the start. "I think it was just the way he smelled," she says. "He smelled like my family. It was a smell of familiarity. I'm speaking not just metaphorically but olfactorily. They say that once a woman takes a whiff of her infant you can blindfold her and march twenty babies in front of her and she'll pick hers, and that's how it felt to me. I felt like I was blindfolded and took a smell and said, 'This is the guy.'"

Capshaw giggles a lot when she talks, and indulges in girlish squeals; her hair is sometimes reddish brown and sometimes blond, her eyes are a keen, pale blue, and, though she has a fetching sexy-pixie air, one senses a will of steel beneath the wiles. She is not a sophisticate or a fashion nut, and she doesn't pretend to be. Today she is wearing coveralls over a leotard, and we are tramping around Spielberg's verdant Pacific Palisades neighborhood with their youngest child, a very blond two-year-old boy named Sawyer, tucked in a stroller. Clearly, she has taken Spielberg in hand, managing the house here and another in East Hampton and the five kids (one each from previous marriages, two from their own, one adopted). They have been married for two years and have lived together for four. And the winning of Spielberg was a long campaign. Capshaw even converted from Methodism to Judaism, a move widely thought to have been contrived as the final snare. Both Spielberg and Capshaw deny any ulterior motive, of course, and Capshaw says, "When I converted, Steven was delighted, but then all the people in his family who were supposed to fall to their knees in exultation didn't say a word, because they so wanted me to know that it didn't matter to them."

Capshaw says she had long been drawn to Judaism; she liked its emphasis on the family. "We were watching *Indiana Jones and the Temple of Doom* the other night on television," she says. "And I turned to Steven and I said, 'What happened to my career after that movie?' He said, 'You weren't supposed to have a career. You were supposed to be with me.' And it's true." She peers at me for a moment, and perhaps she reads some consternation in my face. "Oh, I absolutely feel that way," she says. "I think you have to have a great deal of ambition—these careers of our A-list ladies don't happen by accident. And if they do they don't sustain. And I didn't do the things you have to do. My focus was on Steven and a large family."

Just now, their three-year-old daughter, Sasha, is running around the Spielberg living room naked, wearing a plastic knights-of-the-Round-Table helmet, brandishing a rubbery sword, and screaming at the top of her lungs. Her father is standing by the fireplace, and he is on the telephone with Robin Williams. "I've only been playing Syndicate," Spielberg is saying, "and it's much harder to play. They put a lot more graphic design into some of the bullets. And I haven't got far enough into it yet, but I hear there's air cover. And there's also supply drops and there's also air strikes. We only played two countries, and I got my ass whipped in the second country. So I've got another seventy-five countries to go. So you want to do a mission today? O.K. Let's do it. Let's do one mission."

The house we are in is huge, white, airy, and Mediterranean in style, and it sits on five and a half acres of palm trees and gardens, along with several large outbuildings—a screening room, an office, a guesthouse. Douglas Fairbanks, Jr., once lived here, and so did David O. Selznick when he was making *Gone with the Wind,* and Cary Grant when he was married to Barbara Hutton. Spielberg has renovated much of it, but parts of the original structure remain. On one living-room wall is a small Modigliani, and, on the adjacent wall, a big, luminous Monet. Under that is a table, which, like most of the other furniture in the house, is in the Arts and Crafts style (much of it by Gustav Stickley), and on the table are three scripts under glass: originals of *Citizen Kane, Casablanca,* and Orson Welles' radio broadcast *The War of the Worlds.* Everywhere else you look there are Norman Rockwell paintings.

There is a mystery here, and it is, finally, the mystery that makes *Schindler's List* so hard to fathom. What is on the screen is overwhelming—tremendously moving; insightful about the nature of evil and even the nature of goodness. And yet here is the man who made it, an overgrown boy in a baseball cap, with a sweet, happy wife and five lovely kids and, behind him, a childhood whose sufferings were so much milder and more banal than the sufferings that popular mythology insists that an artist must undergo. Here he is, playing video games.

I remember something Kathleen Kennedy told me: "Steven has trouble with a level of intimacy. He gets close to people to a point, and then it begins to break down, because I don't think Steven is always comfortable communicating his feelings. His inability to trust very many people creates a certain amount of personal loneliness for him. But I also think it comes from just wanting to be by himself and be close to some creative, inanimate world he can live within, rather than deal with the real world and real people. I've sometimes witnessed him doing this thing: I see him withdrawing, and he's going into a place where he's more comfortable. He goes to that place, and it is completely devoid of other people and other pressures—it's almost Zen-like. And he comes out with extraordinary things. He goes there just like a monk. And he doesn't even know what it is."

What it is, perhaps, is a kind of sandbox, and, once he is in it, everything is mutable—subject only to the laws of play. Spielberg understands those laws instinctively, and he can apply them to anything. Whatever subject you throw at him, large or small, great or mean—the Holocaust or Casper the Friendly Ghost—is taken back into the sandbox and played with until he has made it marvellous.

Play is a kind of manipulation, and Spielberg is an unusually deft manipulator. Richard Dreyfuss likes to tell a story about a long night near the end of the shooting of *Jaws,* during which Spielberg kept Dreyfuss wide awake by going through the movie scene by scene and explaining how else he might have shot it—how it might have been, for instance, an art film, a film that would call attention to Spielberg's own directorial technique instead of to where the shark might pop up next. Spielberg's talent is protean, overlush: he can tell your story better than you can, and then tell it a different way, better still. When he is producing, he flits from project to project like some pollinating insect, sinking proboscis-deep into the fantasy at hand, and then going on to the next.

But, of course, there *is* a difference between Casper and the Holocaust, and even between his other great films—*Jaws, Close Encounters, E.T.*—and *Schindler's List.* It is too easy to say that the difference lies in the subject matter. Rather, the difference lies in the quality of emotion that Spielberg brings to it. *Schindler's List* is angry. And the anger in it, one feels, is not like the other Spielberg emotions. The terror in *Jaws,* the wonder in *Close Encounters,* even the longing for love in *E.T.*—all those things come, in some way, from the boy playing in his sandbox; they are beautifully manipulated, but manipulated all the same. The anger in *Schindler's List* is not. It feels earned and vital; it feels as though it took even Spielberg by surprise.

And it leaves him in a difficult situation. For if you talk with him, watch him work, observe the way he lives, you know that he still resides in the sandbox—and that it is going to take something very unusual to make him rise from it again.

He knows it, too. "I'm kind of in a pickle," he says. "And I'm looking forward to not getting out of it for a long time."

A "World" Apart

PETER BISKIND/1997

S TEVEN S PIELBERG, WEARING DESIGNER Army-surplus
pants, a brown shirt, and smoky glasses with wire frames, is sprawled in a
director's chair watching a video monitor. He is on location at Bellefontaine,
in Pasadena, a collection of imposing stone buildings built in the style of
the Italian Renaissance and a part of the Mayfield Senior School, a posh
educational institution for Catholic girls run by the Sisters of the Holy
Child Jesus, which is receiving about $5,000 a day to host two days of pro-
duction. Spielberg is shooting in a cavernous room paneled in rich dark
wood that is passing for the bedroom of John Hammond, who is played
by Richard Attenborough, returning for a cameo appearance in *The Lost
World,* the sequel to history's highest-grossing behemoth, *Jurassic Park.*
Instead of the obligatory hunt prints, on the wall hang photographs of,
well, dinosaurs.

Spielberg has not been behind the camera for three years, since he directed
Schindler's List, the film that finally won him an Oscar and the respect that
all those billions he earned for the studios somehow never managed to do.
But it's not exactly like he's been idle. Between *Schindler's List* and now,
he's joined forces with Jeffrey Katzenberg and David Geffen to start a new
studio, DreamWorks SKG. And he and his wife, Kate Capshaw, have just had
a seven-pound-twelve-ounce baby girl, Destry, their third child together.

Slight and frail, with a tangle of thinning snow-white hair, Sir Richard,
or "Dickie," as he is familiarly known around the set, is attired in pajamas

From *Premiere,* May 1997. Reprinted by permission of the author.

and a purple robe with red piping. He is propped up on a mound of pillows in a bed with a carved-wood headboard. An IV stands nearby, along with an oxygen cylinder and bunches of flowers. Attenborough is speaking in a conciliatory tone to Jeff Goldblum, who is reprising his role as chaos maven Ian Malcolm. Goldblum is a mess. He is wearing a greasy, black leather jacket one size too small, is badly in need of a shave, and looks as if he has spent the last four years sleeping on hard wooden benches in bus terminals. If you saw him walking down the street toward you, you'd cross over to the other side.

They're shooting every director's nightmare, a long exposition scene — five and a half pages of script — that occurs early in the movie, a necessary evil intended to explain the premise of *The Lost World:* why there are still dinosaurs roaming about an island off Costa Rica, when we were assured in the original that they were bred lysine deficient and thus couldn't survive for very long without their booster shots.

David Koepp, the screenwriter, is hanging around to fix any glitches that may arise in the dialogue. He has long, sandy hair, wears horn-rim glasses and Top-Siders — if his career as a screenwriter, or now as a director as well (*The Trigger Effect*), ever flags, he could make a nice living playing young lawyers in the avalanche of pictures adapted from John Grisham novels. Occasionally he mutters wry asides under his breath that make those who can hear them smile. He explains that since *Jurassic Park,* the powers that be have hushed up the unhappy adventures on Isla Nublar and all but Malcolm have kept mum. But of course no one believes Malcolm's story, and his career is in ruins as a result. Says Koepp, "He's the guy selling videos of alien encounters on the street corner."

Koepp goes on to explain that there is a second island, Isla Sorna, Site B — somehow neglected in the first movie — where the dinosaurs were manufactured and now run riot after the breeding facilities have been destroyed by a hurricane. Hammond himself has been ousted from the corporation InGen by his nephew, Peter Ludlow, played by Arliss Howard. The bad guys are intent on capturing and exploiting the remaining dinosaurs, while Hammond, who has had a change of heart, wishes to protect them, to study them for the good of mankind.

It is the last week of shooting, save for some pickups in Hawaii. Christmas is just around the corner, and the cast and crew are giddy with anticipation. *The Lost World* is not the first production to use the Bellefontaine campus, but, alas, the Mayfield girls do not seem to be taking the filming in stride; rather, they contribute to the disorder by congregating in the corridor and pressing their teeny upturned noses against the glass-paned French doors, making little squeaks of excitement at the sight of Goldblum, who is now, courtesy of *Independence Day,* somewhat of a star.

Meanwhile, Attenborough's Hammond is trying to persuade Goldblum's distinctly unfriendly and sarcastic Malcolm to go down to Isla Sorna and help him out. Malcolm would rather have hot needles sunk into his eyeballs than look at another raptor. Spielberg explains that the point here is "to get Malcolm from 'John, how can you even ask me to go back?' to 'I'm going back.'" Attenborough flicks a spot of lint or dandruff off his robe and says, "Now it's only a matter of time before this lost world is found and pillaged...." Goldblum sneers and says, "How did you manage to go from capitalist to naturalist in four years?"

Spielberg is worried about this scene. There was a lot of exposition at the beginning of *Jurassic Park* as well—genetic engineering, paleontology, chaos theory—"but that was compelling stuff," he says, frowning. "People don't know a lot about paleontology, know next to nothing about genetic engineering, so all that exposition was enthralling. You learned something. I even did some of it in animation, like one of those Frank Baxter films—*Our Mr. Sun* or *Gateway to the Mind*—that I saw as a school kid.

"But now that we've been educated in Hollywood's version of how dinosaurs are created by man, it's a tougher challenge to justify why these characters, who wouldn't ever imagine themselves returning to that nightmare alley, decide to go back. And that takes a lot of chat, to put it mildly, chat-chat-chat-chat, to explain the second island, what justifies somebody like Jeff Goldblum going back. It's not unlike William Holden being asked by Jack Hawkins, in *The Bridge on the River Kwai* after that horrendous ordeal of escaping from the Japanese prisoner-of-war camp, to lead an elite commando group back in. It's just a lot more construction than I'm used to as a storyteller."

Spielberg rises to his feet, his fatigues puddling around his orange sneakers, and engages his director of photography, Janusz Kaminski, who shot *Schindler's List,* in a lowkey debate about the lighting. He wants more, Kaminski less. The director tells a story on himself: "Once I did a TV show where I lit the windows so brightly that Ralph Bellamy, who was sitting in front of them and had to deliver three minutes of dialogue, was invisible from the waist up. But it was a ghost story, so I left it in."

"This isn't a ghost movie," snaps Kaminski, who is wearing a knitted skull cap.

While the gaffers fuss with the lights, Spielberg takes a moment to examine his trousers. "Kate bought me these pants," he says. "They have seventeen holes in them. Is that why they're so expensive?"

Cris, his assistant, takes a look. "They're distressed, from Fred Segal."

"You mean somebody else has already worn them? They look like they've been dragged by a horse across Pebble Beach."

Koepp says that it was Goldblum who suggested the plot device that explains why Malcolm agrees to go back: Hammond tells Malcolm that he has persuaded Sarah Harding (Julianne Moore), a paleontologist, to go down and observe the dinos. She also happens to be Malcolm's girlfriend, and he is horrified. Goldblum turns his back on Attenborough and strides angrily toward the door, where he pauses, turns around, and punches the air with his finger for emphasis, roaring, "You sent my girlfriend to the island alone? It's not a research expedition, it's a rescue mission!" Spielberg has him do it over and over. Goldblum whispers, he barks, he jabs his finger in the air. His hands are large, like Ping-Pong paddles. Almost sadly, Spielberg shakes his head no and says, "The finger is becoming the star of the scene." Goldblum does it again, without the finger.

Spielberg is pleased. "Wonderful! Cut. Print."

"One of the things Steven does is, he keeps rolling and doesn't break and say, 'Take two,'" explains Goldblum. "His attitude is, actors' engines are like lawn-mower motors, and each time, you have to pull the rope and start them up again. So once you've got them started, it's better to just keep them going."

But it's late, 8 o'clock in the evening, and Spielberg's motor is running down. "C'mon, guys," he says, "let's keep going. I have baby duty at ten, ten to midnight. Then I get to go to sleep."

Schindler's List was a watershed for Spielberg, not just because he tackled a big, serious subject but because he did so in an original way. Sure, he was attacked for applying to the Holocaust narrative strategies that worked in a movie such as *Jurassic Park*; for relegating the Jews to being extras in their own tragedy; for picking through the skeletal bodies of the camps, the mounds of hair and gold teeth, the soap and the lampshades, and finding the proverbial needle, an inspirational story with a heartwarming happy ending. But until that point, the last ten minutes or so of a three hours-plus picture, he put a series of chilling, indelible images on the screen—not just the Holocaust picture-postcard "Wish you were here" from Auschwitz but a strange spectacle of pain more akin to the Theatre of Cruelty than the Hollywood image bank of Nazi iconography that Spielberg himself had glibly exploited in his Indiana Jones series. Nothing in his other pictures, except perhaps the darkest moments of *Empire of the Sun* and *Indiana Jones and the Temple of Doom,* had prepared us for this. This was a new Steven Spielberg, one who had truly shed his Tinker Bell wings and was just as inclined to sprinkle ashes as fairy dust on his creations.

So for those who thought that Spielberg had turned a corner with *Schindler's List,* the news that he would direct *The Lost World* came as a bit of a surprise. Except for the Indiana Jones films, he had resisted doing sequels, even of *Jaws.* "That film was physically a nightmare, and I didn't want to go back on the water again," he says. "If they weren't drafting me, and they certainly couldn't, then I wasn't going to return voluntarily. I wasn't General MacArthur on that movie, I was more like the kid in *The Red Badge of Courage* that runs." But afterward, when the studio went ahead without him and torpedoed the franchise with three ridiculous fol-low-ups, he regretted his decision. Says Kathleen Kennedy, his longtime producer, the *Jaws* sequels were "inferior, frankly, and many people think he still had something to do with them. So there's a proprietary creative interest to protect and ensure the quality."

With *E.T. The Extra-Terrestrial,* there was a different reason. "E.T. was a very personal film for me," he says. "It was a movie that I absolutely cher-ished in my heart. I know it has become a much-abused icon, but at the time, it was my first personal film, the opposite of *Jaws.* I didn't want to do anything that would blemish its memory with a sequel that would not be—could not possibly be—its superior. So despite all the letters and per-sonal requests to make a sequel, I didn't want to mess with something that I thought was almost a perfect little movie.

"I never felt the same way about *Jurassic Park.* I didn't think it was a perfect film, and it wasn't so close to my heart that I needed to protect the integrity of a follow-up by preventing anybody else from doing one, which I certainly had the right to do. Among the films that I really think are good movies that I've directed, it's not even in the top five. But there was such an outpouring of demand from the public—thousands and thousands of letters—and so, after all those years of denying them the sequel to *E.T.*, I couldn't face the same nine-year-old, now saying, 'Okay, so you're not going to make a sequel to *E.T.*, I understand how personal it was to you, so why are you not making the sequel to *Jurassic Park*?' And I had no answer to that. I also didn't want to do a serious movie after *Schindler's List*. Coming back from those three years of not directing, I didn't want to jump into the deep end of the pool, I wanted to step into the shallow end and get used to the water. I wanted to do something familiar. So all those reasons conspired to get me to say yes to this."

But returning to familiar material is not without drawbacks. "One of the toughest things about a sequel is the expectation that goes along with it, that you're gonna top the first one," says Spielberg. "And therein lies all of my anxiety. We worried about that every time we made another Indiana Jones picture. But we wound up realizing you really can't top yourself. You just tell a different story and hope the new MacGuffin is as compelling as the last MacGuffin."

The project got a much-needed boost when Michael Crichton came on board to write a sequel to the best-seller on which *Jurassic Park* was based. "When Michael told me that the basis for his new book was going to be a complete lost world, a perfect dinosaur ecological system, and then about the human incursion into a real prehistoric land, I got very excited," the director continues. "As a popcorn muncher when I was a kid, I always loved those kinds of movies—*King Kong*, even some of the B's, like *Dinosaurus!* and the Jock Mahoney film called *The Land Unknown*."

Koepp, who got cowriting credit (with Crichton) on the original and sole credit on this one, set to work on a script that would excite Spielberg. "One of the problems writing for Steven," Koepp says, "is that he's done so many big, memorable films. You're always saying, 'Oh, that's just too Indiana Jones.'" And then there's *Jaws*, which haunts pictures like *Jurassic Park*, the *Die Hard* series, *Speed* and *Speed 2*, even *Independence Day*. *Jaws* is not only the first big action-adventure spectacle, it is the best. Even though its writing process was lengthy and chaotic, the *Jaws* script featured three male leads that were vividly individuated, and it was fleshed out by three strong actors—Robert Shaw, Richard Dreyfuss, and Roy Scheider—who more than held their own with the shark.

Jurassic failed the *Jaws* test miserably, perhaps a victim of '90s-style make-nice filmmaking, in which characters' rough edges are rubbed smooth and no villains are allowed, save for cardboard terrorists or Colombian drug lords, of which *Jurassic* offered neither. The Hammond character in Crichton's novel is a ruthless money-grubber, but in the film, that went out the window, and Hammond, played by the avuncular Attenborough, became a crusty, benevolent type, like Disney's Scrooge McDuck, even though he put his grandchildren in extreme jeopardy. The characters, and the actors who played them, were simply overwhelmed by the dinos.

The problems posed by pictures like *Jurassic* and now *The Lost World* are the opposite of the problems posed by *Jaws*. In *Jaws*, the effects were primitive, and much of the time they didn't work. Spielberg had to do without much of the shark footage, forcing audiences to rely on their imagination. He adopted a less-is-more approach that worked remarkably well. As he famously put it, *Jaws* went from being "a Japanese Saturday-matinee horror flick to more of a Hitchcock thriller." The virtue of this approach was that it enabled him to focus on the characters. But now that special-effects technology has advanced so far that anything is possible, the characters must fend for themselves.

"In writing *Jurassic Park*, I threw out a lot of detail about the characters," says Koepp, "because whenever they started talking about their personal lives, you couldn't care less. You wanted them to shut up and go stand on a hill where you can see the dinosaurs. When we announced the sequel, I got this packet of letters from an elementary-school class somewhere outside San Francisco, and one of the kids wrote that we should add a stegosaurus and this and that, but 'whatever you do, please don't have a long, boring part at the beginning that has nothing to do with the island.' In other words, the premise of these movies is so exciting the usual cat-and-mouse game just doesn't work. The kid is only eight, but he's right, and I kept his letter on my desk. On my tombstone it'll say my name, the years I lived, and then, IT TOOK TOO LONG TO GET TO THE ISLAND."

While Crichton was writing his *Lost World* novel, Spielberg and Koepp kept bouncing ideas back and forth. Recalls Koepp, "The first thing you do is say, 'Okay, if I was going to go see a movie like this, what scenes would I really demand be in it? What would be really cool?' Steven operates from images. He'll call up and say, 'I had this idea for a shot.' It's not even a shot. It's part of a shot. 'What do you think of that? Is that part of our story?' I'll think, 'Now how does that relate to anything?' And then I try to figure it out. I really like working with directors like that because they tend to leave a lot of the other stuff, dialogue and so on, to you. They provide these sparks."

Much of the Crichton novel was eventually tossed. "I couldn't find a lot of story narrative in the middle part," explains Spielberg. "But his set-up was excellent and he certainly put us on the right road." Spielberg also retained the big set piece in the middle of the book, in which the laboratory trailer—really two trailers connected by a rubberized umbilical cord—are pushed over a cliff by the angry rexes.

Both the Sam Neill and Laura Dern characters have been dropped and replaced by what promises to be a more pungent ensemble. There is a rumored surprise in the third act, too, in which the bad guys transport the dinosaurs to the mainland in an elaborately designed Rex-proof boat. Spielberg is unwilling to leak the details, but suffice it to say that nestled against the side of the soundstage on the Universal lot where he has been shooting, there are two badly dented Union 76 balls.

The "message" of the sequel is somewhat different from the original as well. *Jurassic* had a classic horror-movie moral: Mad scientists mess with God's work at their peril. In *The Lost World,* the scientists are ecologically correct good guys, the dinos endangered species. "Although terrible things were happening in *Jurassic,*" says production designer Rick Carter, "I don't think you ever felt the terror very deeply, because everything had this Hollywood veneer, which is how the theme park presented itself. Here, there are darker intentions and darker problems to deal with. I think it's *Jurassic Park* post-*Schindler's List.* Spielberg was the guy who was not Martin Scorsese, not Francis Coppola. He never really accepted himself as an artist on that level. But I just don't think it's the same Steven Spielberg now. This world *is* lost and the people in this movie are trying very hard to protect that which they believe in, but the forces they're up against are too big and powerful and convoluted. Luckily, they succeed, but the only way they succeed is to pull out the smallest of victories."

Adds Spielberg, "The first movie was really about the failure of technology and the success of nature. This movie is much more about the failure of people to find restraints within themselves, and the failure of morality to protect these animals." He pauses, then laughs. "I liken myself to the hunters that go after the animals. They'll do anything for money, and so will we."

There are two T-rexes in *The Lost World,* a mister and missus, and one of them, all 15,000 pounds or so, is reclining in a soundstage on an enormous dolly, like the gun carriage of an old World War II howitzer that runs on tracks. The models, puppets, or robots, as they are variously called, are startlingly lifelike constructions that cost, in the case of the rexes, an estimated $1 million apiece. Each is computer-assisted and manned by a team of as many as ten puppeteers. The head of a rex alone weighs about 1,000 pounds, and can pack two G's of wallop moving in an arc from full left to full right, which is enough to total a car. They are extremely unwieldy; it can take as long as two days to turn a rex around, say, from pointing north to pointing south.

The models are the work of Stan Winston's shop, the same folks who provided the puppets for *Jurassic.* That film had been the occasion of considerable bloodletting among the various effects specialties. The initial intent had been to employ Winston's life-size robots along with the go-motion technology (an animation process more advanced than stop-motion photography) of Phil Tippett, who went all the way back to *Star Wars.* At the time, CGI (computer-graphics imaging) was in its infancy, and nobody thought the whiz kids at Industrial Light & Magic could simulate on a computer a dinosaur that would convince anyone older than a toddler that it was real. Says ILM effects supervisor Dennis Muren: "We had four months or five months of tests to see if we could make a computer create an image that looks like lizard skin and not like plastic. Then we had to get the motions right." The gallimimus stampede that ILM came up with convinced Spielberg that CGI was the wave of the future. Though he kept Winston's robots, he discarded the work that Tippet's team had done, which was considerable. (A rule of thumb in *Jurassic* is, if you see a close-up of a dino, or a medium shot in which the creature is standing behind a bush that obscures its nether parts, it's a robot. If you see a long shot of the whole creature walking or running, it's CGI.)

According to special effects supervisor Michael Lantieri, who worked on the pioneering *Who Framed Roger Rabbit, Jurassic,* and, most recently, *Mars*

Attacks!, "Lots of people suggested that *The Lost World* should be all CG, because now they've done all-CG movies like *Dragonheart* and *Toy Story*. But we realized that the mix brings something to the life of the creatures that we don't think can be gotten just mechanically or just digitally." For the moment, anyway, peace has broken out, and *The Lost World* is a comfortable amalgam of Winston's robotics and ILM's CGI.

There are several new dinosaurs in *The Lost World:* "compies," which are like chickens from hell; an adult and baby stegosaurus; a pachycephalosaurus (otherwise known as a head butter); and a dead parasaurolophus. Other choices, like a super-raptor, were considered but discarded. "The super-raptor was a little too much out of a horror movie," says Spielberg. "I didn't want to create an alien."

To make the *Lost World* CGI dinos look more like animals than they did in *Jurassic,* ILM animators visited Marine World Africa USA and videotaped the elephants, rhinos, and reptiles. "We were trying to actually have the muscles and flesh and fat pockets under the animal's flesh move, as you would see on the side of an elephant that was walking by you," says visual effects producer Ned Gorman. "And Steven asked for a higher level of integration of the dinosaurs into the environment. So when you see dinosaurs running across a meadow, ours are going to be kicking up dust and dirt."

In *Jurassic,* there are a number of cheats that become visible if the film is run frame by frame. Says Lantieri, "In some cases you could see when we cut from a walking CG element to someone in a suit to a hydraulic puppet. In this movie we're doing some blends right in frame, where we actually go from a puppet to a CG item without any kind of a cutaway. What you see is neither a mechanical nor a computer image, but something that starts out as one, blends into another, and is so seamless that you can't tell which one is which."

And while CGI technology has improved since *Jurassic,* so have Winston's models. "We've made a lot of progress in terms of making the robots behave and interact and touch human beings that we couldn't have done in the first movie," says Lantieri. "We actually tear some things apart for real. In the first movie we built an Explorer that rolls over and crushes itself with the children in it, but there's no dinosaur in the shot. In *The Lost World,* we did a shot in which the rex bites through the real windshield, almost picking the car off the ground, and tears it to pieces. It lends a realism to the film, allows us to not have to rely too much on CG except for really unbelievable things that couldn't be done otherwise."

But the advances in robotics come at a price. The cost of CGI is going down—even when the enormous overhead of a shop like ILM is added in—whereas the cost of Winston's work is going up. "On the set," says one source on the CG side who declined to be identified, "[robots require] more personnel to keep the things going than they did before, and a whole air-conditioned room just for the computers. You can look at the robots and say, 'That's better than a year ago or two years ago.' But they still can't walk. Were robotics really working, you would be seeing a big machine walking out on the freeway and removing cars that are stuck in traffic. And you don't see those kinds of things, because you just can't do it."

Not that CGI is cheap. Says Spielberg, "It still runs you between $250,000 and $500,000 to put anything into a computer, even a small, uncomplicated dinosaur, and that's before you generate a single shot. If you've got a dinosaur just walking around, it's $80,000 for eight seconds. If the dinosaur is splashing in a puddle or kicking up tufts of dirt, it's $100,000. If there are four dinosaurs in the background of that shot, it's $150,000."

And robotics still has distinct advantages over CGI. It gives the actors something to act against, instead of thin air, and once you build a model, you can shoot it from as many angles as you wish for no more than the cost of the film, whereas with CGI, every new angle is a new shot that could carry a six-digit price tag. "Anything that you can touch and feel is better," says Winston, who is sanguine about getting the robots to walk. "It's not, like, 'Forget this, we'll never do it.' It gives us something to shoot for."

But the handwriting is on the wall. If the technology doesn't retire the mechanical-effects folks, the economics will, the way the cheesy Hanna-Barbera cartoons of the '60s helped to end the golden age of Disney animation. A few years down the road, they will become the real dinosaurs, living in Florida, retired. *Jurassic* and *The Lost World* will probably go down as the last classics of the robotics-CGI mixed-media era. Examining a rex up close, running your fingers over the pebbled skin, feeling the delicate tissue around the eyes as soft as tapioca pudding, is to be astonished at the artistry that goes into these models. After the picture is shot, the rexes are disassembled. The hoses and hydraulics can be used again, but after three months or so the wonderful foam-rubber skin just rots away.

The nerve center of *The Lost World* is Spielberg's home at Amblin, an enclave of adobe buildings Universal built for its wunderkind in the early

'80s for an estimated cost of $3.5 million in an effort, some speculated, to counter the lure of Warner Bros. honcho Steve Ross, who was assiduously courting him. Now it is also the temporary headquarters of DreamWorks. There is no love lost between Katzenberg and Disney on the one hand, and Geffen and former Disney number two Michael Ovitz on the other. So it is amusing that on the very afternoon in December that Ovitz's departure from Disney is announced, DreamWorks is throwing a lavish Christmas party. *Quelle coïncidence!,* as the French would say.

When he headed up production at Disney, Katzenberg was famously dedicated to reducing production costs, and some of this philosophy has rubbed off on *The Lost World*'s director. Despite the broad palette of potential effects available to Spielberg, he resisted the impulse to, as he puts it, "over-torque *The Lost World,*" watching the budget carefully, perhaps through the eyes of a part owner of a newborn studio. "Universal would have given me $130 million to have made a sequel to *Jurassic Park,*" he says. "I don't have a lot of people who are going to say no to me in the films I make, so I'm the one who has to be responsible. There's a lot of things I wanted to do that I couldn't do, because I'm my own worst nightmare of a producer. I had 59 CG shots in the first film. I limited myself to 75 in the second film, which is kind of small when you consider that the film we produced last year, *Twister,* has 350 composited opticals. We brought the film in six days ahead of schedule and under $74 million."

Spielberg is of the opinion that bloated budgets are ruining Hollywood. "I think that we're at DefCon Three right now. Everybody is looking to their neighbor to see what they're making. There's always some highwater mark, and every year it inches up. It's not going to be too long before an average film, without marketing, is going to cost $55 million. It is getting to the point where only two kinds of movies are being made, the tentpole summer or Christmas hits or the sequels, and the audacious little Gramercy, Fine Line, or Miramax films. It's kind of like India, where there's an upper class and a poverty class and no middle class. Right now we are squeezing the middle class out of Hollywood and only allowing the $70 million-plus films or the $10 million-minus films. And that is going to spell doom for everyone.

"The only way out is that everybody has to attack these big budgets. Actors who are rich enough as it is, and they all know who they are, should stop taking $20, $25 million a picture and start gambling on their own talent, gambling on gross first-dollar points [a percentage of the studio's gross take, before most costs are factored in], and the trust they have in the filmmaker and the script they've obviously committed to. They'll make their money and more, based on their larger slice of the pie. Directors, too, should stop taking the huge up-front money. That's what Tom Hanks and I are doing on *Saving Private Ryan,* my movie after next. He's not taking any money up front, and neither am I. Now, to be fair, I haven't taken a salary in many, many years—I've just always gambled on my points— and that gives me the right to say that it hasn't made me any poorer. The agents will say, 'Okay, my client will make your movie for no money up front, but if the film doesn't make him the money he would have earned as a salary, you have to guarantee the remainder.' That's cheating. That's cosmeticizing the whole formula. I think we've all got to take some risks, the same risks that young filmmakers are taking by baring their souls to us on film. Sometimes I wonder, 'What business are we in? Are we in the business of making money, or are we in the business of making an impression with our talent?' It depresses me when a young actor will actually crave a part in a movie but turn it down because a second movie has offered more money."

Spielberg finished principal photography for *The Lost World* in December. In February, while the film was still in postproduction, he began *Amistad,* a historical epic about a slave rebellion aboard a ship in the 1830s, based on an actual incident. In June he is supposed to go right into *Private Ryan,* the Hanks picture set against the background of World War II. It's a tough schedule for someone who doesn't have to work and has nothing more to prove. *Amistad* and *Private Ryan* are both DreamWorks pictures (*Private Ryan* is a coproduction with Paramount Pictures), and it may be that he is just doing his part to get the studio up and running. Kennedy says it is just an accident of scheduling, based on Tom Hanks's brief window of availability. "I could have retired at any time over the last sixteen years," says Spielberg. "But I feel driven to work on the projects that I want to work on. I'm only 50 years old and I'm not ready to retire. The minute I feel I have achieved my goals, then I'll probably stop. But I don't know what my goals are. And I just love the work too much to lay back on the laurels that other people bestow on me."

He scoffs at the idea that there is some relation between the two dinosaur pictures and *Schindler's List.* "I'll tell you how *Schindler's List* changed me as a filmmaker, how I beat myself up in the making of *The Lost World*. I found myself in the middle of the sequel to *Jurassic Park,* growing more and more impatient with myself with respect to the kinds of films I really like to make. And often feeling that I have stuck myself in Doc Brown's DeLorean and gone back in time four and a half years, and that I was just serving the audience a banquet, but I wasn't serving myself anything challenging. I found myself saying, 'Is that all there is? It's not enough for me.'

"If *The Lost World* is successful enough to justify a third film, you'll probably see me executive producing it, but you won't see me directing it. At the same time, I promised myself after I made *Schindler's List* that I wasn't going to make one film after the next just like it, because *Schindler's List* can be as limiting as *Jurassic Park* can be. So I went to a historical drama, because it's very compelling for me, but I also would like to do a love story. And I still have a mad chocolate craving to direct a conventional musical. There's a lot of different things I haven't done yet."

Five-Star General

STEPHEN PIZZELLO/1998

OVER THE PAST HALF-CENTURY, World War II has been one of cinema's favorite subjects, spawning a genre that rivals the Western in sheer breadth. Countless films have been made about the granddaddy of all global conflicts, a roll call that runs the gamut of patriotic, action-oriented epics (*Sands of Iwo Jima, Twelve O'Clock High, The Great Escape*), searing documentaries (*The Sorrow and the Pity, Shoah*), biographical portraits of larger-than-life heroes (*Patton, MacArthur*) and villains (*Hitler*), romantic dramas (*From Here to Eternity, Casablanca*), spy thrillers (*Saboteur, Eye of the Needle*) revisionist satires (*Catch-22*), comedies (*Mister Roberts*) and even musicals (*South Pacific*).

Given the staggering number of pictures set during the "Good War," it would seem that a fresh perspective on this monumental event would require the attention of a truly gifted auteur with a unique sensibility. Enter Steven Spielberg, who was recently named the "most influential director of the 20th Century" by *Time* magazine. Spielberg demonstrated an affinity for the era with *1941*, the *Raiders of the Lost Ark* trilogy and *Empire of the Sun* before stunning the world's moviegoers with *Schindler's List*, a masterful dramatization of the Holocaust. The filmmaker and studio mogul has returned to his favorite historical period with

From *American Cinematographer*, August 1998. Reprinted by permission.

Saving Private Ryan, an intense, strikingly authentic epic which uses the bloody D-Day invasion as its backdrop.

Hollywood has rendered the pivotal Normandy battle before, most notably in the 1962 all-star CinemaScope spectacular *The Longest Day,* which earned Oscars for both black-and-white cinematography (by the team of Jean Bourgoin, Walter Wottitz, Henri Persin, and Pierre Levent) and special effects (Robert MacDonald and Jacques Maumont). But few filmmakers have demonstrated Spielberg's skill with large-scale action and the mechanics of suspense, and the director maintains that his rendering of the Omaha Beach massacre is "as unflinching as *Schindler's List*" in its depiction of wartime horrors.

Spielberg recently took time out of his busy schedule to answer AC's questions about his latest celluloid adventure.

AMERICAN CINEMATOGRAPHER: *Why are you so drawn to the World War II era as a setting for your films?*
STEVEN SPIELBERG: I think that World War II is the most significant event of the last 100 years; the fate of the Baby Boomers and even Generation X was linked to the outcome. Beyond that, I've just always been interested in World War II. My earliest films, which I made when I was about 14 years old, were combat pictures that were set both on the ground and in the air. For years now, I've been looking for the right World War II story to shoot, and when Robert Rodat wrote *Saving Private Ryan,* I found it.

AC: *On the surface, World War II is a classic conflict between good and evil, but this picture addresses some philosophical issues which aren't quite so clear-cut. The soldiers who are sent out to rescue Private Ryan are conflicted and openly critical of their mission.*
SPIELBERG: From an historical perspective, the Second World War seems pretty cut-and-dried, or black-and-white. But inside a war, and inside combat, it's technically chaotic and personally very contradictory. When we look back from the standpoint of history, we can say, 'Oh yeah, World War II clearly set the good and bad apart from one another.' But inside combat, the issue is never that clear. To the soldiers fighting the war, it can be very confusing.

A C : *What are some of your favorite war movies? Did those particular films affect your approach to* Private Ryan *either visually or dramatically?*
S P I E L B E R G : In terms of features, the World War II pictures that inspired me the most were William Wellman's *Battleground* [1949], Sam Fuller's *The Steel Helmet* [1951] and Don Siegel's *Hell Is for Heroes* [1962]. I didn't really draw from those films aesthetically, but they made a big impression on me while I was growing up in Arizona and watching a lot of TV. I haven't studied World War II films, but I'm very familiar with them because they were a part of my formative years.

In truth, on *Private Ryan* I tried to take the opposite approach of nearly every one of my favorite World War II movies. Films that were made during the actual war years never really concerned themselves with realism, but more with extolling the virtues of winning and sacrificing ourselves upon the altar of freedom. Those were the themes of many World War II pictures, which also were designed to help sell war bonds. I love those movies, but I think Vietnam pushed people from my generation to tell the truth about war without glorifying it. As a result, I've taken a much harder approach to telling this particular story. From a visual perspective, I was much more influenced by various World War II documentaries—*Memphis Belle, Why We Fight,* John Ford's Midway movie and John Huston's film on the liberation of the Nazi death camps—than I was by any of Hollywood's representations of the war. I was also very inspired by [photographer] Robert Capa's documentary work, and the eight surviving stills he took during the assault on Omaha Beach.

A C : *Your right-hand man, Janusz Kaminski, told me that the two of you like to challenge each other artistically, and that your relationship sometimes takes on an air of friendly competition. Do you agree with that assessment?*
S P I E L B E R G : I don't see our relationship as being competitive. We are collaborators and friends, and we give each other tremendous emotional support. Because we have so much mutual respect, neither of us wants to let the other down. We've developed our relationship over the course of four movies together, and we're about to do a fifth one, *Memoirs of a Geisha.* Janusz is the first brother I've ever had on a set; I feel closer to him than any other collaborator I've had in my career.

AC: *How would you compare your visual approach on* Private Ryan *to what you've done together on previous films? Do you consider this picture to be a departure?*

SPIELBERG: The whole movie has a different style than anything I've done before. It's very hard and rough, and in the best sense, I think it's extraordinarily sloppy. But reality is sloppy—it's not the perfect dolly shot or crane move. We were attempting to put fear and chaos on film. If the lens got splattered with sand and blood, I didn't say, 'Oh my God, the shot's ruined, we have to do it over again'—we just used it in the picture. Our camera was affected in the same way that a combat cameraman's would be when an explosion or bullet hit happened nearby.

AC: *About 90 percent of* Private Ryan *was shot with handheld cameras. How did that strategy influence your role as director? Did it affect the amount of control you had over the images?*

SPIELBERG: I still had a lot of control because I was watching everything on video monitors; I could always do something over again if I didn't like it. I was also recording the takes so I could pore over the playbacks to see if things were working or not. On *Schindler's List* and *Amistad*, I had video assist, but no playback. Because we had so many physical effects working during the production of *Private Ryan*, every department needed to watch the playbacks to see if they were doing their jobs. On this film, I departed from my 'purist' mode and brought in modern technology.

AC: *I understand that you didn't storyboard any of the movie. That must have made things a bit challenging, given the film's elaborate battle scenes. How much improvisation were you able to do?*

SPIELBERG: I had a very strong screenplay, and the actors and I were certainly following that as a blueprint. But in terms of my approach to the combat sequences, I was improvising all of them. I just went to war and did things the way I thought a combat cameraman would have. I had a very good advisor for the battle scenes: [retired Marine Corps Captain] Dale Dye. He served three tours of duty under fire in Vietnam, and he was wounded several times. In order to capture the realism of combat, I relied on Dale, as well as several World War II combat veterans who also served as consultants.

One thing that really helped me was that we shot every battle scene in continuity. For example, I started the Omaha Beach sequence in the Higgins boats, worked my way out of the 'murder holes,' moved on to the beach obstacles and the 'sandy shingle,' and finally proceeded up the Vierville draw.

A C :   *How did you handle the dangers of the battle sequences, which involved explosions, gunfire squibs and other hazards?*

S P I E L B E R G :   We had crack safety teams and set safety supervisors, and our pyrotechnical work was supervised by some of the best 'powder men' and women I've ever seen in the film business. We were slaves to their long-winded but necessary explanations of where the squibs and explosions were hidden, and we made completely certain that only stuntmen were positioned anywhere near an explosion. We had [approximately 750] members of the Irish Army helping us stage the retaking of Omaha Beach, and we kept them well away from the dangerous areas.

A C :   *You shot the D-Day scenes at a beach location in Ireland. What kinds of benefits or drawbacks did you experience there?*

S P I E L B E R G :   I was a bit disappointed that the beach we used wasn't as broad as the real Omaha Beach in France. I tried to use certain wide-angle lenses to extend the length of the flats on the sandy beach before the soldiers reach the shingle. I used wider lenses for geography and tighter lenses for the compression of action.

We were very lucky with the weather, though. D-Day took place in very inclement conditions, and many of the soldiers who fought there were seasick before they even reached the beach. During the four weeks that we were shooting the Omaha Beach sequence, which comprises the first 25 minutes of the film, we had very rough seas and bad weather—it was overcast about 90 percent of the time. That was a miracle, because we were shooting at a time of year when there's normally bright weather and the tourists are flocking. We were handed a huge break.

A C :   *How did you balance the large-scale action with the human drama of the characters? The camera basically stays with the soldiers during the entire picture, but you must have been constantly tempted to set up epic, God's-eye views of the battlefield.*

SPIELBERG: I did a few of those, but not many. I tried to create a motivation for the God's-eye shots by having a character holding the high ground to justify the point of view. There were a couple of times when I went up in an unmotivated way in order to show more of the action, but the movie is pretty much shot from the frightened viewpoint of a 'dogface' who's hugging the sand and trying to avoid having his head blown off.

AC: *You used a variety of techniques—stripping the protective coatings from your lenses, flashing the film stock, applying the ENR process and desaturating the picture's colors—to give* Private Ryan *an air of absolute authenticity. How did those strategies come about?*
SPIELBERG: To present war as 'up close and personal' as we possibly could, we really deglamorized the technology we were using. The images we got involved a combination of several elements—film stock, processing and a deconstruction of the slickness that you usually get with modern lenses. It was Janusz's idea to strip the lenses, flash the film and use ENR; it was my decision to desaturate the colors. I came up with that notion while watching the color 16mm Signal Corps footage that George Stevens had done during the invasion of France. I was very taken with the desaturated look of that film; I have a feeling it was shot on Ektachrome stock.

AC: *You also used 45- and 90-degree shutters instead of the usual 180-degree configuration.*
SPIELBERG: Not all the time—we varied our approach. We used different shutters to create different realities, and we occasionally did speed changes in conjunction with shutter-degree changes. All of the special techniques we used were intended to make you feel as if you were right in the middle of combat, as opposed to watching it like an armchair civilian.

AC: *Why did you choose to shoot* Private Ryan *in the 1.85:1 format rather than a widescreen format?*
SPIELBERG: To me, widescreen formats like CinemaScope were a Hollywood invention of the 1950s. I find widescreen to be an artificial aspect ratio, whereas 1.85 more closely approximates the way the human eye really sees, in the sense that we see as high to low as we do from side to side. If I had to make a choice, I'd rather see from high to low. I think the most human perspective is [the range] from 1.66:1 to 1.85:1. The slickest format

for theaters is 2.35:1. I've chosen 1.85:1 for my last four pictures because they were intended to be more lifelike.

A C : *Your shooting ratio on this film was approximately 4 to 1, which is quite low. Was that mainly due to the fact that you had a lot of logistically complex setups that could only be done a few times?*
S P I E L B E R G : Actually, some of the more complicated setups had a higher ratio, but our average for the film was about 4 to 1. I had great actors, an amazing effects crew and terrific stunt performers, so quite often I was able to get things exactly the way I'd envisioned them in the first three or four takes. I rarely walked away from a scene until I got what I wanted, and I'd say that I got what I wanted from those complex setups about 80 percent of the time.

A C : *Did you face any particular challenges during the editing?*
S P I E L B E R G : Mike Kahn [who earned Academy Awards for his work on *Raiders of the Lost Ark* and *Schindler's List*] was just wonderful in the editing room. His rhythms are the best in the world, and he tries to throw the audience off of their expectations. When you expect something to be sort of slow and clear in terms of a scene's geography, you might instead get lost; at other times, you might feel as if you're lost when you suddenly realize where you are and how you can get out of the jam. In World War II, the enemy wasn't working from the same script as the Allies; the two sides had their own screenplays, and they were always improvising. I tried to be as improvisational in my production of a war film as wars are when they're actually fought. We didn't want to telegraph anything, and we also wanted viewers to be just as surprised as the combat G.I.'s were when the enemy threw something new at them. I think some of that is the product of deft editing.

A C : *In addition to the Omaha Beach sequence,* Private Ryan *features a climactic battle scene in a fictional French village called Ramelle.*
S P I E L B E R G : That was a very complicated sequence which took weeks and weeks to plan out on paper. We didn't storyboard it, but we wrote it all out. Dale Dye got involved, and he really screwed my head on straight by reminding me not to let the audience down after giving them such a visceral experience in the Omaha Beach scenes. We had to properly book-

end the picture, and this time more emotionally. Dale helped me a great deal by showing me the firepower of the weapons that the Germans were using, or what the effect of an artillery round would look like on the ground—and not by Hollywood standards, which is usually larger than reality. Every time I wanted a large fireball or explosion, Dale would ask me what round was fired to create that effect, and he would invariably say, 'Go half that size, they were never that big.' He was a really good person to have around, because he was able to scale the reality down to what he was accustomed to in Vietnam—just as the World War II veterans we talked to or had on the set could tell us what they were accustomed to.

AC: *Speaking of realism, it's been widely reported that you put your key actors through a week of bootcamp hell during preproduction. What led to that decision on your part?*
SPIELBERG: Dale Dye and Tom Hanks talked me into it. After I hired him, Dale told me he'd done that on other pictures, including *Forrest Gump*. To prepare for *Gump*'s few short scenes in Vietnam, Tom had gone through Dale's boot camp. In retrospect, I think it was a good thing to do. The actors arrived both willing and able to win a war.

AC: *You're known for working very rapidly during production. Was there any particular advantage to that kind of pace on this show? Did it lend extra intensity to the shoot?*
SPIELBERG: Absolutely. We worked fast but carefully, and we wound up a few days ahead of schedule on this show. A war is fought fast, and I really wanted to keep all of the actors off-balance. I didn't want them to be able to read 75 pages of a novel in their trailer before they were called back for the second setup of the morning. I wanted to work fast enough so that they always felt as if they were in combat, they always felt as if they were under fire, they always felt as if they were in jeopardy. In order to keep the actors so involved in the story, I had to keep them on the set, which meant shooting the film even faster than I normally do. War doesn't give you a break, and I didn't want the production of *Private Ryan* to give them one either.

Crossroads: Steven Spielberg

KENNETH TURAN / 1998

EVERYONE CALLS HIM STEVEN; within the busy cata-
combs of Hollywood, no further identification is necessary. His
record as a popular culture taste-master speaks for itself; through
the end of 1997, seven of the 20 highest-grossing films bear his
mark as either director, producer or executive producer. And in
1998, Steven Spielberg did it again, re-creating World War II to
both critical and box-office success in *Saving Private Ryan,* the
favorite for this year's best picture Oscar.

Sitting in a comfortable conference room in his DreamWorks
compound just days before his 51st birthday, Spielberg talks with
the aplomb and maturity that come from having been a public figure for more than half of his life (not to mention being the father
of seven children). Underneath a large poster for *Men in Black*
(not the film he executive-produced but an early Three Stooges
two-reeler), Spielberg provided a straightforward perspective on
his own work and the industry that reveres him.

QUESTION: *I want to start with the studio system, where it has been, where
it's going. When you started at Universal, it was close to its last days. What's
the difference in Hollywood between then and now?*
ANSWER: Huge differences. I think basically it was a lot calmer. It was a
sweeter place to exist within. When I first got started, there didn't seem to

From *Los Angeles Times,* 28 December 1998, © 1998 by *The Los Angeles Times.* Reprinted by
permission.

be this kind of hysteria and true nail-biting anxiety before a film opened. Films opened quietly, there weren't full-page ads touting the three-day box office in the trades. It just didn't seem as frantic as today.

Q: *One of your strengths as a filmmaker, both as a producer and a director, is knowing what audiences like. With executives relying on testing a great deal, that's become something of a lost art. Is this a good thing?*
A: The movies that I personally direct I don't test. I haven't tested a movie since *Hook* in 1991. I think tests are deceiving. Even though the critical community vilified me and trounced that film, the test scores were some of the highest that had ever been gotten by a movie. People who got in to see *Hook* for free, in the one test screening, liked the movie a hell of a lot better than people who wound up having to pay for it and didn't think it was worth five or six bucks.

When people say, "How do you define your success?" I feel the one thing that I've achieved as a filmmaker is I don't test my movies—and it's not because I'm so certain they're going to succeed. *Amistad* certainly could have used a couple of tests; it might have benefited had I tested it. But I don't have to go through the anxiety of knowing that the test is on Friday—"Oh, my God, I have to go to San Jose, I've got to sit with an audience." You don't know what that does to my giblets.

If I've ever earned anything, it's the right to say to the studios, "Please, don't even ask."

Q: *The movie business is turning into a fascinating two-track system, with the big studio films and the independent films. Twenty years ago this didn't exist. How do you feel about it?*
A: I think the independent revolution is the most exciting thing that's happened since the French New Wave. The independent film has always been with us, but it's never had this commercial reception.

Q: *I think Miramax was one of the companies to prove that you could make real money with these films.*
A: Miramax is actually my favorite company in town. I think it's amazing that they didn't narrow their range to European pickups or low-ball financing of very talented filmmakers; they also will occasionally make the Roger Corman films, the ones that go boo in the night. I like the way they're stretching. It means they don't take themselves that seriously.

Q : *Why did you want to start a studio? What couldn't you get that you wanted to get?*

A : I had been thinking about doing something with Amblin to give myself more proprietary ownership in not only the negatives but the real estate. I'd actually been in conversation with Mike Ovitz, who was my agent at CAA, on privatizing Amblin and turning it into an independent entity. It's because I woke up one day and realized that I really didn't work for myself and never had. I had achieved success beyond my wildest dreams, but I'd achieved that working for everybody in Hollywood.

I was very happy to do that for the rest of my life, but starting my own shop, including distributing my own pictures, did nag at me a bit. So when Jeffrey [Katzenberg] suggested that I go into partnership with himself and David Geffen, it wasn't something that I just began thinking about the day Jeffrey left Disney. I wanted to feel what it was like to go into business for myself. I've never really had my own place; I hadn't had *Cheers.*

Q : *Now that you have a company, does that impact the films you pick?*

A : Not at all, I promise you. It really is just a galvanic skin response to what I read or what I hear. It just literally is, "Oh, I'd love to go see that picture." It's the same way I'll go to see a movie like *Celebration.* I adored *Celebration,* and I think if [Danish director] Thomas Vinterberg had told me that story and come to me with that concept of shooting a movie in available light, I would have found the financing for him to make that picture, and I would have been very happy to put either DreamWorks name or a smaller, independent distribution branch of DreamWorks on it and release it. So I'm just open to anything.

Q : *So do you envision having an independent film subsidiary of DreamWorks at some point?*

A : Absolutely, I do. Right now I've got a larger appetite than our business plan allows me to have. Our plan only lets me make a maximum of nine live-action movies a year. Frankly, I have not been able to find more than six that I would really stand behind and claim pride of ownership. So I always wonder how studios can make 35 films a year and stand behind each and every one of them with a great deal of pride.

Q : *Well, obviously, I don't think they can.*

A : I don't think it's possible. And it's also a lot of work. You wouldn't even have a life if you're making 32 films a year. So when we formed DreamWorks,

I said to Jeffrey, "Look, don't ask me to go up from four films a year at Amblin, which I've done for 13 years, to 24 films a year, or even 14 films a year." At the time I had five kids—I have seven now—and I said, "I just can't do that."

Q : *Talk a bit about budgets. It seems that they go up every year. What's behind this?*
A : A lot of the costs are natural due to cost-of-living increases and wage increases, costs that follow a curve that you can chart from the time films began. And the use of money and what money can buy is a lot less than what money used to buy. When I look back at making *Jaws,* I see I spent almost $10 million, more than twice its initial $4-million-plus budget. But looking back at the 155 shooting days it took to make that picture, I know that today the film would have cost probably close to $140 million, and it's only been 23 years. And there were no stars in *Jaws,* the shark was the star, so it would have cost $140 million in 1998 without stars.

Q : *But can this go on forever? I mean up, up, up?*
A : It can go on until it hits critical mass, which is when they make another *Titanic* for $300 million and it earns $30 million domestically. And if two other films that each cost $150 million that same year both do $60 million or $70 million domestically. Then you'd have a recession inside the film business. I think it would take something that traumatizing to get Hollywood to figure out some way to cut costs, like issuing some kind of common stock among the profit participants, dividing up the pie better so we're all in it together.

Q : *One of the reasons I worry about big budgets is that when a film costs a lot of money, studios get nervous and some films end up dumber than they need to be.*
A : I don't know that that's correct, generally speaking. I know that we worked very hard not to dumb down *Deep Impact.* And sometimes, in a way, I have heard that same argument from the director of the film. I've heard directors much harder on their own films than the suits watching the dailies.

Q : *Really?*
A : Let's not kid ourselves. Directors of mainstream or independent films want success. They're not making pictures just so they can show up on

the Sundance Channel. We all want the same thing, and so I've found filmmakers actually giving me the speeches that characteristically I'm supposed to give them. They're the ones saying to me, "Did you see the dailies today? Wasn't that awful? I think I missed the mark with that character. I want that character not to die in the end. God, I think I've lost half my audience. Can I have the money to go back out and breathe life back into that guy so people will come see the movie?"

I've had directors asking me to change elements of their film that first attracted me to the picture, but now they've gotten cold feet based on having seen the stuff cut together. And I've found myself in situations encouraging directors, telling them it was a good idea—try not to worry so much.

Q : *You mentioned all the trade ads and the focus on grosses. Is this infecting directors more than is good?*
A : I'm a Pollyanna about this, so everything I'm about to say will never come true, but it's a dream I've always had. I would love it if studios stopped boasting about how much money their movies made. It would be so wonderful if it didn't become the Olympics every Monday of every holiday weekend. I would just love for that not to be the zeitgeist of why we're doing this.

Q : *Expand on that a little bit. What are the bad effects of the way things are now?*
A : I just am afraid about audiences being so hip to what a movie does. If it's advertised in very colorful adjectives how poorly a film did, it cuts off a whole segment of people who read magazines and newspapers and watch television, people who might have really intended to see that picture because the film got great reviews. But because of how much money it didn't make, they may be less likely to see it next weekend.

Q : *I think that's very true. Filmmakers are always joking about how their maiden aunts in Dubuque know all about the grosses.*
A : Listen, I got calls from relatives consoling me on the *Amistad* grosses on the second weekend. I got really nice calls the first weekend saying, "Gee, it did really good in so few theaters," and the second weekend it was, "Gee, it did so poorly in so many more theaters." I said, "Hey, have you seen the movie yet?" "Uh, no." "But you know it did poorly the sec-

ond weekend?" "Yes." "Are you going to see the movie?" "Well, of course, because you made it."

q : *There's another thing I wanted to ask you about costs, especially vis-a-vis DreamWorks. You've done some co-productions with other studios. What's the reasoning behind that?*
a : We have no philosophy about finances; it's on a case-by-case basis. With *Private Ryan,* I got the script from my agent, but Paramount owned the movie. I wanted very much to do it for DreamWorks, and Paramount agreed to split it. The Tom Cruise movie I'm going to make next is a similar situation; it originated at Fox. And by the way, I am making *Memoirs of a Geisha.* Everyone's printing that I'm not, but I am. I just did not want to come out during the millennium with a small Asian movie when there will be the biggest Mardi Gras we have ever seen between October and January. So I pushed it back, but only a year.

q : *Do you have the feeling that you could make any film you wanted to?*
a : No, not really. I wouldn't want to do a comedy, I don't think I'd be very good at it. If something that read funny on paper came to me, I'm sure I'd find some way to ruin it. *1941* was supposed to be a comedy, but it turned into a Demolition Derby. *E.T.* has really good comedy because the context is drama, I'm not selling it for its laughs. So I feel safer experimenting and doing things that I think are funny, and if it doesn't get a laugh, nobody came for them so I'm off the hook.

But there are genres that I haven't quite gotten into yet. I'd like to, but I haven't made a love story yet. A real love story. Oddly, I'd like to make an old-fashioned musical. Sing and talk, talk and sing. And dancing.

q : *Would you like to be able to make a small film that everyone in the world wasn't watching and saying it's the next Steven Spielberg film?*
a : Well, it'll never happen. The only time I'd ever make a sleeper again is if I go out of style and people are looking the other way and something slips through the big 747s. Every time I've attempted to make a small film, the problem is—I don't care what company I make the picture for— they're going to sell the movie as if it's a big movie. I do have a very small movie that I do intend to direct written by my sister, Anne, and the thing that scares me about it is people are going to be looking at it through mag-

nifying glasses. They're not really going to let it be the light confection that it is meant to be.

Q: *Are you as satisfied with* Private Ryan *as most critics are?*
A: I'm very satisfied with it. There's nothing I would have changed, even though the bookends, the beginning and end in the cemetery, have gotten some criticism. I really did that for the veterans, and those two scenes actually affect the veterans more than the Omaha Beach landings. I feel a little bit vindicated by the amount of mail and number of people who stop me when I'm going somewhere. If they're men over 70, they'll always comment about the bookends of the picture being the most poignant moments for them.

Q: *I don't know anyone who wasn't impressed by the opening Omaha Beach sequence in* Private Ryan. *How did it feel to be making that sequence?*
A: I shot the whole sequence in continuity, starting in the boats and ending on the push into Tom Hanks' eyes. And because every shot formed the next shot, and because I'd done a lot of research as to what that must have been like and used my imagination based on what people were telling me and what I was reading, I didn't storyboard anything.

We shot four weeks just for the first 25 minutes of the movie, and on the second week I turned to Tom Hanks, and I said, "Despite you being in this movie, nobody's showing up for this picture." I was convinced of that.

Q: *Why?*
A: I didn't think this would be tolerable to audiences. I had always had a line, a line that I never crossed, that was my own measurement of my own good to bad taste. For myself, I never crossed that line, but I presumed that the audience had crossed that line 19 shots ago. And this isn't like the end of the schedule where suddenly you're having this horrible attack of guilt. This was the beginning of the picture, in the second week, when I thought this was going to be inaccessible.

I thought we'd have a good opening—though not to the level we had—simply because Tom was in the movie.

I thought the second weekend it would be over. And so every weekend this summer I just sat there with my mouth falling open. It was amazing.

I'd said to my whole cast midway through the shooting, "Don't think of this movie as something we're going to go out and make a killing on but just as a memorial. We're thanking all those guys, your grandparents and my dad, who fought in World War II." And so we had kind of noble ambitions but never really any commercial ones. Which is why the budget was relatively low for a film that size.

Q: *Your budgets have a reputation for being reasonable.*
A: I'm my own worst producer is why. I take things away from me. Listen, I stopped running into people who would take things away from me after my second movie. After the success of *Jaws*, the people I craved to be my kind of strict parent suddenly looked at me like I knew what I was doing, and I didn't know what I was doing. And so I had to sort of do it to myself.

Q: *We started out talking about what's changed within the studio system. For you, what's remained the same about the movie business?*
A: What's remained the same is the passion for it and the fact that you have to really fight your natural instincts, which is to be a father and a husband, because the movie business is such a powerful magnet.

For me, nothing's changed from the first day when I was 12 years old and showed an 8-millimeter movie I made to the Boy Scouts. The reaction the Boy Scout troop had and the feeling that gave me inside is no different than the feeling I have today when an audience has the same reaction to something made by hundreds of people and for a lot more money.

People don't believe me when I say this, but it's absolutely true: Whenever I have a movie coming out, I am the same nervous blob of misshapen Jell-O I was when I first began showing those little 8-millimeter films to teeny audiences. That hasn't changed, and it's a very good thing, because I think all of us do our best work when we're the most frightened.

Steven the Good

STEPHEN J. DUBNER/1999

STEVEN SPIELBERG HAS CREATED an alternate universe, in life and in the movies, of populism, patriotism and good trumping evil. It has made him the most successful filmmaker in history—and it may have kept him from achieving a certain kind of genius.

Even when he is a shade queasy, Steve Spielberg has no trouble with self-reflection. He has the bearing of a man who has come in for his annual physical knowing he's in good shape. He is queasy just now because his jet is taking off, bound for New York from Los Angeles, and Spielberg is rather afraid of flying. So, cradling a mug of cinnamon-stick tea, he concentrates on the question at hand—a question concerning the nature of his character—and responds by cheerfully reciting the moral code he learned long ago: "A Boy Scout," he says, "is trustworthy, loyal, helpful, friendly, courteous, kind, obedient, cheerful, thrifty, brave, clean and reverent."

And how does Spielberg measure up today?

"Let's see," he says. "I'm trustworthy, I'm loyal, I'm sometimes helpful, I'm sometimes friendly, I'm always courteous, not always kind, not always obedient, not always cheerful, mostly thrifty as a producer, not brave at all, always clean and *very* reverent."

Reverent indeed, and in all the right directions: toward God, country, family, and entertainment for entertainment's sake. It is hardly surprising that Spielberg owns 25 works of art by that other master of reverence, Norman Rockwell. "Aside from being an astonishingly good storyteller,"

From *New York Times Magazine,* 14 February 1999. Reprinted by permission of the author.

Spielberg says, "Rockwell spoke volumes about a certain kind of American morality."

He might well have been describing himself, of course. For more than 25 years, Spielberg has been an astonishingly good storyteller, and his films have come to represent a morality that it seems churlish to argue against, a morality of populism and patriotism, a morality derived more from intuition than intellect, a morality that yearns above all for goodness to trump evil.

In the process, Spielberg has become, for better or worse, a sort of public oracle. With his 1993 film *Schindler's List,* he singlehandedly brought the Holocaust to the attention of Middle America. *Amistad,* released in 1997, reopened the wounds of the slave trade, while last summer's *Saving Private Ryan* reminded a forgetful citizenry just how bad the Good War truly was.

"I've never made a movie that I consider immoral," he says. "I've never made a film that I could say, 'You know, I wish I hadn't made that picture because it led people astray.' And I'm real proud of that."

Spielberg is also proud of his motivation for making movies. "The majority of my films," he says, "I have made to please people."

He is, in a sense, an antiauteur; it is hard to imagine Martin Scorsese or Francis Ford Coppola or even the Coen brothers saying such a thing. But Steven Spielberg is driven by a need for approval—from his family, from his peers and especially from his ticket buyers. When I ask him who he thinks his core audience is, he says, "At this point, it's pretty much everybody, which I think is great, because every comic wants to fill up the house with laughing, stomping people, and I'm a whore like any other standup who wants big laughs."

This is the kind of talk that makes his friends smile and his critics cringe. Spielberg's desire for approval, the critics say, is what breathes sentimentality into his films, or inspires him to substitute moral simplicity for nuance. They chafe at his do-good instincts and argue that his cinema of accommodation has taught the entire world to view history as he sees it: in black and white, with musical accompaniment.

But Spielberg's grip on the national consciousness is too firm for such criticism to have had much effect. Freely toggling between history-based dramas and his "popcorn movies," he is the most popular filmmaker in the world and the king of an entertainment empire whose esthetic—a sort of right-minded, irony-free, thrill-seeking esthetic—has permeated the cultural landscape. His creations live on not only in classroom discussions but also in theme parks, on lunch boxes, in TV commercials. His reach is so great and his power so boundless that when people in Hollywood talk about him, it sounds as if they are talking about God, with one difference: people are not afraid to badmouth God. "I don't think it's politically correct to stand up and say anything against him," says Sid Sheinberg, former president of MCA and a longtime mentor of Spielberg.

His reverence has been repaid with interest. Even his detractors, who assault his films off the record, acknowledge that Spielberg is a ferocious multitasker, an idea machine and an unusually canny businessman who has also managed to become a devout family man and a hardcore mensch. "The thing about Steven," says his friend Tom Cruise, "is that he hasn't let go of a decency I've seen so many others lose."

Spielberg fully understands the height of his pedestal. "I do think I have a personal responsibility as a family man to use my filmmaking opportunities to put out there stories that have some sort of redeeming social value," he says at one point, his brow serious. But when asked if movies really need to have a moral imperative, he says, "I think even movies that are pure escape give people a chance to look at someone up on the screen and say, 'Man, I wish that was *my* mousse in Cameron Diaz's hair.'"

These are the two sides of Steven Spielberg: the reverent grown-up who knows when to say the right thing and the exuberant kid who loves a good yuk. Both sides are sincere and both are necessary, for Spielberg knows he cannot feel good about himself unless everyone else already feels the same way. For an artist, this is a tricky formulation, since what is good for the heart isn't necessarily good for the art.

Spielberg's flight to New York—to visit Max, his 13-year-old son from his first marriage, to Amy Irving—came on a Friday in early December. I had spent the last three days with him in Los Angeles, watching him do business and trying to learn just what kind of a good guy he really is.

We first met up early Tuesday morning at the offices of Dreamworks Interactive, which designs computer games for Dreamworks SKG, the 5-year-old entertainment company founded by Spielberg, Jeffrey Katzenberg, and David Geffen.

When I arrived, Spielberg was in full-throttle consultation with four designers working on a science-fiction game whose hero must vanquish a band of bad guys. These bad guys, Spielberg explains, "want to race-purify the universe—kind of like, you know, *those* guys."

Dressed in beige jeans and a nappy maroon sweater, he is still sporting the soldierish haircut he got in honor of *Saving Private Ryan*. Under his sweater, he wears a set of fake dogtags, another memento. As the designers show him their progress, he peppers them with suggestions. He is relentlessly upbeat. He lavishes praise on a new dinosaur game, spun off from his blockbusters *Jurassic Park* and *The Lost World,* but sucks in his breath when the designers boast about the 20 varieties of "dino damage" that haven't yet been inflicted.

"Ooh—just don't make it too bloody," he says, "because then parents won't let the kids play with it." The designers look crestfallen; Spielberg quickly finds something to compliment: the intricate animation of the velociraptor's tail. "Oh, that's fantastic! We didn't do that in either of the movies—we should have."

Now he asks about the sales figures for another spinoff game, *Small Soldiers*. The numbers, he's told, are very good. Although the film didn't do well at the box office, video rentals and sales of *Small Soldiers* toys and games are so strong that Dreamworks is making a sequel, in large part to broaden the ancillary franchise.

Among other things, Spielberg is very good at making money. While he is generally considered to be courtly in creative matters, his reputation as a negotiator is far less benign. "It's as tough to make a deal with him as anyone in history," says Peter Bart, the editor in chief of *Variety.*

As a director, Spielberg has the sweetest of sweetheart deals, forgoing a salary in exchange for a share of the gross that reportedly reaches 50 percent once a film hits a certain box-office level. As a producer—he has produced or executive-produced more than 40 films in the past 15 years, including *Back to the Future, The Flintstones* and *Men in Black*—he reportedly receives at least 10 percent of the gross. Then there are TV rights, ancillary sales and video rentals (again, Spielberg's cut is among the highest in the business). From *Jurassic Park* alone, which grossed $951 million, Spielberg took home a reported $294 million.

The movies are only the engine of Spielberg's entertainment machine. There are the TV shows and cartoons he has produced, a joint venture to build futuristic video arcades and, opening in May, a Universal Studios theme park in Orlando for which he is a creative consultant. All told, he is worth an estimated $2 billion, which has led to many whispers that his taste for money exceeds his taste for art.

"Like most very successful, very creative human beings, he likes the idea of getting paid a lot of money," says David Geffen. "But I wouldn't say it's the focus of his interests." As evidence, Geffen points to Spielberg's rampant philanthropy and to his investment strategy. "He has an enormous bond portfolio," Geffen says, "which is to say he has no appetite for risk."

Now Spielberg climbs into his green Ford Explorer and sets out for the Universal Studios lot, which has been his home for more than 30 years. His next meeting is with James Acheson, the costume designer for a film Spielberg will direct next year, *Memoirs of a Geisha,* based on Arthur Golden's best-selling novel.

Acheson and his assistant leap up like mice when Spielberg enters, but within a few minutes, he has put them at ease. He has that effect on people. Acheson walks Spielberg through dozens of kimono sketches, many of which, practically dripping with dragons, are too garish for Spielberg's taste. "I think we need to make it less Disney, more Degas," he says.

Geisha, because it is owned by Columbia Pictures, has presented a bit of a complication for Spielberg. As a partner in Dreamworks, he is supposed to be its movie rainmaker. But as a director, he has always freelanced among different studios, and Dreamworks was formed with his partners' understanding that he would continue to do so. *Saving Private Ryan,* for instance, was a co-production with Paramount, which owned the script, and Spielberg has just agreed to direct two films in co-production with 20th Century Fox. "Having half of something Steven is excited about," Katzenberg says, "is better than having none." Still, such deals have led to sniping within Hollywood that Spielberg is more concerned with his own directing career than the future of Dreamworks or, conversely, that he is more robber baron than rainmaker, plucking other studios' plum pictures for himself and his fledgling studio.

But in the case of *Geisha,* Spielberg's partners didn't *want* the film. "I tried to talk him out of it," says Geffen. "I don't think it's good enough for him."

So next year, the star of Dreamworks will direct *Memoirs of a Geisha* for Columbia Pictures. Spielberg, Geffen, and Katzenberg all say they're fine with this arrangement, but Spielberg cannot hide his disappointment at his partners' lack of desire for *Geisha*. On the other hand, he knows that, as of last year, the only Dreamworks film to have lost serious money was one that he directed, *Amistad*.

When he's between films, as he is now, Spielberg spends his days at Amblin Entertainment, the production company he founded in 1982. He will re-main here until—or if—Dreamworks finally builds its own studio com-plex. Efforts to do so have long been stymied by environmental concerns and bureaucratic wrangling. "I will not believe it," Spielberg says, "until I see a shovel go into the ground."

Amblin is a low-slung Southwestern compound—"a Taco Bell construc-tion," in the words of Sid Sheinberg—designed by Spielberg himself and built on the former site of the *Leave It to Beaver* house. Unlike those of Beaver's house, the doorways of Amblin all have mezuzas.

Spielberg's office is comfortable, plenty pricey but hardly ostentatious: mission furniture, Tiffany lamps, Rockwell paintings, a huge flat-screen TV, an overflowing trophy shelf and framed photographs of Spielberg with, well, everyone. The only faces I don't recognize in the pictures are those of his children. He has seven all told: Jessica Capshaw, the 22-year-old daugh-ter of his wife, the actress Kate Capshaw; his son Max; three children born to him and Kate (daughters Sasha and Destry, 8 and 2, and a son, Sawyer, 6); and two adopted children, Theo, 10, and Mikaela, 2, both of whom are African-American. "We wanted Theo to not be the only black child in the family," he says when I ask why he and Capshaw adopted again once they started having children.

Spielberg is, by all accounts, an exemplary father and husband. His love for Capshaw borders on infatuation, and he is preternaturally jealous. Capshaw has just starred in and co-produced a Dreamworks film, *The Love Letter,* that called for a fair amount of lovemaking. Whenever Capshaw showed Spielberg the dailies, she surreptitiously excised her sex scenes. But one day he accidentally saw the unexpurgated version—which made him, in Capshaw's words, "extremely wiggy."

After showing me around his office, Spielberg pops in one videotape, a director's reel, and then another, of a comedian. He likes the first reel; the second is too low-tech to make a call. Didn't the comedian's agent know the reel was going to Spielberg? "Oh no," he says, "we never use my name, because if I specify I want to see something, the prices go up right away."

The weight of his very name, he admits, can be a burden. That is why, when Spielberg recently saw a play that he hated, he wouldn't leave at intermission, worried about the signal it would send. That is why Spielberg asks me not to name the cinematographer he recently fired from a Dreamworks film, for fear of tainting his career.

Now Tom Stoppard drops in for a visit. He and Spielberg have been friends for some time. Stoppard wrote the screenplay for *Empire of the Sun*, and doctored *Indiana Jones and the Last Crusade*, for which he received about $120,000. Once the film took off, Spielberg sent Stoppard a $1 million thank-you bonus.

After Stoppard comes lunch, delivered from the Amblin kitchen. Spielberg is having broccoli, edamame, a tall glass of carrot-spinach juice and some vitamin E. He is on an anti-cancer, weight-losing kick, prescribed by Goldie Hawn. He has recently taken up cigars but he has always been caffeine-free (except for the occasional chocolate bar), and has never done drugs of any sort. His college roommates, he explains, were ardent drug users. It was Spielberg's job to cart them—and their cat, Daytripper, who leapt from a fourth-story window after being fed LSD—to the emergency room whenever they overdosed. "That really helped keep me off drugs," he says. "I'm also a control freak, and I was afraid if I took any marijuana and got really stoned, I would lose control of my life. It's as simple as that."

His mother, Leah, backs up his story. "He's very Boy Scout-minded, you know," she says with a sort of bewildered chuckle. "He's really a throwback to my generation."

Over lunch, we talk movies. Spielberg sees more than 100 new films a year and seems to recall them frame for frame. (He has a notoriously acute visual memory.) He waxes on any number of his old favorites: *It's a Wonderful Life*, *Lawrence of Arabia*, and *The Godfather*, which he considers the best film by a living director. "I've never made a movie anywhere near as good as *The Godfather*," he says, "and I don't have the ambition to, either. If it happens, it happens."

This is a surprising confession. It is partly self-deprecation, but Spielberg also seems to be admitting that he has more of an appetite for uplift than a certain kind of artistry can accommodate. *The Godfather*, after all, is a film whose violence never dares wane; it crescendos with Michael Corleone ordering the murder of his own brother-in-law and leaves the audience with the uneasy feeling that evil leads simply to more evil. Both *Schindler's List* and *Saving Private Ryan,* meanwhile, end not in the killing fields but many years later, in the cemeteries, with survivors paying respects to their rescuers—the cinematic equivalent, some critics felt, of putting ketchup on a perfectly good steak.

A strange thing happens when Spielberg discusses his own work. His degree of self-criticism seems a direct reflection of each film's box-office performance. You will not catch him complaining that the audience "didn't get" a film; if it didn't do well, it generally didn't deserve to. On *Empire of the Sun,* he says, "I was a visual opportunist—I just feel there's a patent lack of story and relationship." With *Amistad,* he says, "I kind of dried it out, and it became too much of a history lesson."

When talk turns to *Schindler's List,* he visibly brightens. *Schindler's List,* after all, changed everything. Until then, Spielberg was seen as a phenomenally talented Peter Pan, growing up just long enough to try a *Color Purple* or an *Empire of the Sun* before dashing back to the safety of his popcorn movies.

His motivation for making those earlier serious movies was simple: to be taken seriously. But *Schindler's List,* he says, "is the most personal film I've ever made, because it was something I was so ashamed of."

The "it," of course, was being Jewish. As a scrawny kid in gentile suburbia, he couldn't stand being disliked for something he had no control over. "It wasn't so much that I wanted to be popular or wanted to meet girls," he says. "I just didn't want to get hit in the mouth." Well into adulthood, he was happy to ignore his Jewish identity. But Kate Capshaw converted to Judaism before their marriage, in 1991, and they became, as Spielberg puts it, "time-permitting practitioners of Judaism." They decided to raise their children as Jews, including Theo and Mikaela. And when Spielberg began to see Judaism as more blessing than curse, he was finally ready to make *Schindler's List,* which he had been flirting with for nearly a decade.

He was convinced the film would lose money, even though it cost only $22 million. A three-hour, black-and-white movie about the Holocaust, after all, would hardly seem to warrant a broad constituency. In an interview a few years earlier, he had addressed the difficulty of making a feature film about the Holocaust: "It has to be accurate and it has to be fair and it cannot *in the least* come across as entertainment."

Spielberg may have intended *Schindler's List* as the opposite of entertainment, but the film grossed $321 million worldwide and engaged audiences as only entertainment can, coaxing them to cry and shudder, leaving their hearts more heavy than broken. Yet the film so reflected Spielberg's intensity for the subject that it nearly stunned his critics; seemingly overnight, he was reborn: Oscar winner, public Jew, a filmmaker who could, for the most part, balance his competing passions for rigorous storytelling and moral uplift.

After *Schindler,* he took a three-year break from directing to spend more time with his family. "I got extremely antsy," he says, "probably contributing, in small part, to my agreeing to form Dreamworks."

Then he shot three films within 12 months. Each of them was designed, in part, to please someone in particular. He made *The Lost World* to fulfill his promise to Universal for a *Jurassic Park* sequel, but also to satisfy his young fans who wanted an *E.T.* sequel. "I'm not going to risk the memory of the first one to give people what they think they want," he says. "I just said, *Lost World* will be kind of giving them what they want without having to give them *E.T. II.*"

The Lost World was followed by *Amistad.* "Well, we were already talking to Theo about slavery and where he came from and who his great-great-grandparents might have been," he says. "So when I heard the story, I immediately thought that this was something that I would be pretty proud to make, simply to say to my son, 'Look, this is about you.'"

Saving Private Ryan was also aimed at strengthening a family tie. "That movie was for my dad," he says. "When I first read the script, I said, 'My dad is going to love this movie.'" For most of his life, Spielberg had a rocky relationship with his father, Arnold, a computer engineer in the industry's earliest days. Steven, the oldest of four and the only son, was always much closer to his free-spirited mother than to his workaholic father. He blamed Arnold outright for his parents' divorce, when Steven was in his late teens. But they have grown close of late, and Steven offers a commensurately more generous view of their shared past. He acknowledges that it was Arnold who jump-started him as a preteen filmmaker, and that it was Arnold, a radio operator on a B-25 during World War II, who was responsible for Steven's lifelong infatuation with the war.

Saving Private Ryan began, Spielberg says, "simply as a badass World War II movie." But talking to veterans during research "sobered me up," and he decided to push the film toward the grimmest realities: fear, boredom, killing.

The harshest killing by far befalls Private Mellish, a tough Jewish soldier who is knifed through the heart, slowly, by a German soldier who shushes Mellish like a baby as he leans on the blade.

"I made that up on the spot," Spielberg says when I ask about it.

But why did he choose the Jewish soldier?

"Believe it or not," he says, "I chose the Jewish soldier because all the other squad members were accounted for, and I'd already shot their whereabouts." Tom Hanks, the star of *Saving Private Ryan,* recalls watching Spielberg shoot the scene. "The blood drained out of my body," Hanks says. "I could not believe what he had done."

Spielberg says that his alter-ego in the film is Corporal Upham, the cowardly pacifist. Hanks disagrees. "I think who Steven *fantasizes* himself being is Mellish," he says, "who pulls out his Star of David, and says, 'Juden, Juden,' as the German P.O.W.'s are going by. I think Steven, for his Jewishness, wants to be that guy who, when the time comes, can pop a guy in the mouth with the butt of his M1."

At 9 the next morning, Spielberg is at his desk trying out a new computer game, European Air War. It is a gift from Robin Williams, whom Spielberg calls "my software pimp." The impeachment hearings are on TV. Spielberg is a friend and supporter of President Clinton, and is thoroughly disgusted with Kenneth Starr, Henry Hyde, and the rest.

He asks his assistant, Kristie Macosko, to bring in some cigars. We're not due anywhere for a half-hour, so he lights up a Davidoff and plops himself down on the couch. In rapid succession, we cover Bill Clinton, the coming Oscars, and the state of Dreamworks. Spielberg says he has forgiven Clinton for the Lewinsky mess and still considers him a moral leader. "Morality is defined not just by a sexual dalliance," he says. "What hurt me is what hurt a lot of his friends, which is that he didn't confide in any of us. But I never came out and asked him if it was true, so he never had to lie to me. Whenever we were together, we talked about family and all sorts of stuff, but we never talked about the elephant in the room." Spielberg laughingly denies the rumor that Dreamworks will someday hire Clinton. "I think he should maybe run a great university or be in charge of a foundation." What about the 2000 election? "I thought about Bradley the last time he almost ran, but right now I'm favoring Gore, because I think Gore has the ambition and the energy, and he's got a great big fat heart, which I hope doesn't bite him in the butt, because he does lead with his heart. He's a real mensch."

Now I ask about *Private Ryan* and the Oscars. No comment. Before winning two awards for *Schindler,* Spielberg had been famously spurned by the Academy. He was the comicbook kid who tried too hard to be serious — and made far too much money to garner a single underdog vote. In 1976, Spielberg was so confident about *Jaws* that he invited a news crew to record his glee as the Oscar nominations were announced on TV — and then his name wasn't called. He has since trained himself to ignore the din. "My two best sports," he says, "are shooting skeet and blocking anticipation."

As for Dreamworks, Spielberg disputes the notion that the young studio has not lived up to its promise. The past year was a good one, he points out, and expectations were too high to begin with. What people forget, Spielberg says, is that when Dreamworks was formed, he had production deals in play with several other studios. "I couldn't suddenly say, 'Thanks, guys, for supporting me for 15 years as a producer, but I'm starting my own studio, and good luck on these projects.' "

Spielberg also brushes off the idea that he started Dreamworks to aid Jeffrey Katzenberg's revenge against Michael Eisner, who fired Katzenberg from Disney. "I didn't throw myself over the barbed wire so Jeffrey could have what *he* wanted," Spielberg says. "I threw myself over the barbed wire with Jeffrey and David so we could have what *we* wanted."

What Spielberg wanted was a proprietary stake in his own business. That is the upside of Dreamworks; the downside, he says, is that after a lifetime of working for father figures at other studios, he now has to be his own father figure. When I ask him about the headaches of being a mogul, he grimaces. "God, I hate that word," he says. "It almost reminds me of *mongrel,* some kind of a debaucher." Anyway, he explains, Dreamworks is essentially Amblin writ large. (His two top production executives from Amblin, Walter Parkes and Laurie MacDonald-Parkes, are still in place at Dreamworks.) As an executive at another studio puts it, "Steven is still the idea man, and though no one ever quite says it, Jeffrey's doing all the grunt work, while Geffen sort of lurks in the wings and lobs in a ball or two when he is inspired to do so."

Kristie pops into Spielberg's office: time to leave. He is taking me on a tour of the Survivors of the Shoah Visual History Foundation. It is three minutes away by golf cart—the only Holocaust-studies center, it seems safe to say, ever situated on a Hollywood studio lot.

The Shoah Foundation is one of two cornerstones of Spielberg's philanthropy, the other being the Righteous Persons Foundation. "Among all the things I've done professionally," he says, "these are the two things I'm most proud of." He began the Righteous Persons Foundation with the profits of *Schindler's List*—"I was unwilling to keep it because it was blood money"—and it has since dispensed $37 million to Holocaust and Jewish-continuity projects.

In the past, Spielberg was a pell-mell philanthropist, and he was eager to have his name prominently attached to his gifts. These days, he is far more circumspect. "A rabbi sat me down," he explains, "and told me, 'You know, if you put your name on everything, it goes unrecognized by God.' I said, 'Really?' So over the last 10 years, 80 percent of what I give is anonymous and the other 20 percent is only where my name can help attract other moneys."

Our three-minute ride turns into 10, then 20. The road to the Shoah Foundation has been rerouted, so Spielberg backtracks again and again. He finally finds his way onto the Shoah lot—seven trailers surrounded by chain-link fencing. The operation has the feel of a displaced-persons camp, which is accidental but perhaps not inappropriate. Michael Berenbaum, the foundation's president, walks us into the first trailer and halts Spielberg in front of a tote board listing the number of Holocaust survivors and witnesses from around the world who have told their life stories on videotape (nearly 50,000 so far).

Some testimonies are being used to teach schoolchildren; others have been turned into documentaries: *The Last Days,* a film about five survivors from Hungary, has just been released. For the most part, though, the testimonies will be painstakingly indexed and then disseminated by fiber-optic cables to Holocaust museums and archives. The chief consultant on the fiber-optic network, it turns out, is Arnold Spielberg.

As we wend through a battery of employees working at computers and video stations, Berenbaum mentions that Spielberg's father just landed a big donation from Unisys. "Oh, that's great," Spielberg says. "I'm always looking for something to congratulate my dad on."

And there, in the next trailer, is the man in question. "Dad! We were just talking about you!"

Arnold Spielberg is 82, stocky and hale, wearing a plaid shirt and khakis. He and his son chat for a few minutes—they have the same rat-a-tat cadence—and then Berenbaum resumes the tour. "If I wanted to," Spielberg tells me, "I could easily write one check to cover this entire project, but—."

Berenbaum cuts him off: "But then it would be *Spielberg's* foundation, and Spielberg is associated with many, many great things, but all of them fantasies." Spielberg explains: "What we're trying to do here is recreate social studies in America. We're also available to anyone who wants to rubber-stamp our technology—to spearhead the search for the genealogy of African-Americans as former slaves, who would like to create a social-studies curriculum having to do with the genocide of the American Indian, anything having to do with racial intolerance or just plain intolerance."

In serious conversation with Spielberg, "tolerance" and "intolerance" are among the most common words to crop up. Despite his success, he says, he still feels like an outsider, indelibly stamped by his childhood. Indeed, his movies add up to one long argument for tolerance, a plea to accept the outsider. *E.T. The Extra-Terrestrial* has Elliott, a young loner, recognizing that E.T. is more kindred spirit than alien. *Close Encounters of the Third Kind* was, above all, a quest for peace among men (and, again, aliens). More recently, *Saving Private Ryan* was rewritten, at Spielberg's insistence, from a swaggering World War II movie into a melting-pot ensemble drama: the Jewish soldier, the Italian soldier, the Scripture-quoting sharpshooter.

It is this morality of tolerance, his critics say, that turns his characters into stereotypes or leads Spielberg to crown the wrong heroes. Why, he was asked after *Schindler's List,* did he make a Holocaust film whose hero was a redeemed Nazi? Even David Geffen feels that *Amistad* was less about slavery than "about white people saving black people."

These are, in effect, new twists on an old line of criticism. It used to be said that Spielberg and his best friend, George Lucas, infantilized the movies with their cartoonish, thrill-seeking, sequel-generating mentality. That charge stuck, particularly since half of Hollywood immediately began imitating them. But the latest wave of Spielberg criticism—that he massages history in order to get his tolerance fix—hasn't yet found its legs, in large part because his vision has not become a trend.

Why is it that no one else is making films like Steven Spielberg's? It could be that it's simply too soon for imitators. Or it could be that no one else is able to.

Back at Amblin, Spielberg walks into a roomful of people and stone-age gadgetry: a production meeting for a *Flintstones* sequel.

The director, Brian Levant, breathlessly marches Spielberg through a parade of drawings and models. "Oh, that's so great, that's so clever!" Spielberg says. "Now I have a question. Is Steve Wynn-Rock in the script a nice character?"

"No," Levant says, "he's our bad guy."

"Then you can't call him Steve Wynn-Rock," Spielberg says, "because Steve's a very good friend of mine."

No problem, Levant says. Spielberg proclaims: "Um, great! Gee. When do you start?"

"When *do* we start?" Levant says with an awkward laugh. "Well, that's a very good question. We don't have a green light."

A pregnant moment. The film is being produced by Universal — Spielberg is just "a neighborly adviser," as he puts it — and Universal has been in upheaval since its chairman, Casey Silver, was fired a week earlier.

"Well," Spielberg says, "Stacey's making all the decisions with Ronnie Meyer right now, since Casey left, so you're going to have to get them down here." Spielberg hollers into the next room: "Kristie — is Ronnie Meyer in town? If he is, ask if he'd come down this afternoon with Stacey and look at this *Flintstones* stuff."

The skids greased to perfection, Levant grins. Spielberg grins back, asks Levant to slip him a copy of the budget and heads out. Kristie is already dialing Ron Meyer.

A quick lunch and then downstairs for a meeting with Gore Verbinski, who directed *Mousehunt* for Dreamworks. Verbinski, sporting a black turtleneck and creeping sideburns, has come to Spielberg with a pitch for a new film: a remake of a 1950's drama about German P.O.W.'s returning home.

Spielberg listens, nods. He, of course, remembers the original, in great detail. They talk at some length about the plot and the characters. "Frankly, the one thing that scares me here is my politics" — that is, lionizing the German soldiers. "Let me give you a crazy idea," he says suddenly. "Would you ever think of making this picture all in German with American subtitles?"

"Yeah," says Verbinski, somewhat unenthusiastically, "like a *Das Boot*."

"Because then you could make this film for really low-end, get a really great German cast."

"No, I think there's an integrity to that," Verbinski says.

"And you'd make all your money back in your first weekend in Germany alone. Would you be willing to really go short strings on this?"

"Absolutely."

Back upstairs, the *Flintstones* props are still spread out. And now, lo and behold, Ron Meyer and Stacey Snider have stopped by. They look things over, then convene in Spielberg's office.

The minute they leave, Spielberg calls Levant. "Brian, you got a green light, pal," he says. "But you've got to make me a promise, because I don't want the green light to turn yellow. Try to get one million dollars out of the overall budget below the line. All right? Congratulations."

Spielberg loves to say yes, especially to younger filmmakers. He says he will never forget the opportunity that Sid Sheinberg gave him in 1969, signing Spielberg to a seven-year contract at a time when Hollywood did not consider youth a good thing. He is particularly supportive of women. Two of his former secretaries, Kathleen Kennedy and Bonnie Curtis, are now producers, and Spielberg has hired any number of female directors for Amblin and Dreamworks movies. "Steven is the single most active mentoring director in Hollywood," says the director Robert Zemeckis. "He has taken responsibility for the power he's been given, which I guess you could suggest is the very definition of humility."

Now Spielberg is pawing through his in-box as Kristie awaits orders. A pair of charity requests. (Yes to both.) A request for an interview from a journalist who panned *Amistad*. (He'll do it, because he thought the criticism was smart.) The guest list for a coming V.I.P. screening of *Close Encounters*. (Julia Phillips, one of the film's producers, hasn't been invited. Spielberg hasn't seen her in years, and in 1991, she assaulted him in her infamous Hollywood diatribe *You'll Never Eat Lunch in This Town Again*. But Spielberg tells Kristie to invite her; he likes to keep his friends close and his enemies closer.)

And then he turns to me and says, "By the way, Tom Cruise and I are officially now going to make a movie together."

The deal was finalized last night. This makes Spielberg very happy. He and Cruise are longtime friends and neighbors but have never worked together. The film, *Minority Report,* is based on a story by the science-fiction writer Philip K. Dick. It will be set in the year 2080, in an America so anarchic that the Government, forearmed with the knowledge of murders that haven't yet happened, takes it upon itself to murder the murderers. Spielberg calls *Minority Report* the most cynical film he will have made—but yes, it has a happy ending, he says, and yes, it's a popcorn movie, "but a gourmet popcorn movie." He'll shoot it this fall in Los Angeles so he can be near his family; *Geisha* will follow in the spring.

Later, I ask Spielberg what happened to the film about Charles Lindbergh that he had planned to direct.

He answers by explaining how *Schindler's List* and the Shoah Foundation have reshaped his thinking. "They've given me more of a moral responsibility to make sure I'm not putting someone else's agenda in front of the most important agenda, which is trying to create tolerance," he says. "We'll probably make *Lindbergh,* but one of the reasons I've considered not being the director is that I didn't know very much about him until I read Scott Berg's book and I read it only after I purchased it, and I think it's one of the greatest biographies I've ever read but his America First and his anti-Semitism bothers me to my core, and I don't want to celebrate an anti-Semite unless I can create an understanding of why he felt that way. Because sometimes the best way to prevent discrimination is to understand the discriminator." — *su film*

The long day ends at the Dreamworks animation complex, where the consuls general from 50 countries have been invited for a preview screening of *The Prince of Egypt.* Spielberg pulls up in his Explorer, a big green shark in a sea of diplomatic sedans. Pete Wilson, the outgoing Governor of California, is escorted to him.

"Hey, Governor," Spielberg says. "How you doing?"

"Good to see you," says the Governor. "You're very kind to do this."

"Listen, thank *you* for coming," Spielberg says. "It's great that we have the whole world here tonight, in one room. I wonder if I should start soliciting for Shoah donations."

The two men share a laugh, then head inside. The Governor is approached by the stray diplomat; Spielberg, meanwhile, is immediately encased in a circle of flesh, five deep, the consuls general from Croatia and Gambia, Guatemala and France. They are exceedingly well dressed; he's wearing scruffy corduroys and a suede jacket, a dead cigar cupped in his hand. They tell him that they love his movies, that he should shoot his next one in their countries, that he should dramatize the lives of *their* repressed people.

These men and women, powerful in their own circles, clearly recognize that Spielberg's power dwarfs theirs by a frightening multiple. His power, after all, is unlimited by reality. The stories he tells have come to represent not just escape from an imperfect world but a facsimile of a more perfect world—where the lamb lies down with the lion, the discriminator with the discriminated. And in that world, they know, Steven Spielberg is the king.

After driving his children to school on Thursday morning, Spielberg heads for the set of *E.R.* Djimon Hounsou, who played the leader of the slave revolt in *Amistad,* has just landed a recurring role, and Spielberg wants to wish him well. Here, too, Spielberg is treated like royalty, for he was a founding producer of the show.

On the drive back to Amblin, I ask Spielberg if perhaps his need for approval, his pressing desire to say yes, ever gets him in trouble. One of his frequent collaborators, after telling me of Spielberg's ability to do three or five things at once, all of them well, wondered aloud if his own films might benefit if he shoved a few things off his plate. Even now, when he's not directing, he is developing dozens of films and TV shows and computer games; he is making a European fund-raising tour for the Shoah Foundation; he is still a producer of record on three Saturday morning cartoon shows; he is co-producer of a millennial extravaganza for the White House and helping shape the new Universal theme park. All this must fit around his family obligations, since Kate Capshaw's prime insistence when he formed Dreamworks was that he not become an absentee father.

Every project, Spielberg says now, a bit testily, fulfills a certain desire, satisfies a certain constituency. The films are what he lives for. The Shoah Foundation is a vital outlet for his altruism. The White House was not someone he could turn down. The cartoons and games and theme park "make my kids really proud of me," he says. "They couldn't give a rat's [expletive] about *Schindler's List* or *Saving Private Ryan,* but they care volumes that my name precedes *Tiny Toons* and *Animaniacs.*"

The rest of Spielberg's day is spent shuttling between meeting rooms and his office. He's on the phone much of the time, first with his son Max, then with Christie's in New York, which is conducting an auction of Tiffany lamps.

On the first one, he drops out at $62,000. He bids the next lamp up to $660,000 but again drops out. He finally gets the third one, for $140,000. There's one more lamp he's interested in. The bidding quickly moves to $1.3 million, which scares him off. "God, that's more than I'll pay for a script," he tells the Christie's clerk.

During one afternoon meeting, Spielberg suddenly excuses himself, dashes upstairs, shuts his door. President Clinton is on the phone. Today, his lawyers are making their final arguments before the House Judiciary Committee. Spielberg's door remains closed for 15 minutes. When he emerges, he seems rather subdued.

Was Clinton asking a favor? Seeking advice? Looking for encouragement? Spielberg won't breathe a word, but whatever the President wanted, it's a good bet Spielberg gave it to him.

The next day, on the flight to New York, Spielberg tries to persuade me that his view of the world is not as starry as it once was. Fatherhood, he says, has finally made him grow up, and the impeachment of the President has embittered him. "America will have to yet again wait for good work to be done in our names," he says, his language practically Clintonian.

Concerning the President, he is plainly sincere. But his talk of cynicism is, frankly, not very convincing. If I have learned anything about Spielberg, it is that he, like the President, is a congenital optimist. Spielberg and Clinton, in fact, would seem to have much in common (beyond the fact that they are the same age, 52, and both dodged the draft). They are each driven by their need for approval, and they are very much men of their generation, tolerant to a fault and reverent toward the most righteous causes. They are self-styled outsiders who, by force of talent and personality and ambition, crashed the establishment but still summon the discomfort of the outsider when it serves to motivate them. They are, in short, the leaders we have asked for, and don't know quite what to make of.

The airplane is climbing. The sky is cloudless this morning, the hills of Los Angeles piney and calm. "Out there is Sunland," Spielberg says, pointing. "That's where I shot *E.T.* Out there and in Northridge, which is that way."

Of his own films, *E.T.* is a clear favorite. It is also the closest that Spielberg has come to autobiography, albeit a peculiar one: a boy who is good but lonely, his parents divorced, who discovers true happiness in the realm outside of reality.

I ask Spielberg if he might ever make a film that's truly about himself. Yes, he says, somewhat wistfully. It's called *I'll Be Home*. It's about his family, written by his sister Anne, who was a co-writer of *Big*. Spielberg has considered making *I'll Be Home* for years. "My big fear," he explains, "is that my mom and dad won't like it and will think it's an insult and won't share my loving yet critical point of view about what it was like to grow up with them."

There is a poignant friction at work here: the artist who wants to tell a story, the man who is unwilling to offend. It is a friction that Steven Spielberg may never resolve, but that may keep him exactly what he is: one of the best American entertainers in history.

INDEX